# In Quest of the Jewish Mary

*Tota pulchra es, Maria . . .*
*tu gloria Jerusalem,*
*tu laetitia Israel,*
*tu honorificentia populi nostri.*

You are all beautiful, O Mary . . .
You are the glory of Jerusalem,
You are the joy of Israel,
You are the honor of our people.

—SECOND VESPERS FOR THE SOLEMNITY OF THE FEAST OF THE IMMACULATE CONCEPTION. (BASED ON JUDITH 15:9)

# In Quest of the Jewish Mary

*The Mother of Jesus in History, Theology, and Spirituality*

**Mary Christine Athans, BVM**

Maryknoll, New York 10545

Third Printing, March 2014

Founded in 1970, Orbis Books endeavors to publish works that enlighten the mind, nourish the spirit, and challenge the conscience. The publishing arm of the Maryknoll Fathers and Brothers, Orbis seeks to explore the global dimensions of the Christian faith and mission, to invite dialogue with diverse cultures and religious traditions, and to serve the cause of reconciliation and peace. The books published reflect the views of their authors and do not represent the official position of the Maryknoll Society. To learn more about Maryknoll and Orbis Books, please visit our website at www.maryknollsociety.org.

---



Manufactured in the United States of America.

Manuscript editing and typesetting by Joan Weber.

---

**Library of Congress Cataloging-in-Publication Data**

Athans, Mary Christine.
In quest of the Jewish Mary : the mother of Jesus in history, theology and spirituality / Mary Christine Athans.
p. cm.
Includes bibliographical references and index.
ISBN 978–1–62698–004–4 (pbk.)
1. Mary, Blessed Virgin, Saint. 2. Catholic Church—Doctrines. I. Title.
BT603.A84 2013
232.91—dc23

2012038593

*To Mary,*
*the Jewish mother of Jesus,*

*to*
*my Irish mother, Mary,*

*and to*
*Mary Frances Clarke,*
*founder of the Sisters of Charity of the*
*Blessed Virgin Mary.*

# Contents

# Foreword

**EUGENE J. FISHER**

As I write, it is Yom Kippur, the day on which Jews seek atonement, turning back to God in repentance and reconciliation with God and with anyone whom they may have offended or injured during the course of the year. On this day the Torah scroll in the synagogue is covered in white, symbolizing the purity of a new start and a new birth in living out the law of God written on the hearts of each Jew by the *Shekhinah*, the Holy Spirit, the living Presence of God on earth. These are most appropriate sentiments for the reader to bring to this remarkable book, the fruit of a lifetime of dialogue and spiritual meditation, scholarship and teaching. The reader of this book will come away with a renewed appreciation not only of Mary, the Jewish mother of Jesus, but of the history of the Catholic Church and its relations with Jews and with other Christians. Readers will be renewed in their understanding of the role of Sacred Scripture in their lives as individuals and as members of the people of God, in covenant both with the One God of Israel and with God's people, the Jews.

The author takes the reader through the different ways in which Mary has been imaged and understood by the greatest thinkers of the church, from Patristic times through the Renaissance, Reformation, and Enlightenment, to the present new look at Mary as a Jewish wife and mother of both Jesus and the church itself. In each age the image and understanding of Mary reflects and distills Christianity's understanding of itself, its role in the world, and the relationship it has had with both biblical Israel and contemporary Jews. The image of Mary in the church also reflected the church's understanding of the role and nature of women in the church and in the world. Mary Christine Athans's work and analysis provide a unique new lens for many Catholics, male and female, on the history of the church, how we came to be, theologically and institutionally, what we are as people of God, and how such a fresh look at our development as a church might free us to renewed efforts to be what we have been and are called to be by God.

The above may sound like too much for a single work to accomplish in relatively few pages, but readers, I believe, will come to the realization that it is no exaggeration. Athans brings to bear a wealth of insights from contemporary biblical, historical, and theological scholarship, the scholarship that lay at the heart of the *aggiornamento* of the Second Vatican Council and of the vision of a reformed and renewed church that was the essence of the conciliar debates and statements, the stories of which she narrates and analyzes with precision. The challenge of understanding Mary as a real—which is to say *Jewish*—human being, was and is also the challenge of re-understanding the church not simply as an ideal "mystical body" but as a community of believers struggling in our individual lives and as a whole to live up to what God calls us to be in the world and to do for the world, just as the biblical prophets and Jesus challenged the Jews of their times to live fully and unreservedly not only the letter but the spirit of the divine word revealed to them as a people and written in their hearts by the Spirit. It is a challenge to return the church to history, to wrangle with the issues, concerns, and very real human needs of our times. For we, like the Jews, have not been called into being as people of God simply to pray in the Temple or worship in our churches, but to change the world, to prepare humanity for the coming of the reign of God.

This joint Jewish/Christian task is also, this book vividly reminds us, a joint task of the women and men who make up our communities. The new image of Mary, the Jewish mother of our Jewish Jesus, calls us back to the roots of who and what we are as people of God. Athans takes her title from the nineteenth- and early twentieth-century search, largely the work of Protestants, for the "historical Jesus." While this search, as she shows, had its flaws, its goal was worthwhile. That goal, however, only became possible when Protestant, Catholic, and Orthodox Christians turned, after the great tragedy of the Shoah, for the first time in the history of any of our churches, to a true dialogue with Jews. Much of the revisioning of the church that took place in the Second Vatican Council, this book shows, as have numerous others, was possible only because of the radical re-understanding of Jesus as a Jew made possible by the dialogue between Jews and Christians after the Holocaust.

Athans also takes into account the significant body of work of Christian feminists, especially since the council, and how this work has reordered our understanding of what the church is and what it might be. Taking seriously Mary as a model for women in the church today is possible, she shows, if one takes seriously Mary in her full humanity as a Jew.

There is a personal touch to this book that helps to make it come to life for the reader. The author weaves into her summaries of multidisciplinary studies of the new questions that have arisen for the church since the Second World War numerous vignettes of her own life as a woman religious, a leader of ecumenical, interreligious, and Catholic-Jewish dialogue, and as a professor of theology. These personal narratives both exemplify and move forward the scholarly points she is making so that the book is at once enormously informative and, simply put, a great read, indeed, a page turner.

Athans concludes with a deeply moving evocation of a thirty-six day retreat she made following the *Spiritual Exercises* of Ignatius of Loyola, placing herself in the role of

Mary praying Hebrew prayers from Jesus' and Mary's time. This brings the Catholic reader, whether male or female, into another world, both different and wonderfully familiar, challenging us in ways unexpectedly moving and enabling us to journey with her over the centuries and into the very real, very Jewish world of the founders of our church. It is a prayerful and exciting journey, and readers will close this book with a sigh, refreshed and ready to take on life's tasks with a new appreciation for their potential to benefit themselves and others, invigorated by a sense of the Shalom of Mary and her Son.

EUGENE J. FISHER
Distinguished Professor of Catholic-Jewish Studies
Saint Leo University

# Prologue

I can still recall a hot, dry Friday evening in August 1970 in Phoenix, Arizona, when I stood nervously in the hallway adjacent to the sanctuary at Temple Beth Israel. Having recently been appointed executive director of the North Phoenix Corporate Ministry, a cluster of five Protestant churches, one Catholic church, and two synagogues (one Conservative and one Reform), I was invited to preach the sermon during the Friday evening Sabbath service at one of "our synagogues."

Not only had I never preached in a synagogue, I had never even attended a service on Shabbat. I had toured synagogues with groups of students, attended a "model" Passover Seder, enjoyed meals in the homes of Jewish friends, and been involved in social justice projects and theological dialogues with rabbis, but Shabbat services were new to me. Garbed in a yellow sleeveless dress with a white Peter Pan collar and wearing my "nun pin," I was oblivious to the fact that some synagogues require women to wear long sleeves. (With the rabbis in their black robes, I probably would have looked less out of place in the long black habit I had worn a few years earlier.) Suddenly, a dear, elderly rabbi approached me with a smile. He told me that the last time he was in Israel, he had gone to the synagogue in Capernaum where Jesus had preached—and he wanted me to know how happy the congregation was to have me with them that evening! With a sigh of relief, I joined the procession of rabbis into the sanctuary.

With that Shabbat service my spirituality changed forever. As I sat on the *bimah* (the dais in the pulpit area near the Ark), listening to the cantor chant in Hebrew and the rabbi read from the Torah scroll, I realized for the first time that—

despite all the changes throughout the centuries—this was how Jesus and Mary prayed. This was how they worshiped when they lived on this earth! With that Shabbat service I knew there was no way for me to understand Christianity unless I could somehow "get inside" Judaism—because Jesus and Mary were Jews. For them, liturgy and spirituality were rooted and grounded in the synagogue, and it would be impossible for me to try to understand something of their prayer life, their encounters with God, apart from it. The beauty of this ancient tradition of prayer gave me a new appreciation of God's love for the Jewish people. It was a pivotal moment in my life.

Throughout the years I have preached sermons in other synagogues, attended Shabbat services regularly, celebrated Rosh Hashanah, fasted and prayed all day on Yom Kippur, danced under the stars on Sukkot, and celebrated other Jewish holy days and holidays. I traveled to Israel with the Conservative rabbi, his family, and people from "our two synagogues." I am grateful for many opportunities to be a part of their life cycles and liturgical celebrations: Friday night Shabbat dinner in a Jewish home, joining a family for Bar or Bat Mitzvah celebrations, attending a *bris* (circumcision) or a funeral. I have attended camp with Jewish high school students where I learned their prayers in Hebrew, dialogued with them about our traditions, and joined in their Israeli dancing. In Phoenix I was either "the Temple nun" or "the synagogue Sister," depending on whether I was at the Reform or the Conservative congregation. I loved these grass-roots experiences. In interfaith relations there is no substitute for experience. Even more, there is no substitute for praying together, if we are to understand one another.

In subsequent years I have studied and written extensively on Jewish-Christian relations.[1] I have developed ways in which Jews and Christians can dialogue with one another and even pray together. In 1992 I had an enriching opportunity to teach for a semester at the Ecumenical Institute at Tantur in

Jerusalem. Each of these experiences has enhanced my prayer and my understanding.

But the pivotal event will always be that hot Shabbat night in August in Phoenix. The opportunity to pray in the synagogue deeply enriched my approach to God. My heart found a way to connect with Jesus and Mary in their prayer lives in a way that continues to influence my spirituality to this day. That experience enabled me to grow in a deep love and appreciation for the Jewish people and their ongoing covenant with God.

# Acknowledgments

How does one ever thank all of those persons who helped to make a book possible? If it takes a village to raise a child, it takes a community of scholars to write a book! I am especially grateful to John Pawlikowski, OSM, Eugene Fisher, and David Fox Sandmel for reading the manuscript and offering valuable and sage advice. I was blessed to have three rabbis, Michael Balinsky and Victor Mirelman in addition to David Sandmel, who cautioned me regarding unwarranted conclusions, and challenged me on specifics. Happily they provided clarifications, offered suggestions, and more than once confirmed my intuitions regarding Hebrew prayer that might possibly have been a part of Mary's life. To all of them, *todah rabah!*—Thank you very much!

In addition, English professors Margaret Ann McGinn, BVM, and Marjorie Carey read large portions of the manuscript and prodded me to sharpen my focus and stay on target. Mary Stokes, BVM, rescued me when my rusty French needed more accurate translation and specificity. Two liturgical scholars helped to beautify the book: Dominic Serra assisted me in searching for a favorite prayer for the frontispiece, and Eileen Crowley suggested the beautiful cover art. Bill Creed, SJ, an expert in the *Spiritual Exercises,* offered suggestions in the sections on Ignatian contemplation. Each of these generous people was indispensable in his or her own way.

Without Therese De Lisio this volume might never have been completed. Terry is a theologian, a liturgical scholar, and a tech whiz! Her knowledge, scholarly and editorial competence, kindness, and patience in the last six months have been truly invaluable to me. Thank you, Terry!

The patience and kindness of Robert Ellsberg, publisher of Orbis Books, cannot be overestimated. His wisdom and amazing understanding were an extraordinary source of encouragement to me. I am more than grateful for his confidence in me and in this project which has been dear to my heart for many years. Any errors in the volume, of course, are my own.

I would be remiss if I did not acknowledge that this book was seeded in my experience as executive director of the North Phoenix Corporate Ministry (NPCM)—a cluster of five Protestant churches, one Catholic (Jesuit) church and two synagogues (one Conservative and one Reform) in Phoenix, Arizona, which worked together in education, social justice, liturgy, and communications. As coordinator of the interfaith activities for those seven congregations my world opened to the joy of interreligious living and especially to an appreciation of Jewish prayer. Without that opportunity, this book would never have been written.

If the NPCM was a key professional and pastoral experience, my doctoral studies at the Graduate Theological Union in Berkeley, California, provided academic excitement and challenge in Jewish-Christian studies. I will always be grateful to Joseph P. Chinnici, OFM, adviser, dissertation director, and longtime friend. More than anyone, his example of integrating history, theology, and spirituality has been a model for me.

Opportunities for Jewish-Christian dialogue continued at the University of Illinois at Urbana-Champaign, the University of San Francisco, the Saint Paul Seminary School of Divinity of the University of St. Thomas (Minnesota), and more recently at Catholic Theological Union and Loyola University Chicago. Participation in the Catholic-Jewish Scholars Dialogue of the Archdiocese of Chicago, the Chicago Board of Rabbis, and the Jewish Federation of Metropolitan Chicago has provided a lively experience of growing in both knowledge and relationships. I am grateful to the communities at all of these institutions; they have contributed to the writing of this book.

I first began lecturing on "Miryam of Nazareth: The Jewishness of Mary, the Mother of Jesus," at St. Catherine's College (now University) in St. Paul, Minnesota, in 2001. "Searching for the Jewish Mary" has been the subject of my lectures at Xavier College Preparatory in Phoenix, Arizona; the Garaventa Center for the Catholic Intellectual Life and American Culture at the University of Portland (Oregon); and the Gannon Center for Women and Leadership at Loyola University Chicago. In each of these settings, and others as well, I gleaned new insights and received encouragement to explore the topic with new enthusiasm.

My family has been ever so supportive. I thank gratefully my Greek father for his love of philosophy and politics, and my Irish mother for her poetry and piety. Our home was open to all faiths, and we grew up with a real appreciation and reverence for the Jewish tradition. My sister, Cathie, my brother, Cyril, his wife, Von, and the entire family have always been there when I was in need. My religious congregation, the Sisters of Charity of the Blessed Virgin Mary, have loved me and allowed me to be creative these many years. I am grateful. My long grounding in Jesuit education and Ignatian spirituality has challenged me to live always *Ad Majorem Dei Gloriam*—for the greater glory of God. May this book be a small contribution to God's greater glory!

# Introduction

## Mapping the Quest

I recall a delightful cartoon in *The New Yorker* or another magazine, sometime during a December in the 1960s. The cartoon depicted a worried and exhausted Joseph leading a very pregnant Mary along a rocky road on the back of a donkey. They were following a road sign that pointed to Bethlehem. Instead of portraying Mary in contemplation or discomfort, she was attentively reading the book *How to Be a Jewish Mother.* Ironically, while this cartoon was humorously anachronistic, it also depicted a historical truth. Mary was indeed a Jewish mother!

Learning about the historical Mary is difficult due to the meager amount of information available to us in the scriptures. In Part I we ask why Mary has been portrayed as so "un-Jewish" through the centuries. The Jewish Mary faded rapidly as a figure in Christian art and history. Our introductory Chapter 1 discusses the obstacles in the search for the Jewish Mary, particularly in the ways Mary has been portrayed in the recent past. In order to recover the Jewish Mary, however, we have to explore many of the detours taken over the past two thousand years. Fortunately, pathways have emerged in the second half of the twentieth century that provide new avenues, allowing us to recover, in part, the Jewish Mary of scripture and of first-century Judaism. One of these paths is the invitation to reflect on Mary in the context of Jewish-Christian dialogue and feminism.

Probably more than any other woman in history, the mother of Jesus has been the subject of untold works of art, music, poetry, history, doctrine, and popular piety. Chapters 2 and 3 present a historical overview of these portrayals of Mary over the centuries, including the controversies about her role in the Catholic Church through Vatican II. Mary was indeed mythologized throughout the years. As scripture scholar Elisabeth Schüssler Fiorenza suggests, a "deconstructive approach" is necessary if we are to understand Mary as a Jewish woman today.[1] However, she reminds us that a "hermeneutics of remembrance" is important as well.[2] It is to be hoped that these chapters provide the tapestry background against which we can reflect on the past and move toward the future.

The challenge in Part II is to recover the Jewish Mary. We begin in Chapter 4 by asking why we are searching for "the Jewish Mary" *now*. Following Vatican II, there was an explosion of new approaches to Mary. Although research and writing on Mary continued to be categorized under the specific categories of historical studies, biblical scholarship, theological teachings, feminist theology, and spirituality, scholars began to dialogue across disciplines regarding Mary's unique role. This multidisciplinary methodology and the variety of insights that have resulted have provided new possibilities for uncovering the "real Mary" of first-century Judaism.

In Chapter 5 we ask whether the search for the Jewish Jesus has helped us to find the Jewish Mary. In the nineteenth and early twentieth centuries, the "quest for the historical Jesus," largely a Protestant enterprise, had negative implications for the Jewish Mary, mostly because of the paucity of scriptural material and the lack of interest on the part of Protestant scripture scholars. A Jewish "quest for the historical Jesus" emerged, but Mary was neglected there as well. Catholics were not allowed to use modern methods for scripture study at that time, with the result that Catholic descriptions of Jesus and Mary were largely confined to doctrinal terms.

Pope Pius XII opened up the field of scripture studies to Catholic scholars in his 1943 encyclical *Divino Afflante Spiritu*. The discovery of the Dead Sea Scrolls soon thereafter led to new approaches in scripture scholarship and interfaith dialogue. A better understanding of the composition of the Gospels has enlightened us in terms of interpretation of the scriptures. Christian scholars "rediscovered" the Mishnah, the foundational document of the Talmud, whose oral tradition from the first century parallels the writing of the Gospels. Learning about life in the period called Second Temple Judaism, the era in which Jesus and Mary lived, offers us new possibilities. According to Bernadette Brooten, archeological excavations of synagogues provides evidence that women in the first century possibly had a more significant role in Judaism than previously believed, at least in some communities.[3]

In an effort to be more specific about the kind of Judaism that Mary might have practiced, we also ask if the Pharisees can tell us anything about the Jewish Mary. New research suggests that Jesus very likely had more in common with some Pharisees, both in thought and ritual practice, than the Gospels suggest. We discuss the "quest for the historical Pharisees" as well as the similarities and differences of their teachings and practices to that of Jesus. If Jesus embraced, at least in part, some Pharisaic ideas and practices, might they have been a part of Mary's life and prayer as well? How might that affect the women in Jesus' life, including his mother? Hebrew scholar Tal Ilan offers a recent thesis that women may well have been members of the Pharisee sect.[4] Could this tell us something about how Mary, and other women who were members of the early Christian movement, lived and prayed?

I am indebted to the work of many scholars in my effort to describe Mary's first-century Jewish milieu. Elizabeth Johnson's excellent volume, *Truly Our Sister: A Theology of Mary in the Communion of Saints* (2003), gathers groundbreaking research and describes how Mary might have lived as a woman in Galilee during the first century. She concludes her book with an inspiring mosaic of Mary in scripture

Jewish writers have also made distinct contributions. Miri Rubin's comprehensive historical study *Mother of God: A History of the Virgin Mary* (2009) focuses on Mary from the first through the sixteenth century. Edward Kessler's article, "Mary—The Jewish Mother," explores Mary as mother from a Jewish perspective. Israeli scholar Avital Wohlmann reflects in "Why the Silence Today Regarding the Jewishness of Mary of Nazareth? A Jewish Woman Responds."[5]

Last, in Chapter 6 we reflect on Jewish spirituality and Hebrew prayer, and the way Mary may have prayed. After reflecting on Jewish spirituality, we ask how Mary might have prayed as a Jewish woman of her time. Using the method of Ignatian contemplation, I share my own meditations in Mary's voice, offering reflections whereby Hebrew prayers and rituals that were very likely extant in the first century may give us insights into Mary's life of prayer. It is to be hoped that these meditations will encourage readers to discover the Jewish Mary, while providing a deeper appreciation of ways to find God in their own prayer life.

As I have shared my hope for this book with my friends, several have remarked, "What you are writing in your meditations is *midrash*." According to Jewish scholar Edward Kessler, *midrash* is the "Hebrew word for asking, searching, inquiring and interpreting." Although it is "a commentary on a particular book of the Bible," it is often an elaboration that offers development. "Thus, *midrash* is not simply an attempt to understand the biblical text but to make sense of it, i.e. to create meaning, not simply to offer biblical exegesis."[6] *Midrash* can take differing forms: ethical teaching, fables, anecdotes, homilies, and allegories.[7] Sally Cunneen states that "*midrash* means a sustained searching of the biblical texts to bring out their hidden meaning in new words."[8] Many scholars believe the infancy narratives to be *midrash*. Jesus' parables are considered by some writers to be *midrash* as well. The *midrash* I offer elaborates on Mary as a Jewish woman and invites reflection on how she might have prayed in her Jewish milieu. It is my hope that this will provide new ground not only for understanding Mary, but also for understanding ourselves.

## THE REASON FOR MY QUEST

This is the kind of book that must be read with both the head and the heart. I recall as a student in high school and college that books on Mary seemed to fall into two categories. There were the doctrinal studies about her from the fathers of the Church, Saint Thomas Aquinas, and the popes about her motherhood, her immaculate conception, her assumption into heaven, and the various titles attributed to her. Often these works seemed antiseptic, lacking all inspiration.

There were also devotional works that seemed to be filled with hyperbole, such as the writings of St. Louis de Montfort. Many, in the style of the times, were overly sentimental, adorned with portrayals that were, for want of a better word, sugary! Vigil lights and flowers adorned altars, and shrines dedicated to her showed a queenly figure weighed down with velvet robes. I yearned to know this woman who held such a unique role in the history of Christianity, but I did not find her in the theology texts and the pious books I read or in the images I saw.

Understanding Mary, I believe, requires an integration of history, theology, and spirituality. It must be grounded in an authentic theology but must also portray her in her historical context as a Jewish woman of courage, strength, and prayer. How else could she have survived the countless challenges that she encountered? Having embarked on this "quest for the Jewish Mary," I believe that I am finally on the right path. I invite you to join me on this journey.

## COMMENTS

Three explanatory comments may be helpful as we begin our quest. First, I will not use Mary's Hebrew name, Miriam, or the Aramaic variation Mariam throughout this book.

Gospel translations and Christian writings for two thousand years have named her Mary. I have chosen to stay with this familiar term, although I appreciate the fact that she would have been known as Miriam in her time.

Second, there continues to be dialogue and sometimes controversy regarding how we refer to the scriptures in our own and other traditions. The term *Old Testament* is considered pejorative by many today because it implies that what is old is outdated and no longer useful. It has contributed to the notion of supersessionism—the belief that since the coming of Jesus, God's covenant with the Jewish people is no longer valid. Some scholars use First Covenant or First Testament or *Tanakh*—a Hebrew acronym for the whole of the Hebrew Bible (the Torah—or the Pentateuch, the Prophets, and the Writings). I have chosen to use Hebrew scriptures and Christian scriptures, although in the latter case I am mostly referring to the Gospels. I am fully aware that the Christian scriptures include the Hebrew scriptures. Denial of that fact would leave one guilty of Marcionism (explained later). However, *Hebrew scriptures* seems the most appropriate way of referring to the scriptures Mary would have known in her time.

Third, I have taken some poetic license in the meditations in Chapter 6. Often there is no certitude as to whether a prayer or ritual was definitely a part of Jewish life in the first century. Although some of the prayers noted are rabbinic, some scholars suggest that they might have been part of the oral tradition in the first century. Where there is a question as to the authenticity of certain sources used, I have provided endnotes to explain why I believe it is reasonable that such a prayer might have been extant in the first century. Often there is disagreement among scholars as to the origin of a particular prayer or practice. My hope is that, after my searching and choosing, you will allow me the benefit of the doubt in these meditations when using particular prayers as possibilities in Mary's life.

# PART I

# SEARCHING FOR MARY OVER THE CENTURIES

# Chapter 1

## Initiating the Search

*Obstacles, Detours, and New Pathways*

No doubt Mary has been a central figure in Catholic teaching and devotion. Children growing up in Catholic schools in the pre-Vatican II period recall the blond, blue-eyed statues of Mary that peered down on them in classrooms, statues that were crowned each May to the tune of "Bring flowers of the fairest, bring flowers of the rarest. . . ." As a reward for good performance in class, students sometimes received holy cards picturing a Nordic virgin or a Renaissance Madonna. Most Catholic children were given a rosary at the time of their First Communion, so they could participate in this Marian devotion.

Even Jewish children, if they lived in a largely Catholic environment, were sometimes fascinated with religious articles such as the rosary. My dear friend Marsha Yugend, later killed tragically in an accident, was one of two Jewish girls in her public school in Little Falls, Minnesota. She had many Catholic friends and recalled that, at about age nine, when she was searching for a birthday gift for her mother, she selected a beautiful rosary similar to one that her Catholic friends often had with them. Her mother gently explained that Jews did not use the rosary. The event sparked Marsha's curiosity regarding this Catholic devotion. Little did she realize that years later she would become a leader in the Christian-Jewish dialogue in Minnesota.

Depending on one's ethnic origin, Catholic families often set up small shrines decorated with flowers in their homes during the month of May to honor Mary in her special month. Mary adorned birdbaths on the lawns of some homes. What became known as a "Bathtub Mary"—an old bathtub sunk halfway into the soil and decorated so that it formed a kind of grotto for a statue of Mary—graced many front or backyards in the 1950s and exist in some neighborhoods today. Plastic statues of Mary became a familiar addition to the dashboard of cars so she would protect motorists on the road. These visual representations, some copies of artistic masterpieces and others cheap religious articles, underscored the Western European image of the mother of Jesus that dominated Christian spirituality for centuries.

## AN OBSTACLE FOR SOME CATHOLIC WOMEN: "THE PERFECT MARY"

In the aftermath of World War I, the bishops of the United States wrote a pastoral letter in which they described Mary as "the perfect woman and surpassing model of motherhood."[1] During the 1940s, 1950s, and early 1960s, American Catholics, particularly young women, were presented with an image of Mary as a humble, submissive figure on whom all Christians—especially women—should pattern their lives.[2] Catholic children grew up learning poems such as "Lovely Lady dressed in blue," and "Mary-like in soul and body, Mary-like in mind and heart." Images of Mary, influenced by the statuary in Catholic schools, contributed to the stereotypes of Mary. A blond, blue-eyed Mary was represented standing on the world with a crown of stars on her head and crushing a snake (Satan) with her heel.

Many Catholic girls in the pre–Vatican II period matured with this image of the perfect Mary they were to emulate, but she seemed so far out of reach on her pedestal that sometimes they developed a kind of love-hate relationship with her. They loved her and aspired to be like her, this most beautiful and serene woman who had so fascinated God that he made her his mother. But at the same time these young women were told never to do anything that Mary would not do, nor to dress in any way that Mary would not have dressed. One who accepted that image could feel doomed to a joyless social existence. It was hard to think of Mary chewing gum, or going to a beer party in shorts, or riding in the back of a convertible under a full moon on a balmy summer evening. But if Mary would not do such things or go to such events, should we? The perfect Mary, for some, produced either guilt or gloom, and neither was much fun. Catholic women did not really "hate" Mary, but her intrusion into their social life was sometimes resented.

If Mary was depicted as humble and submissive, how could one be independent and assertive and still be Mary-like? Catholic women continued to be caught in the Eve-Mary dichotomy, taught in the early church, and still popular through Vatican II. Eve, according to some of the fathers of the church, had led humanity into a world of sin because she succumbed to Satan; Mary, by accepting God's invitation to be the mother of Jesus, led humanity on the path to redemption. As late as 1963, Leon Joseph Cardinal Suenens of Belgium, known as a liberal among the hierarchy at Vatican II, wrote, "Woman has the awe-ful choice of being Eve or Mary . . . either she ennobles and raises men up by her presence, by creating a climate of beauty and human nobility, or she drags him down with her in her own fall."[3]

When I was in college, a wonderful, well-meaning priest and mentor once said to me: "I never worry about a fellow if he is out with a good girl." I was horrified, and I said so. Why was the woman always seen as the temptress, and the man did not seem to have to shoulder any responsibility in a relationship? This is the imagery of Mary that many Catholic girls resented, and against which many Christian feminists have rebelled.

## DETOURS OVER THE CENTURIES

The quest for the Jewish Mary has taken many detours over the centuries. It is impossible to understand the radical shift in coming to understand Mary since Vatican II unless we reflect on the historical development of beliefs about her, artistic expressions of her, and how people prayed to her in the past. Throughout the centuries Mary became almost completely removed from her historical context as a Jewish woman in the first century. She was adopted by various cultures and divorced from her background as presented in the Christian scriptures.

Elisabeth Schüssler Fiorenza, in her volume *Jesus: Miriam's Child, Sophia's Prophet,* acknowledges that her "deconstructive approach to Mary" can cause "emotional upheaval among Catholics . . . who have cultivated Mariology and Marian devotion for centuries."[4] I believe that this *via negativa* approach, however, is essential if we are going to appreciate the picture of Mary that is emerging today. There is no substitute for exploring the theology and devotionalism regarding Mary in historical context and how that was understood and honored over the centuries if we are going to learn how she is coming to be appreciated as a Jewish woman in our era. The purpose of this overview is not to reject previous ideas and images about Mary, many of which were and still are inspiring and comforting to people. Rather, the hope is that as we have rediscovered scripture since Vatican II, we can view Mary as a strong Jewish woman, a model who can inspire women in the twenty-first century.

## NEW PATHWAYS: HISTORY AND SCRIPTURE

History is a key component that allows persons, churches, and nations to claim their identity. In tracing our lineage we come to know not only where we came from but who we are. In recent years DNA tests have allowed some people to discover ancestors who appeared to be very unlikely persons on their family tree. New discoveries in scripture scholarship, archeology, and other sciences have provided a different kind of DNA whereby we can rediscover our ancestors in faith. Among them, I would suggest, is the Jewish Mary. This does not mean a denial of understandings of Mary in history, doctrine, and devotion in the past. That, too, is part of our lineage. Today, however, we have new tools to use when exploring the question, Whatever became of the Jewish girl who agreed to become the mother of Jesus?

Very little is known about Mary from the scriptures. There are only about fifteen passages in the Gospels that refer to her—sometimes not even by name. Although rooted in history, the Gospels are literary and theological documents. They were written in the later first century, each from a specific vantage point. Many of the favorite stories some of us learned about Mary—the names of her parents, her early years in the Temple, and her marriage to Joseph, which come to us from the Protevangelium of James and other apocryphal literature—were probably written in the second century, as closely as scholars can determine. These stories were often embellished or imaginative works and are not accepted as canonical by Catholics or Protestants. It seems that the Christian community, longing to know more about its founders as memories of them were fading in a Greco-Roman world, glorified those who had gone before them.

Legends and myths need not be totally rejected; they may enlighten us about the inner life of a person or the deeper meaning of an event. Suffice it to say that the apocryphal documents were not accepted by the early church as authentic church teaching. However, most of what could be known about the "Jewish Mary" in the canonical Gospels unfortunately became buried in exalted images of her that emerged over the centuries (detailed in the historical overview in Chapters 2 and 3).

With the advent of the Enlightenment in the seventeenth century and its emphasis on rationalism, the relationship between reason and revelation became a focal point for interpreting scripture. Some schools of thought dismissed all scripture as fantasy. By the nineteenth century modern scientific methods for interpreting scripture were developed but were used mostly by Protestants. This approach was forbidden to Catholic scholars by Pius X in his encyclical *Pascendi Dominici Gregis,* which condemned Modernism in 1907.

As we reflect on new approaches to Mary in the twentieth century, we cannot overestimate the importance of the Catholic "rediscovery" of scripture. With Pius XII's encyclical *Divino Afflante Spiritu* (1943), Catholic scripture scholars were finally able to use historical-critical methods for interpreting scripture. This opened up a new world for understanding life in the time of Jesus. The discoveries of the Nag Hammadi documents in Egypt and the Dead Sea Scrolls in the Qumran caves near the Dead Sea in the same decade were life-changing events for the study of the Hebrew and Christian scriptures. Suddenly ancient documents from the first century and earlier became available, shedding new light on life in the intertestamental period. Jewish, Catholic, and Protestant scholars began exploring these exciting materials together. They shared their research and insights on an ecumenical and interfaith level, which enriched them all. New understandings of life in first-century Judea emerged.

The bishops and the theologians attending Vatican II were the beneficiaries of this remarkable dialogue in scripture scholarship. Enlightened by these new approaches presented to them by the *periti* (experts), they were responsible in good part for understanding the church anew as "The People of God," the title of Chapter II of *Lumen Gentium (The Dogmatic Constitution on the Church)*. In that same document Mary regained her status as one with us among the redeemed in Chapter VIII, which was titled, "The Role of the Blessed Virgin Mary, Mother of God, in the Mystery of Christ and the Church."

Scripture studies were also the basis for the new approach to Jewish-Christians relations in the Vatican II document *Nostra Aetate (The Declaration on the Relationship of the*

*Church on Non-Christian Religions)* and its powerful Article 4 on the church and the Jewish people. It is my belief that these two ground-breaking documents, *Lumen Gentium* with its chapter on Mary, and *Nostra Aetate* with its Article 4 on the Jewish people, contributed to a new appreciation of Mary as a Jewish woman in the life of the church.

## QUESTIONS FOR FURTHER EXPLORATION

As we map our quest we must also ask: What are the essential paths to explore? This includes, as noted above, studying how archeology, biblical studies, and allied fields have affected our understanding of the mother of Jesus. It would be critical to ask whether devotion to Mary in the early centuries was influenced by the cult of the goddesses in the Greco-Roman world. Also, Jews in those early years, in an effort to prove that the Christian interpretation of Judaism was invalid and that Jesus was not the Messiah, included passages in the Talmud clearly uncomplimentary to Mary. What effect did that have on Jewish-Christian relations over the centuries? Although these questions are not the primary focus of this study, we must not avoid these considerations or fail to discuss their implications when searching for a Jewish Mary.

In what way has Vatican II fundamentally reconfigured Mary's role in the Catholic Church in theological perspective? Has feminist theology influenced the discovery of a Jewish Mary? How can an understanding of Jewish prayer enhance our appreciation of Mary and our own prayer life today? Reflecting on these questions is essential to our effort to comprehend the radical changes that took place in the post–Vatican II era that contributed to a serious attempt by scholars to understand Mary as a Jewish woman. How was she challenged by her experiences and her God to live a Spirit-filled life with an extraordinary mission—to be the mother of Jesus, the Incarnate Word of God?

Can devotion to Mary enlighten us in terms of our own spirituality? Devotion to Mary tells us as much about ourselves as it does about Mary, suggests historian Joseph P. Chinnici.[5] Theologian Anne Carr has reflected, "The theology of Mary and her image in the Church may ultimately tell us more about the Church than about Mary."[6] Elizabeth Johnson, expanding on Karl Rahner, states: "By honoring Mary we are ultimately saying something about ourselves, namely, that God has addressed us with a word of grace and called us to discipleship."[7] Exploring how Mary was understood and honored over the centuries, and how she is coming to be appreciated as a Jewish woman today, has implications not only for theology, spirituality, music, art, and poetry, but also for the role of women in society, for Jewish-Christian relations, and for one's prayer life today.

## JEWISH-CHRISTIAN RELATIONS AND THE FEMINIST DIALOGUE

Why has there been an awakening to the Jewishness of Mary in recent years? An important factor, I argue, is the emergence of second-wave feminism concurrently with the growth of Jewish-Catholic relations resulting from the Vatican II document *Nostra Aetate* and its Article 4 on the relationship of Catholics to Jews. These two movements created the atmosphere for women to explore Mary in a new light.

The conversations that evolved between Jews and Christians after *Nostra Aetate*, particularly between Jewish and Christian women, have opened up new vistas for an appreciation of Mary as a Jewish woman. One example of such dialogue is a creative group in Minnesota that continues to this day to provide insights on the grass-roots level regarding how theology and feminism can be lived among women active in their respective synagogues, churches, and mosques.

## FEMINISTS IN FAITH AND MARY

In the spring of 1985 I was invited to serve as one of the "founding mothers" of a group known as the Feminists in

Faith in the Minneapolis/St. Paul metropolitan area of Minnesota. We were all women for whom faith was an important component of our lives—rabbis, Catholic sisters, Protestant ministers, professors at colleges or universities, involved professionals in local churches and synagogues. In addition to our commitment to our traditions, we were also concerned about the roles of women in our religious institutions. We met monthly. Usually we studied a book or article and discussed it from the Jewish, Catholic, and Protestant perspectives. We shared, laughed, and sometimes cried. We supported one another in the challenges we experienced.

Within a few years Muslim women were invited to join the group. We discovered that Mary, the mother of Jesus—a *Jewish* woman who has an important role in *Christianity* and *Islam*—could indeed be a link in the chain and enhance our relationships. I am convinced that the conjunction of feminist scholarship with the Jewish-Christian dialogue resulting from Vatican II was a catalyst for rediscovering the Jewishness of Mary. Muslim participation in many Jewish-Christian dialogues in recent years has broadened the discussion and offers yet a further opportunity to acquire new insights into Mary.

This group illustrates for us that feminism and faith are not only the territory of the academy. Integrating conviction about the importance of women's issues and relating them to our religious institutions on the grass-roots level is integral to raising consciousness regarding the concerns of women in religion and society. An example of an effort to encourage this kind of dialogue is the book *The Faith Club: A Muslim, a Christian, a Jew: Three Women Search for Understanding*.[8] Although Mary, the mother of Jesus, appears only briefly in the volume, Mary as a Jewish woman, revered in Christianity and Islam, continues to be a link for religious women in different eras.

## TAKING THE FIRST STEPS IN OUR QUEST

We begin the quest, therefore, aware of the challenges, and knowledgeable about the obstacles that we will continue to encounter. We will be studying Mary as a Jewish woman, but the opportunity to explore ideas about her will not only be academic. We will make every effort to see her in a broader context, and ask ourselves what the practical implications can be for our interfaith relationships. We will also explore how this new appreciation of Mary can affect our personal prayer lives today. Let us begin the journey by reflecting on the paths our ancestors in the faith took in their search for Mary.

# Chapter 2

# Mary in History, Doctrine, and Devotionalism

## From the Early Church Through the Renaissance

I recall giving a talk in a Protestant church some years ago about Catholicism and encountering a dubious response when we discussed Catholic reverence for Mary. Finally, I smiled and said: "I don't quite understand. If you have such an appreciation for Jesus, I would think you would want to know more about his mother. For example, Rose Fitzgerald Kennedy was an intriguing figure to many people simply because several of her children attained prominence—one even became president of the United States. Why wouldn't the same apply to Mary, the mother of Jesus?" With that, several of the people sat back, relaxed, and listened. The mother of a major figure in history, especially one who made a beneficial contribution to civilization, is often the subject of admiration.

### THE EARLY CHURCH

After the death of Jesus, Christians came to believe that he had risen from the dead. With the second generation of believers, however, questions arose regarding Jesus' lineage, his early years, and his mother. As the number of eyewitnesses to Jesus and his disciples diminished, members of the early

Christian communities knew that the oral tradition would be dwindling, so they began to write down their reflections about Jesus, usually from the vantage point of a particular group or community. The four canonical Gospels were most likely written in the last third of the first century. The infancy narratives in Matthew and Luke, many scholars believe, were developed in the latter part of the writing process to enhance the stories of Jesus' birth and to support claims that he was the messiah. Quotations of the Hebrew prophets regarding the longed-for savior were incorporated into the infancy narratives because the authors believed these would support their claims.

In addition to the canonical Gospels (Matthew, Mark, Luke, and John), which claimed apostolic origin and were finally authenticated by the church in the fourth century, another form of literature arose in which stories of the lineage and life of Jesus were embellished far beyond what could be claimed as rooted in the beliefs of the early church. These *apocrypha* (manuscripts of questionable authenticity) often provided imaginative accounts of the lives of Jesus and Mary. Some of these documents, written in the second and third centuries, although not canonical, influenced the tradition of the church. Three of these documents written in the second century are next discussed. Among others, they challenged the church to define its teachings on Mary: The Protevangelium of James; the section of Origen's *Contra Celsus* that includes the accusation of the illegitimacy of Jesus; and the Infancy Gospel of Thomas.

### *The Protevangelium of James*

Best known among these writings regarding Mary is the Protevangelium of James.[1] Although this book claims to be written by James, the brother of Jesus who died circa 62 CE, scholars agree that it was written sometime in the mid-to-late second century. It was known to several of the fathers of the church such as Justin, Clement of Alexandria, and Origen. This proto-Gospel, which is a highly imaginative account of Mary's life, names her parents as Anne and Joachim and describes how this elderly couple became pregnant with their only child. It elaborates on Mary's childhood at home and the story that, at the age of three, Joachim and Anne took her to the Temple:

> And the priest took her and kissed her and blessed her, saying, "The Lord has magnified your name among all generations; because of you the Lord at the end of days will manifest his redemption to the children of Israel." And he placed her on the third step of the altar, and the Lord God put grace upon the child, and she danced for joy with her feet, and the whole house of Israel loved her.[2]

When Mary reached puberty and could no longer reside in the Temple, an elaborate process was established whereby the elderly widower Joseph, who had children by a previous marriage, was designated to be her husband and care for the virgin Mary.

In the Protevangelium of James, the story of the annunciation has two parts: first, Mary hears a voice at the well, and an angel later appears to her at home. When Joseph discovers Mary's pregnancy, he feels betrayed and angry and weeps, as does Mary. When both claim that they have not had intercourse, the high priest puts them to a test, which they pass. Shortly after that, en route to Bethlehem, Mary gives birth to Jesus.

The virginity of Mary before, during, and after the birth of Jesus is described graphically in the Protevangelium by the Hebrew midwife and another Hebrew woman named Salome, who is doubtful that Mary could still be a virgin. After Salome examines Mary physically following the birth of Jesus, her hand is consumed by fire. An angel appears who directs Salome to touch the child Jesus. Her hand is immediately restored.[3] These amazing stories became part of a

Marian mythology that contributed to conviction regarding the virgin birth.

### *Celsus on the Illegitimacy of Jesus*

Although the second-century document of the pagan philosopher Celsus is no longer extant, we know from Origen's work *Contra Celsum* that Celsus popularized the Jewish polemic regarding the illegitimacy of Jesus. According to Origen, Celsus asserts that

> Jesus had invented his birth from a virgin. . . . He had been born in a certain Jewish village of a poor woman of the country, who gained her subsistence by spinning, and who was turned out of doors by her husband, a carpenter by trade, because she was convicted of adultery . . . and that she bore a child to a certain soldier named Pantera.[4]

For some Jews, striving to retain their identity in an empire becoming increasingly Christian, this allegation that Jesus was born of an adulterous union became an explanation for his birth. The story was repeated in the Talmud and in the *Toledoth Yesuh* (c. sixth century), which became popular among Jews in the Middle Ages and was even read in Yiddish in modern times. Some feminists, such as Jane Schaberg in her book *The Illegitimacy of Jesus,* have adopted this interpretation of Jesus' origin (discussed further in Chapter 4 herein).[5]

### *The Infancy Gospel of Thomas*

There was a desire on the part of those in the early Christian movement, particularly by the second century, to fill in the gap in the Gospel of Luke regarding Jesus' early boyhood. None of the Gospels offered any information from the time the family returned to Nazareth from Egypt until the trip to Jerusalem at Passover when Jesus was twelve. The Infancy

Gospel of Thomas was one effort to describe Jesus as a child prodigy who did amazing deeds. Some were destructive actions, such as killing off uncooperative playmates, and others were miraculous and/or beneficial, such as the familiar story of Jesus forming twelve sparrows from clay on the Sabbath. When questioned by one of his elders for working on the Sabbath, he clapped his hands. To the amazement of all, the birds immediately came alive and flew away.

Two episodes in this document refer to Mary. When Jesus was six years old, his mother sent him to the well to fill a jar with water. Due to the jostling of the crowd, the pitcher broke. To remedy the problem, Jesus removed his cloak, filled it with water, and took it to his mother. "And his mother was amazed and kept in her heart all she had seen" (Infancy 9:1–2).[6] The second reference to Mary is very similar to the Lucan version of finding Jesus in the Temple at age twelve (Lk 2:41–52). However, the scribes and Pharisees ask Mary: "Are you the mother of this child?" When she says yes, they exclaim: "Blessed are you, because the Lord God has blessed the fruit of your womb. For such present wisdom and glory of virtue we have never seen or heard" (Infancy 15:4–5).[7] The fact that the question was not addressed to Joseph but to Mary may indicate that the uniqueness of Jesus' birth was deeply embedded in the tradition.

The earliest reference to the Infancy Gospel of Thomas appears to be in Irenaeus (c. 185 CE). Ron Cameron suggests that it is "Christian missionary propaganda" in order to exalt Jesus above other divine figures.[8] In *The Complete Gospels,* Robert J. Miller claims: "While the Gnostics may have been able to interpret Infancy Thomas for their own ends, it is unlikely that they originally composed the work with the aim of propagating their theological positions."[9]

Of these three non-canonical documents, the Catholic Church found in the Protevangelium of James elements that it built into its tradition, such as the names of Mary's parents, Joachim and Anne. The church did not rely on the so-called proof of Mary's virginity as portrayed in the Protevangelium, and theologians continued the discussion of Mary's virginity before, during, and after the birth of Jesus for years to come. The Protevangelium, however, was likely a catalyst for that theological reflection.

## THE VIRGINITY OF MARY AND THE VIRGIN BIRTH

Theologians of that era, however, had little to proclaim about Mary from a theological perspective. Their focus was Christology, not Mariology. Mary was considered noteworthy only as the mother of Jesus. Ignatius of Antioch (c. 35–107) accepted the belief that Mary had conceived Jesus while a virgin.[10] Justin Martyr (c. 100–164), Tertullian (c. 160–c. 225), and Irenaeus of Lyons (c.130– 200) reflected on Mary's role as an inversion of Eve's role, which they considered similar to the comparison between Christ and Adam. Mary Ann Donovan believes that "this twinned typology is related to the Irenaean desire to join the Old and New Testaments in a single pattern of salvation history."[11] Extraordinary births to women who had not conceived until their elderly years, such as Sarah and Hannah, were considered miraculous, as were the conceptions of quasi-divine figures in Greek and Roman mythology in that era. Therefore, searching for an explanation for the conception of Jesus in the infancy narratives was likely for those hoping to discover more about his origin.

In the world of Middle-Platonic philosophical discourse of that era, the spiritual element of life was deemed superior, and that which was material, especially the sexual, was considered inferior. Therefore, Jesus could not be tainted by having been born of sexual intercourse. As will be discussed further in Chapter 4, it seemed essential to many patristic theologians that Mary was a perpetual virgin.

Justin, in his famous *Dialogue with Trypho the Jew* (second century CE), defends Mary's virginity at some length. He bases his teaching on Isaiah 7:14, using the pre-Christian Greek translation of the Hebrew scriptures, the Septuagint

(LXX), which translated the Hebrew word *almah* (a maiden, or a young girl) into the Greek word *parthenos* (virgin). This would appear to have been an honest acceptance of what some consider today a mistranslation or a misunderstanding. The New American Bible used by Catholics today translates that verse: "Therefore the Lord himself will give you this sign: the virgin shall be with child, and bear a son, and shall name him Immanuel."

Trypho insisted that *parthenos* (virgin) was an incorrect translation of the Hebrew, and many scholars today would agree. Catholic scripture scholar Raymond Brown states: "We have no evidence that in Alexandrian Judaism the LXX of Isaiah 7:14 was understood to predict a virginal conception, since it need mean no more than that the girl who is now a virgin will ultimately conceive (in a natural way)." Brown adds, "Moreover, it is dubious that Isaiah 7:14 was the *origin* of Matthew's tradition of a virginal conception; elsewhere, including chapter 2, it is Matthew's custom to add fulfillment or formula citations to existing traditions."[12] For Justin, however, and for many Christian scholars throughout the ages, this has been interpreted as a prophecy of the virgin birth.

## MARY IN EARLY CHRISTIAN ART

Because the first Christians were Jews, they would have shared the belief that any depiction of the divine or the holy was forbidden according to the first commandment. In addition, they would have rejected cults and probably feared that undue attention to Mary might evoke a suspicion of goddess worship.[13] Therefore, it was not until the migration of Christianity to Greece and Rome that one might expect that pictures of Jesus or Mary would emerge. Because Christianity was undergoing persecution at least periodically until the Edict of Milan in 313, artistic depictions of Mary in that era were unlikely.

George H. Tavard, in *The Thousand Faces of the Virgin Mary,* claims that "there are no traces of pictures of Christ and of his mother in the first two or three centuries of Christianity. The frescos and mosaics in the catacombs date back mostly to the late third and fourth century, when the peace of Constantine lifted all obstacles to the possibility of elaborate decorations of the Christian cemeteries."[14] The catacombs became the sites for honoring Christian martyrs. According to Richard Price, "Invocation of the saints was an essential corollary of the cult of the martyrs, which started in the second century and expanded hugely in the fourth."[15] Because Mary was not a martyr, however, she does not seem to have been a subject for prayer and veneration.

In *Mother of God: A History of the Virgin Mary,* Miri Rubin describes wall paintings from Roman catacombs of the late third and fourth centuries of a woman dressed in robes with a child on her knee; in one instance she is facing what are believed to be the Three Magi on her right. Similar images are found in the catacomb of Peter and Marcellinus, and the *Via Latina* catacomb in Rome from the fourth century.[16]

Geri Parlby, in "The Origins of Marian Art in the Catacombs and the Problem of Identification," explores interpretations of proposed Marian frescos in the catacombs over the centuries.[17] A systematic study of the art in the catacombs did not take place until the sixteenth and seventeenth centuries. A leader in this venture was the Maltese explorer Antonio Bosio (d. 1629), who "recorded almost every fresco, sarcophagus, and artifact discovered in the many catacombs he explored."[18] These records and drawings were published and continue to be a valuable source for research. However, some of the figures who were presumed to be Mary with the child Jesus are questioned by scholars today.

Parlby cautions readers not to discount the fact that images of a mother and a child could well have been part of the funerary art typical at that period, in which members of the family who were buried in a particular tomb were portrayed.

Definitive identification of figures in images is very difficult without inscriptions. Efforts of some artists to retouch the frescos over the centuries have complicated the process. Disintegration of tombs and frescos occurred due to damp conditions in the catacombs. Therefore, certitude in naming the images in the catacombs is rare.

Annunciation scenes in the catacombs are sparse, according to Parlby. There are few Nativity scenes among the frescos, but that seems "to be more than made up for by the vast array of Adoration of the Magi images in both frescos and sarcophagi carving." She suggests that from a theological perspective "the Adoration scene is usually interpreted as a representation of the conversion of the first Gentiles to Christianity." The question has been raised as to whether these images are meant to be symbolic. "Rather than a portrait of Mary introducing her baby son to the approaching wise men, what we may be seeing is an allegorical representation of Christianity, the seated figure a personification of the *Ecclesia* or the Church presenting Christianity to the Gentile nations."[19]

Archeologists and artists, as well as theologians, continue to search for images of Mary from the earliest times. The women in the frescos are all clothed in the garb of Romans of the day. Mary, as a Jewish woman, does not appear to be among the images.

## GODDESS IMAGERY

To what degree did pagan goddess art influence the developing iconography of Mary? As Christianity moved into the Greco-Roman world and Mary received more attention due to discussion of her at the councils, comparisons were made to the goddesses of ancient civilizations popular at the time. Icons of Mary, with Jesus sitting in front of her facing forward, were reminiscent for many Mediterranean Christians of the Egyptian goddess Isis with her son Horus sitting on her lap. Isis, known as the Mother of the God, was considered a mediator, one with healing power who nurtured and healed others. Miri Rubin reflects:

> The reception of early Christianity in Egypt was marked in a number of ways by the presence of this mother goddess. Mary was presented as a local beauty, reminiscent of the ideal of Isis painted on the wall of the house of Fayoum: with large dark eyes under strong eyebrows. Very much like the Isis figure, this Mary sits powerfully on a cushioned seat, her body solid under her light garments, her hair intricately braided, her arms energetically fondling the suckled child. The representation of Mary in Egypt benefited from the prevalence and familiarity of this mother-goddess with the powerful attributes of physical prowess and life-giving energy.[20]

The Greek goddess Artemis/Diana, whose temple at Ephesus was one of the seven wonders of the ancient world, was acclaimed as the ultimate virgin goddess. The Acts of the Apostles states that the silversmiths in Ephesus, who made silver statues of Artemis, believed that Paul's preaching would cause their business to disappear. They instigated a riot in which they cried "Great is Artemis of the Ephesians!" (Acts 19:28, 34). Almost four hundred years later, when Mary was declared Theotokos at the Council of Ephesus, the crowds cried out similarly, "Praise be to the Theotokos!"

John McGuckin, in "The Early Cult of Mary and Inter-Religious Contexts in the Fifth-Century Church," claims "the assimilation of Isis and Artemis [is] the most important single instance of all the many examples of syncretism that the Isaic cult demonstrated. It was this fusing of the 'Great Virgin' with the 'Universal Mother' that made of the late Isaic cult a major force that contended with early Christianity for the allegiance of the masses." However, McGuckin believes, "What is at issue . . . is cross-religious perceptions, rather than real influences and indebtedness."[21]

He adds:

> Mary indeed absorbed iconic aspects of previous goddess cults, but in each instance they are absorptions on a wholly different level of operation than the syncretism witnessed in the pagan cults themselves. . . . Mary as a symbol of cultural assonance is far from being a sign of religious inter-penetration between Christianity and late Hellenistic paganism, but in fact always stands as a symbol of the dramatic missionary strategy of dislocation and replacement which Christianity initiated in its attitude to pagan cult and theology.[22]

Scholars will continue to debate the degree to which images of Mary were influenced by the goddess imagery of the time. Mary's integral role in the theology of the church grew considerably after the Council of Ephesus (431 CE). As the church defined its beliefs in Greek philosophical language, it also adapted its art to the style of the Greco-Roman world. When Mary was acclaimed Theotokos, her image needed to be worthy of the title "bearer of God." An imperial figure of Mary emerged with some of the aspects of a goddess. Although elements of devotion to Isis and Artemis appear to have influenced some artists in their representations of Mary, today Isis and Artemis are studied primarily as figures in history and art. On the other hand, veneration of Mary is alive and well in the twenty-first century.

## PRAYER TO MARY

Prayer to Mary does not seem to have been common in the early patristic era. Most scholars agree that the oldest prayer to Mary extant is the *Sub tuum praesidum confugimus sancta Dei genitrix,* possibly from third- or fourth-century Egypt.

The papyrus fragment with this text written in Greek was discovered in Egypt in 1938 and is the earliest known version of this prayer. The inscription reads: "Under your mercy we take refuge, Theotokos. Do not overlook our petitions in adversity but rescue us from danger, uniquely holy one and uniquely blessed one."[23] As years passed the prayer expanded; one translation is: "We seek refuge under the protection of your mercies, O Mother of God; do not reject our supplication in need but save us from perdition, oh you who alone are blessed."[24] Pre–Vatican II Catholics may remember this prayer as, "We fly to your protection, O holy Mother of God. Despise not our petitions and our necessities. . . . "

The belief that prayer to Mary did not exist before the development of a cult to Mary following the Council of Ephesus, however, is questioned by scholars today. In "Marian Liturgies and Devotion in Early Christianity," Stephen J. Shoemaker suggests that the great Cappadocian fathers Gregory of Nyssa and Gregory of Nazianzus offered examples of intercessory prayers to Mary in the late fourth century. Epiphanius of Salamis (d. 403) condemned the activities of the Kollyridians, who are alleged to have been a group of women "who worshipped the Virgin Mary and allowed women to serve as priests."[25]

## MARY AND THE EARLY ECUMENICAL COUNCILS

Mary does not receive theological attention until the great ecumenical councils, and then not primarily for herself. The theological disputes were centered on Christ. After Constantine summoned the Council of Nicaea (325 CE), Mary's role came under new scrutiny. This focus was partly due to an early christological heresy named docetism (derived from the Greek word meaning "to seem"), which claimed that Jesus did not have a human body. Docetists believed that Jesus' "body" was only a mirage to contain the divine. This heresy was a major challenge to belief in the incarnation. Was Jesus really human? The Apostles' Creed, undated and not of apostolic origin, was based on an Old Roman Creed that stated that Jesus was born of the virgin Mary *(ex Maria virgine)*.

The Council of Constantinople (381 CE), which defined the role of the Holy Spirit, produced the Niceno-Constantinopolitan Creed, which is professed at the Eucharist in Catholic churches on Sundays and special feasts. It says in part: "He came down from heaven, and by the Holy Spirit incarnate of the Virgin Mary, and became man. For our sake he was crucified under Pontius Pilate, he suffered death, and was buried."[26] All of the elements mentioned in this creed—being born, crucified, buried—emphasize that Jesus had human flesh. Although the relationship of the divine to the human in Jesus continued to be a contentious theological issue until the Council of Chalcedon (451 CE) and even later, the ecumenical councils consistently affirmed that Jesus had a human body born from Mary's body.

The question then became whether Mary was only the mother of the humanity of Jesus?—or was she truly the mother of God? Cyril, bishop of Alexandria, believed ardently that Mary should be named Theotokos (God-bearer). Nestorius, the patriarch of Constantinople, was preaching that Mary was Christotokos (Christ-bearer), which implied that she was only the mother of the humanity of Jesus. Cyril convinced Pope Celestine to request Emperor Theodosius II to summon a council to discuss Nestorius's teaching and make decrees accordingly. The emperor finally issued a call for a council to open in Ephesus on Pentecost in 431 CE. The location was auspicious because of the belief that the apostle John had taken Mary to live with him in Ephesus, where she may have died.

Evidence suggests that the common folk of Ephesus in their affection for Mary lobbied for her to be declared Theotokos. Ephesus was one of the largest commercial and cultural centers in the Roman world. Its local populace became an important factor in this otherwise theological dispute. Crowds assembled and demonstrated during the council shouting that Mary should be named Theotokos, affirming the position of Cyril of Alexandria.

The council was embattled from the beginning. The rival factions—Cyril's Egyptian supporters from Alexandria, and Nestorius's from Constantinople—arrived about Easter to lobby for their respective positions. A substantial contingent of Syrian and Roman bishops were delayed. At one point there was not only verbal disagreement but physical attacks as well. After several delays a first session was called. Nestorius refused to attend without the sixty-four Syrian bishops who supported him. His teaching was condemned. When the Syrian bishops arrived, they held a rival council and condemned Cyril. When the Roman bishops finally arrived, they supported Cyril. For a period of time, chaos reigned.

Cyril had an ally in Pulcheria, the eldest sister of the Emperor Theodosius II. She had taken a vow of virginity and, according to Rubin, "Pulcheria's deep identification with the Theotokos, through their shared femininity, only compounded the difficulties that Nestorians encountered in the mingling of woman and God."[27] Pulcheria was stalwart in her orthodoxy and instrumental in influencing her brother, the emperor, to support Cyril's position on the Theotokos.

Eventually, the council declared Nestorius a heretic and he was excommunicated. Although the council never explicitly declared Mary the Theotokos, Cyril's position was vindicated.[28] The assembled crowds roaming the streets were jubilant. At the end of the final session, they accompanied the bishops to their lodgings carrying lighted torches and shouting, "Praised be the Theotokos! Long live Cyril!"[29] Tavard states, "From this point on it was a feature of the central Christian tradition that Mary's virginity and holiness are inseparably tied to the incarnation of the Logos."[30] Mary, as an ordinary Jewish woman who had accepted God's invitation to be the mother of Jesus, seemed to have vanished.

Pulcheria's power grew and her devotion to the Theotokos enhanced her own role as an imperial woman. Upon the sudden death of her brother in 450, Pulcheria became empress. She chose as her consort an aged general and senator named Marcion. After they ascended the imperial throne in Constantinople, Pulcheria arranged for a council to define further the orthodox beliefs of the church. Two decades after Pulcheria had argued vehemently for Mary to be affirmed as Theotokos, she and the Emperor Marcion presided in person at the final session of the Council of Chalcedon (451 CE), which defined the relationship of the divine and the human in Jesus known as the hypostatic union.

Although scholars differ regarding an origin for the development of a Marian cult, a movement supported by Pulcheria and others in the imperial court led not only to exalting Mary as Theotokos, but to enthusiasm regarding Mary herself as an imperial figure displayed in icons still common in Christian art. Mary was depicted as an empress in imperial robes. Icons of the patristic era portray Mary decked in fine garb, holding the man-God, a child-king, in her lap, presiding over heaven and earth. The title Theotokos is still cherished by those in the Orthodox Churches of the East where she is also known lovingly as Aeiparthenos (ever virgin), Panagia (all-holy), and Archrantos (immaculate). Although these titles have never been defined explicitly in an ecumenical council of the Eastern Orthodox Churches, they are used frequently in liturgy and personal prayer.[31]

This devotion was impressed on me as a child. My father was born in a village near Sparta, Greece, and raised in the Greek Orthodox Church. He had great devotion to Mary. Years later he married my Irish mother and became a Catholic, but he never lost his Greek Orthodox spirituality. During an era in the Catholic Church when we were encouraged to say the family Rosary, I recall gifting my dad with rosary beads on various occasions—but he always seemed to "lose" them. In later years I realized that he was never comfortable with the Rosary, but he probably had more appreciation for Mary than the rest of our family. His death was a huge loss for us. When we went to the funeral home to view his body before the wake, there was the initial shock of seeing him in the coffin. After a moment of silence, we noticed that the Irish funeral director at Whitney Murphy Funeral Home had put a rosary in his hands. We all laughed and said, "Papa—we got you in the end!" I am sure that the Panagia was there to welcome him to everlasting life. The Eastern Orthodox Churches continue their distinctive devotion to Mary.

## MARY IN THE MIDDLE AGES

### *Devotion*

In the medieval period Christianity became immersed in a feudal world of lords and vassals. The code of chivalry portrayed "the lady" as a woman put on a pedestal and worshiped from afar. In time, Mary was transformed into our Lady—Notre Dame. She became the lady par excellence of the feudal era.

Cathedrals and shrines were erected in her honor. Three times a day bells rang over cities, towns, and fields. Lords and peasants alike paused to recite the Angelus: "The angel of the Lord declared unto Mary, and she conceived of the Holy Spirit." The Memorare prayer seeking Mary's aid—attributed to Bernard of Clairvaux—and the Rosary—"the poor man's psalter" for the illiterate—became common prayers. Christians petitioned Mary for good crops, health, wealth, a spouse, and safety in childbirth. People fervently believed that Mary was their patroness and protector.

Devotionalism abounded. Litanies to Mary were created. Hymns were composed. Passion plays captured the imagination of illiterate people. The medieval antiphons—the "Salve Regina" and the "Alma Redemptoris Mater"—which emerged in the eleventh century, plead for Mary's assistance in gaining God's mercy. During that same period the cult of the Mater Dolorosa (sorrowful mother) grew in western Europe. Jacopone de Todi (c. 1230–1303) wrote some of the most poignant vernacular poems about Mary in Italian. According to Marina Warner, his hymn on the sorrows of Mary, "Donna del Paradiso" (lady of paradise), "gave unique voice to her suffering in the Easter tradition."[32] When Mary meets Jesus on the road to Calvary, he speaks to her in his pain: "Mama, why have you come? You cause me a mortal wound, for your weeping pierces me and seems to me the sharpest sword." Part of her anguished response is, "Son of the laughing face, why has the world so despised thee?"[33]

At a time when infant mortality rates were high, sons were killed in the Crusades, and disease was rampant, women could identify with Mary as the suffering mother. Men, too, might have sought the solace of Mary as mother when the image of God seemed so distant. Typical in the medieval period was the idea of accepting suffering on earth so that one would receive one's eternal reward in heaven. These earthy portrayals of Mary portrayed a mother in her grief.

As Christ was depicted increasingly as the just judge, Mary became the mediatrix. Bernard of Clairvaux (1090–1153) believed that her role was to be the aqueduct of God's grace, the channel through whom God's blessings would flow. She became the approachable one who would intercede for those in distress—accessible and merciful to sinners and those in need. Even today tales abound about Mary as the one who rescues sinners. One bit of folklore describes Jesus, noticing some less-than-desirable folks in heaven, as asking Peter if he is screening people properly at the gates of paradise. Peter's response is: "I do my best to keep them out, Lord, but your mother keeps letting them in through the windows!"

Medieval legends describe how Jews in the Middle Ages were aided by Mary when they were fearful or in need. In the thirteenth century, Alfonso X, the Wise (1221–84), gathered and set down in writing some 420 songs praising Mary, many recounting miracles attributed to her. The *Cantigas de Santa Maria,* originally written in Galician-Portuguese, includes a half dozen songs in which Jews are mentioned. In one, a small Jewish boy had a vision of Mary, who gave him communion. When his father discovers this, he throws his son into the furnace. The virgin protects the boy from the fire. He later receives baptism along with his grateful mother. In another song/poem, a Jewess is near death in childbirth; through Mary's intercession, she delivers her baby. She and her children are later baptized. While it is true that the Jews who are aided by Mary are always baptized, these songs indicate that Mary was clearly perceived as a sympathetic and helpful figure to both Jews and Christians in distress.[34]

Jewish scholar Arthur Green's article "Shekhinah, the Virgin Mary, and the Song of Songs: Reflections on a Kabbalistic Symbol in Its Historical Context," provides an in-depth study of an instance of "Jewish *indebtedness* to Christianity, especially on the level of popular piety" in the Middle Ages.[35] It is a complex issue, which Green approaches with an amazing knowledge of both Jewish and Christian sources too complicated to explicate here. However, he is convinced that the popular revival of devotion to Mary in the twelfth century, particularly in France, evoked the Jewish response of "the unequivocal feminization of the *shekinah* [the indwelling Presence of God] in the Kabbalah in the thirteenth century."[36]

Green focuses particularly on interpretations of the Song of Songs, especially in the homilies of Bernard of Clairvaux, which became one of the most popular texts in Western mysticism through the centuries. Bernard and other Cistercians "include important mariological interpretations of the Song." Indeed, "the entire Canticle is understood as betokening the love between Christ and Mary." In this period of romance, troubadours, personal quest, and an exaltation of "the Lady," Green suggests that "the female figure of *shekinah* may be seen as *a Jewish response to the great popular revival of Marian piety in the twelfth century Western church*."[37]

Although this was a period of persecution of Jews in many areas of Europe with pogroms, the Crusades, and edicts of the Third and Fourth Lateran Councils against the Jews, Mary appears to have exerted some positive influences in Jewish life and spirituality during these centuries.

### *Doctrine*

The major theological argument about Mary in the Middle Ages concerned her conception. The Conception of Mary was celebrated as a feast day in the East as early as the seventh century, but it was mentioned only rarely before the end of the first millennium in the West.[38] By the twelfth century, however, it became a point of division among theologians. Bernard of Clairvaux, despite all his warm and loving devotion to Mary, believed that because she was conceived in a natural way, she had original sin like every other human being. Therefore, one could not celebrate a feast of her immaculate conception.[39] Other famous doctors of the church, such as the Dominicans Albert the Great and Thomas Aquinas, and the Franciscan Bonaventure, agreed with him. Their belief was based on the christological conviction that because redemption had not yet taken place, Mary could not have been born without sin.

The first well-known theologian in the West to defend the immaculate conception was the Franciscan John Duns Scotus. He argued that if Mary was immaculately conceived, it was in anticipation of the merits of her son, Jesus. The Franciscans became defenders of the immaculate conception. Dominicans, while equally devoted to Mary, did not believe the immaculate conception could be accepted as a doctrine. Debates ensued. Tavard explains, "By the sixteenth century theologians were divided into two factions, 'maculists' and 'immaculists.'"[40] The dogma of the immaculate conception was not defined until 1854.

Bonaventure provided a helpful distinction regarding homage to Mary. Rather than use the Greek word *latria* (worship paid only to God), or *doulia* (veneration paid to the saints), he coined the word *hyperdoulia* (veneration greater than that due to the saints but not worship).[41] Mary, highest among the saints, was due special honor and praise, but she was not to be worshiped. This distinction has continued to be the teaching of the Catholic Church throughout the centuries.

### *The Renaissance Mary*

The Renaissance brought a new appreciation of humanism. The vision of the human person became increasingly earthbound, as did images of Mary. The madonnas of artists like Raphael and Botticelli depict Mary with her child, sometimes nursing him at her breast. All were very human and serene, as can be seen in Leonardo Da Vinci's remarkable painting "Virgin and Child with Saint Anne." Michelangelo's study of anatomy enhanced his sculpture, as is evident in the incomparable *Pieta*: Mary with the dead body of Jesus on her lap. The muscles and veins are so real that one would want to touch them. Mary's face reveals a poignant acceptance which seems to transcend the stone out of which it is carved. However, Mary was pictured as a woman of the Renaissance rather than a first-century Jewish mother.

The Renaissance was an era of scientific investigation. The printing press was invented. Greek and Latin manuscripts were rediscovered, opening up the field of biblical studies. Scholars of the Renaissance such as Lorenzo Valla (c. 1406–57) began to use more sophisticated approaches such as linguistic methods to identify the authorship of documents. These sometimes exposed forgeries, such as the Donation of Constantine, purportedly an imperial decree. Errors in the Vulgate—the Latin translation of the Bible by Jerome, which for years was considered sacrosanct—came to light. These sometimes affected how Mary was understood in the scriptures.

New instruments were invented that enabled geographical exploration. New worlds were discovered in Africa, Asia, and the Americas. Mary continued to be a guiding light for Catholics. One need only remember that the name of Columbus's lead ship on his exploration to the New World in 1492 was *La Santa María de la Immaculada Concepción*. And he named the second island he discovered in the Caribbean *Santa María de la Concepción*. Queen Isabella symbolically donated the first gold that Columbus brought her from America for the ceiling of the west apse of the basilica Santa Maria Maggiore in Rome. Mary's influence was attaining global significance, but more as a royal figure than as a Jewish maiden.

## MARY IN THE PROTESTANT REFORMATION

### *Martin Luther and Mary*

Although Protestant reformers decried the exaltation of Mary among Catholics, some did have a special regard for her. Martin Luther (1483–1546) in his earlier years had a warm devotion to Mary. Even after his initial break with the church, his sermons and tracts regarding Mary were positive and even pious. He believed in the virgin birth and the perpetual virginity of Mary. His famous commentary on the Magnificat, written shortly after he had been excommunicated by Pope Leo X in 1521, accepted Mary as Theotokos. Luther wrote, "She is the foremost example of the grace of God." He added glowingly, "It needs to be pondered in the heart, what it means to be the Mother of God." He then asks, "Tell me, was not hers a wondrous soul?"[42]

By Christmas 1530, however, Luther emphasized the separation of Jesus not only from his mother but from the rest of creation. Cunneen notes that Luther seemed to be convinced that the more Mary loses, the more Christ wins. Luther concluded that human beings have in Jesus a greater honor than Mary: "He is more mine than Mary's, for he is born for me, for the angel said, 'To you is born the Savior.'" Luther added, "Our papists . . . retain the mass, the invocation of saints. . . . They sing the words of the angel, hold their triple masses and play their organs. . . . The text says that he is the Savior. And if this is true, then let everything else go."[43] Cunneen believes, "By his diminution of Mary, Luther perhaps unconsciously denied the feminine dimension of the sacred and eliminated the one symbol that had for many embodied it."[44]

### *Calvin and His Followers on Mary*

Primary among the second generation of reformers, John Calvin (1509–64), was further removed from medieval piety. He emphasized Mary's humility but stressed that "it was of more importance to be reborn by the Spirit of Christ than to conceive the flesh of Christ in her womb, to have Christ living in herself spiritually than to nurse him at the breast."[45] Calvin used the biblical image of Mary to exemplify right living. He was not adverse to praising Mary if it was done in the right way. However, he believed that one must *never* invoke her.

Calvin adamantly attacked Catholic practices of devotion to Mary. He preached, "The papists attribute to her enough titles, but in this they blaspheme against God and take from him with their sacrileges what was proper and special to Him. They will call the Virgin Mary 'Queen of heaven,' 'Star to guide poor errant folk,' 'Salvation of the world,'. . . God appropriates nothing in Holy Scripture that is not transposed to Mary by the papists . . . these poor baboons who are no more than vermin crawling on the earth . . . poor earthworms [with their] diabolical audacity."[46] In short, Calvin believed that Catholics had made Mary into an idol. Foundational for all of Calvin's theology is the conviction that all doctrine must be grounded in scripture. He believed that theologians should not speculate beyond that. Liturgy as well as hymns should only include what is actually contained in the scriptural text. From Calvin's perspective, Catholic devotionalism had exceeded all limits.

The first reformers all praised Mary while damning the Catholic devotions that invoked her aid, but their successors did not continue this appreciation of her except for an occasional Christmas sermon. There is only one reference to Mary in the Lutheran *Heidelberg Catechism* (1563). Although the Reformed Churches affirm her role as stated in the creeds in the *Second Helvetic Confession* (1566), Tavard claims that "Mary appears in negative perspective implicitly when the confession bans the use of holy pictures and explicitly when it condemns 'adoration, worship and invocation of saints.'"[47]

A new iconoclasm developed in many Protestant churches, particularly in the Reformed tradition. The rationale was that visual images distracted members of the congregation from hearing the word of God. In the aftermath of the Peasants War (1524–26) and other movements of civil unrest, figures of Jesus and Mary wearing crowns suggested a political statement supporting royalty. Ornate altars became bare communion tables. The pulpit for preaching the word became central. Screens and ornaments were removed. Luther became disgusted with bells, incense, and vestments. More radical reformers banished liturgical chant and ritual.[48] The most extreme Protestant reaction to church decoration and statuary occurred during the era of Cromwell and the Puritan Revolution in England (1649–60). Statues were beheaded and destroyed. Mary's role as queen was no longer considered only theological but took on political and socioeconomic overtones. Mary was soon neglected in Protestant life and thought.

## MARY IN THE CATHOLIC REFORM

Many movements for reform emerged in the Catholic Church in the fifteenth and sixteenth centuries. Groups such as the Beguines and the Brethren of the Common Life were among those who made efforts to countermand the extravagance and corruption in many sectors of church life.

### *Erasmus and Mary*

Humanists such as Erasmus (1466/69–1536) departed from Scholastic theology, which had dominated the universities in the medieval period, and encouraged broader scholarship and a rebirth of classical wisdom. Erasmus was influenced in his younger years by the Brethren of the Common Life and the *Devotio Moderna* (modern devotion). He became an Augustinian Canon in 1487 and was ordained a priest in 1492. As a biblical scholar, Erasmus translated the New Testament from the original Greek and had considerable influence on theological studies. One example that relates to Mary is that instead of translating the Greek word *kecharitomene* in Luke 1:28 as "full of grace," he preferred an expression closer to the Greek original, "being in favor." He was attacked for changing the traditional meaning of this phrase and accused of being in league with the reformers. Although critical of the Catholic Church, particularly the corruption of that era, he never departed from it.

Erasmus highlighted the need for church reform by composing biting satires. In *Pilgrimage for Devotion* he focused on Mary. One of his characters, a Protestant named Glaucoplutus, supposedly receives a letter written by Mary in which she expresses her gratitude to Martin Luther for discouraging prayers to her; she has become overwhelmed with requests. Graef describes Mary's purported plight as articulated by Erasmus: "For it is always she who is asked as if her Son were still an infant in her arms who did not dare deny her anything for fear she might refuse him her milk."[49]

Mary is exhausted by all the lurid petitions she receives, such as "a young nun casts off her veil and asks the Mother of God to defend the reputation of her virginity which she is about to throw away; a businessman going to Spain entrusts to her the faithfulness of his concubine; soldiers planning a robbery ask for a fat haul, a prostitute for rich customers, and priests for a lucrative benefice."[50] Mary commends Luther for reducing the number of petitions she receives but cautions him to reconsider her role in the life of her Son. Although Erasmus in his satires attacked extravagant external devotion to Mary, he clearly believed that Mary was inextricably linked to the worship of Christ and had an important role in the church.

### *Guadalupe*

Mexico also became a center for devotion to Mary. In 1531 a simple Aztec peasant, Juan Diego, who had recently converted to Christianity, had the extraordinary experience of meeting a beautiful woman on the hill of Tepeyac. She gave him instructions "to go the City of Mexico, to the palace of the Bishop who lives there to whom you will say that I have sent you, and that it is my pleasure that he build me a church in this place."[51] Despite variations on the story, it seems clear that it was a startled Spanish bishop of Mexico, Juan de Zumarraga, who first viewed the image of Our Lady of Guadalupe on Juan Diego's cloak: Mary, depicted as an Aztec maiden. The Aztec maiden and the Jewish maiden may have had more similarities than most of the regal portraits of the Renaissance.

### *Ignatius of Loyola*

Mary was an inspiration for efforts at reform in the Catholic Church. One of the religious orders that exemplified this was the Society of Jesus. The story of Ignatius of Loyola (1491–1556) and his conversion to a life of dedication to Christ is well known. He was a vain and arrogant soldier, whose leg was injured irreparably at the battle of Pamplona in 1521, warranting his recuperation at the castle of Loyola. During his time of convalescence he read the lives of Christ and the saints, which effected a transformation that caused him to change his life radically.

In February 1522, Ignatius visited the shrine of the Black Virgin at the Benedictine Monastery at Montserrat. There he began seriously a spiritual journey that would have implications for many future generations. As was the typical custom of knights about to commit themselves to the code of chivalry, on March 24, the vigil of the feast of the Annunciation, Ignatius took off his fine clothing and replaced them with pilgrim garb. He laid his sword at the foot of our Lady's statue and spent the whole night there in prayer, dedicating himself to serve Christ the King under Mary's protection.[52]

Following his spiritual experience at Montserrat, Ignatius spent eleven months at Manressa (March 1522–February 1523), where he examined his life and deepened his spirituality. Mary inextricably became part of his reflections and illuminations.[53] After years of study, the men who gathered around Ignatius in Paris made their first vows in the small chapel of our Lady in Montmartre in 1534. Hoping to go on pilgrimage to Jerusalem, the group rendezvoused three years later in Venice and prepared for holy orders. Ignatius and six of his confreres were ordained to the priesthood there on June 24, 1537.

On the way to Rome in late 1537 Ignatius's devotion to Mary was once again evident. After "praying Our Lady to deign to place him with her Son . . . he was at prayer in a church and experienced such a change in his soul and saw so clearly that God the father placed him with Christ his Son that he would not dare to doubt it."[54] This vision at La Storta was written indelibly in Ignatius's heart. For reform groups within the Catholic Church, belief in and devotion to Mary became strengthened as her status seemed to be questioned or neglected within Protestantism.

Although Ignatius and Luther differed in their attitudes to authority and on practices regarding Mary, both relied strongly on the scriptures, as is apparent in both the writings of Luther and the *Spiritual Exercises* of Saint Ignatius. The latter encouraged the use of visual imagery and the imagination. For example, in the meditation on the incarnation, retreatants are invited to visualize Mary in her consent to God that makes possible the birth of Jesus. This method of actively engaging one's imagination with a reading of scripture helps to provide for a more real and human image of Mary as a Jewish girl rather than as the crowned queen of the universe.

### *The Council of Trent (1545–63) and After*

After several aborted efforts, the Council of Trent was finally convoked in 1545 and met in three sessions continuing to 1563. The council's efforts were directed on two tracks: disciplinary and doctrinal. The only time Mary is mentioned at Trent is in the *Decree on Original Sin,* approved on June 17, 1546. It explicitly excludes her and states: "Nevertheless this same holy council declares that it is not its intention to include in this decree on original sin the blessed and immaculate Virgin Mary, Mother of God; but it declares that the constitutions of Pope Sixtus IV of happy memory are to be observed."[55] Sixtus, the Franciscan Francesco della Rovere, had approved the feast of the Immaculate Conception in 1476 with its own mass and office. Marian devotions were defended during the Council of Trent by Jesuit theologians Peter Canisius, Francisco Suarez, and Robert Bellarmine.[56]

Catholics became defensive about the doctrines and practices that the Protestants denounced. Protestants outlawed the Rosary. In turn, Pope Pius V recognized it and advanced the devotion further by instituting the feast of the Holy Rosary, commemorating the naval victory over the Turks at Lepanto (October 7, 1571), which he attributed to Mary's intercession due to the many Rosaries recited that day. The Jesuit Peter Canisius preached that devotion to Mary would help to repair the damage in the Catholic Church due to the Reformation. Marian sodalities under the direction of the Jesuits flourished in Catholic urban centers in Europe.[57] In the period after Trent, the divide widened between Catholics and Protestants regarding the role of Mary in their respective churches, but no reference was made to a Jewish Mary.

## CONCLUSION

Mary emerged as an iconic figure in the first fifteen hundred years of Christianity partly as a result of legends about her that filled the gaps left by the Gospels. As the church became more Western, the Jewish maiden of the Gospels came to be replaced by the idealized empress. Christological disputes at the ecumenical councils of the fourth and fifth centuries required that Mary's role in salvation be more clearly defined. At Ephesus she was affirmed as Theotokos, which gave license to those who wanted to exalt her further.

Although devotion to Mary seems to have evolved prior to Ephesus, this council's affirmation allowed for the explosion of Marian devotion in the Middle Ages and thereafter.

As the people became more removed from the liturgy, and as monastic communities of women and men developed that had an ardent devotion to her, Mary's approachability became a focus for those of every age and class. Despite her simple Jewish roots, Mary took on the figure of the most exalted woman of each era. Although Mary belongs to every time and place, her historical person cannot be denied. In the post-Renaissance period she was ignored by the Reformers and exalted by the Roman Catholics and Eastern Orthodox Christians. There was little concern for her Jewish roots until the late twentieth century.

# Chapter 3

# Mary in History, Doctrine, and Devotionalism

## From the Enlightenment Through Vatican II

A Presbyterian woman minister friend and I were discussing the role of Mary in our respective churches. At one point with a sparkle in her eye she responded, "Well, at least you Catholics have *one* woman who is important in your church!" It has always mystified me that until recently Mary appears to have been neglected by Protestants except for her presence on Christmas cards. If Jesus is so central to our understanding of Christianity, why isn't there a greater appreciation of his mother in most Protestant churches? On the other hand, many Protestants feel that Catholics have "divinized" Mary; it seems to them as if she has become more important than Jesus. Catholic scripture scholar Raymond Brown described the situation as "Protestant minimalism and Catholic exaggeration in Mariology."[1]

### MARY IN AN AGE OF ABSOLUTISM

How did Europe move from a culture that had been predominantly Catholic to one that also accepted a variety of Protestant churches? How did it adapt to a world where the emperor was no longer the preeminent power, but where kings and queens ruled until the cataclysm of the French Revolution in 1789? In the aftermath of the Reformation, tensions between the churches and the states exploded. The culmination of these conflicts in the Thirty Years' War (1618–48) resulted in the Peace of Westphalia. Sometimes described as the end of the wars of religion, it allowed for the existence of Lutheran and Calvinist churches as well as Catholicism. In that era, however, people could not conceive of any political/ecclesiastical structure other than a nation-state with an established church. It mandated, therefore, that "the religion of the prince is the religion of the people" *(cuius regio eius religio)*. If one wanted to worship as a Catholic or a Lutheran or a Calvinist, one had to find a country or province where the ruler was of that faith. Religious pluralism was still far away.

Catholics continued to look to Christ as king and Mary as queen. Pilgrimages to Marian shrines were advertised. Wilhelm von Gumppenberg (1609–75) published the *Atlas Marianus* in the 1650s. In several volumes it offered brief histories of over a thousand shrines in Mary's honor around the Catholic world.[2] Catholics were encouraged by their clergy and their rulers to join these pilgrimages.

The Catholic dynasties of Europe often chose Mary as their patroness. Maximilian I, who ruled Bavaria from 1598 to 1651, exemplified this commitment. He "not only developed a rich personal devotion to Mary, consecrating himself to her with a vow written in his own blood, but also adopted the Virgin as the chief emblem of his considerable dynastic and confessional ambitions. . . . In 1601, the duke required all Bavarians by law to carry rosary beads constantly."[3]

Devotion to Mary was enhanced by efforts to visualize her physical beauty. José de Jesus Maria (1562–1629), a Discalced Carmelite in Spain, claimed that no other mortal body was as beautiful as hers. "Following Epiphanius . . . he described the Virgin as of average or above-average height, perfectly proportioned, blonde, green-eyed, with curved 'decently dark' eyebrows, a long nose, soft, red lips, white, even teeth, and a face neither round nor sharp, but quite long." Despite his own Mediterranean background, he claimed that "her complexion was without blemish; her face was pale pink, the 'most perfect colour for the human body . . . because it derives from the balance of the four humours.'"[4] Images of a blond, blue- or green-eyed Mary, rather than the Palestinian maiden, clearly predate the nineteenth century.

In the seventeenth-century France was divided between the influence of Jansenism (a kind of Catholic Calvinism that demanded moral rigorism) and the opulent excesses of the Bourbon monarchy flourishing at Versailles. The French School of Spirituality that developed with Cardinal Pierre de Bérulle (1575–1629), Jean-Jacques Olier (1608–57), and Jean Eudes (1601–80) provided new impetus for extravagant devotion to Mary. One of the more radical approaches to Marian devotion was espoused by Louis Grignon de Montfort (1673–1716), author of *True Devotion to the Blessed Virgin*, who promoted the metaphor of slavery as a description of absolute surrender to Mary. He believed one could not approach Christ on one's own; to reach Christ one had to go through Mary.[5]

In the eighteenth century a new focus developed on "the spiritual motherhood of Mary and on her egregious purity, as underscored in the doctrine of her immaculate conception."[6] This laid the groundwork for both the doctrinal and devotional explosion of Marian devotion in the nineteenth and twentieth centuries. With the exception of some Anglicans, those professing Protestant orthodoxy or Pietism were uninterested in Mary.

## THE ENLIGHTENMENT

Negative reaction began to develop among many Christians to both the Baroque spirituality and the arid orthodoxy of the period. That response was due, in part, to an excitement regarding advances in science, the rule of reason, and the so-called inevitability of progress, particularly among many intellectuals. This spirit of the Enlightenment contributed to the rise of deism, with its disregard for revelation, and its image of God as "the Watchmaker," who wound up the universe and sat passively by while it moved along. These rationalists often viewed religion as superstition because it could not be proved by science or reason.

The philosophers of the day, including Rousseau, Locke, and Montesquieu, envisioned a new world. Carl Becker, in his slim volume *The Heavenly City of the Eighteenth Century Philosophers,* describes the *philsophes* gathered in their salons, dressed decorously, debating theoretically the momentous questions of the age: liberty, equality, religious toleration, and a government by the people. He claims, however, that they failed to see the practical implications of their philosophical debates. They never discussed these issues in front of the servants![7]

Skepticism infiltrated religion in this era—even Catholic devotion to Mary. Some Marian feasts were eliminated from the liturgical calendar. Marian devotions were marginal except in Spain and Italy, where the efforts of Alphonsus Ligouri (1696–1787) and the Redemptorists promoted Mary as the mother of mercy.[8] She became even more invisible in Protestant circles during the Enlightenment.

## DISPARAGING MARY: THE FRENCH REVOLUTION AND NAPOLEON

Because of the alliance between throne and altar, religion, as well as the royalty, became a target when the French Revolution (1789–99) erupted. In addition to beheading the king and queen, one of the goals of the Reign of Terror (c. 1792–95) was to destroy Catholicism. Church property was confiscated. Nuns and priests were sent to the guillotine.

A Goddess of Reason and other figures were established to replace Mary and the saints. Images of Mary were identified as symbols of the privileged aristocracy and were broken or burned. An allegorical figure named Marianne, who personified the French Republic, was created. Revolutionaries chanted: "Virgin of liberty, deliver us from kings and popes! Virgin of equality, deliver us from aristocrats." This ridicule of Mary was most evident in a parody of the *Ave Maria*: "Hail Marianne, full of strength, the People are with thee. Blessed is the fruit of thy womb, the Republic."[9]

After Napoleon attained power, however, he believed that Christianity could be the "glue" for his empire. He needed the church to affirm his authority, so he negotiated a concordat with the papacy in 1801. Three years later he invited Pope Pius VII to preside over his coronation as emperor to give credibility to himself and to his empire. Napoleon would go only so far in acknowledging Catholicism, however. He took the crown from the pope and crowned himself!

## MARY IN THE NINETEENTH CENTURY: DEVOTION AND DOCTRINE

With the fall of Napoleon in 1815, not only were kings, queens, and the pope restored to their thrones, but Jesus and Mary were as well. The effort to return to pre–French Revolutionary Europe began. The Vicomte de Chateaubriand's brilliant defense of Catholicism, *The Genius of Christianity* (1802), became popular. A new emphasis on authority emerged, such as the work of Count Joseph De Maistre on the pope. The trend toward centralization gained momentum. Romanticism flourished and the Middle Ages were idealized. There was a devotional renewal in Europe; some referred to it as a "second spring." Missionary work took on new life.

### *Mary on the American Frontier*

In the United States, where multiple ethnic groups migrated between 1820 and 1924, devotion to Mary manifested itself in Italian festas, Irish novenas, French Christmas crèches, and German hymns. Together with devotional renewal and a missionary thrust, a new sense of excitement evolved in the church in America.

Religious orders were restored or refounded (for example, the Jesuits and the Holy Ghost Congregation), and new congregations, many of them devoted to Mary, sprang up on both sides of the Atlantic Ocean. Examples of this fervor in the United States include the Sisters of Charity of the Blessed Virgin Mary, founded by five women who came from Ireland to Philadelphia in 1833 and then accepted the invitation of Bishop Mathias Loras to settle on the frontier in Dubuque, Iowa, in 1843, to teach Indians and immigrants; the Dominican Sisters of the Most Holy Rosary founded in Sinsinawa, Wisconsin in 1847; and the School Sisters of Notre Dame, who established their American foundation in Milwaukee, Wisconsin, in 1849.

For some Catholics, Mary became associated with a kind of frontier imagery, and with virgin territory. Mary had heard a special call from God at the annunciation to move beyond the ordinary boundaries of life, and she accepted the challenge. Did Mary in some way symbolize a Catholic counterpart to the Protestant version of "the errand into the wilderness" and the mission to establish "God's New Israel"? The response of many Catholic men and women who attempted, under the banner of Mary, to move Catholicism to the West during that era presents Mary as a model for this frontier orientation, even though this attempt was coupled, in some instances, with a desire to escape the Nativist riots in the East.[10]

### American Protestants and Mary

Elizabeth Cady Stanton was among the Protestant women activists in the United States who acknowledged that certain passages of the Bible were oppressive for women. She initiated the project, and chaired the committee of women scholars, that launched *The Women's Bible*. Its purpose was to revise passages referring to women or excluding women in the scriptures. It was eventually published in 1898. Stanton was conscious of the fact that women in Catholicism had a role model in Mary; in addition, congregations of women religious in the church provided a feminine dimension she saw as lacking in Protestantism. In her 1885 essay "Has Christianity Benefitted Women?" Stanton stated that the Catholic Church, "in its holy sisterhoods" and "in its worship of the Virgin Mary, Mother of Jesus has preserved some recognition of the feminine element in its religion; but from Protestantism it is wholly eliminated."[11]

Margaret Fuller, also a Protestant woman reformer, saw devotion to Mary as "potentially beneficial to women's social position."[12] She regretted that stories about Mary and works of art featuring her no longer appeared in Protestant churches and homes. Educated women in both England and America began to believe that a social system which idealized motherhood was often one that also victimized women.

Best known among the reformers was Harriet Beecher Stowe, author of *Uncle Tom's Cabin.* With the proceeds of her popular book this daughter and wife of Calvinist ministers traveled to Europe as an "art-pilgrim." She "longed for visual art that affirmed the power and goodness of women." She particularly appreciated the Sistine Madonna of Raphael. She loved "its historical accuracy in representing the dark-eyed Jewish maiden" and was enamored of "the mysterious resemblance and sympathy between the face of the mother and the divine child." She admitted that it affected her deeply and saw in it a depiction of the "idea of sorrow in heaven—sorrow for the lost, in the heart of God himself—which forms the most sacred mystery of Christianity."[13]

In some areas Protestant disdain for Mary was apparently alive and well. In 1865, Martin John Spalding, archbishop of Baltimore, in an article in *Ave Maria* magazine, described "the cold and sneering progressive and evangelical Protestantism which almost shudders at the mention of Mary." Later, he stated, "Had her prophetic vision rested, for even one moment, on the cold and dreary land of Protestantism, it would have been saddened, and she would have turned away her Seer's eye with a shudder! But her mother's instinctive love prevented her from dwelling on this chilling spectacle."[14] Spalding, who was born in Kentucky, and who served as bishop of Louisville from 1850 to 1864, no doubt had negative experiences of evangelical Protestants in the South regarding Mary. Until the ecumenical movement of the twentieth century, Mary was not a likely subject for dialogue between Catholics and Protestants, much less with Jews.

### *Poetic Appreciation of Mary in Nineteenth-Century England*

Amid some of the pious and sentimental verse of the nineteenth century, there appeared the almost mystical poetry of Gerard Manley Hopkins, SJ (1844–89). An Anglican who entered the Catholic Church and became a Jesuit priest and poet, his poem "The Blessed Mother Compared to the Air We Breathe" is an exquisite portrayal of Mary as incarnating Christ anew:

> Of her flesh he took flesh:
> He does take fresh and fresh,
> Though much the mystery how,
> Not flesh but spirit now
> And makes, O marvelous!
> New Nazareths in us.[15]

Hopkins's appreciation of nature aligned him with the Romantic poets but, in Cunneen's words, "drawing on the tradition as he found it, one in which Mary had long stood as a visible sign of the work of the Spirit, Hopkins reimagined Mary in a way that showed her at home in a united, scientifically conceived universe."[16] He writes of the incarnation as a continuing reality and of ourselves as part of the body of Christ.

John Henry Cardinal Newman (1801–90), also a convert from Anglicanism, wrote and spoke poetically about Mary, influenced by his research into the church fathers. His 1849 sermon "The Glories of Mary for the Sake of her Son" described her as a symbol of the church and as the "daughter of Eve unfallen." He preached, "She raised herself aloft silently, and has grown into her place in the Church by a tranquil influence as a natural process. She was as some fair tree, stretching forth her fruitful branches and her fragrant leaves, and overshadowing the territory of the saints."[17] Both Hopkins and Newman evoked simple images of Mary, unlike her royal images of earlier years.

### *Marian Apparitions*

The church has always proceeded with caution regarding alleged apparitions. Edward Schillebeeckx, OP, in his volume *Mary, Mother of the Redemption,* states: "The Church's approbation of an apparition or private revelation is . . . never an infallible proof of its historical truth and authenticity." He adds, "It is merely an official confirmation of the fact that sufficient evidence has emerged from the investigation to enable us to be cautiously certain in our acceptance of the divine authenticity of the apparition on rational grounds."[18] Even if the church has approved of an apparition, it does not belong to the deposit of faith, that is, doctrines to which a Catholic would be expected to give assent. A Catholic, while respecting the authority of the church, is not required to accept the apparition.

Since the eighteenth century the church has generally relied on local bishops to give formal approval, if warranted, to such phenomena. The bishop, after investigation, does not assert as a fact that the apparition has taken place; he only states that it is not contrary to the faith, and therefore, devotion is not prohibited in the place at which the apparition is alleged to have occurred. According to Schillebeeckx, "All the Church declares is that, in her judgment, they are in no way contrary to faith and morals, and that there are sufficient indications for their pious and cautious approval by human faith."[19]

Perhaps the most dramatic events concerning Mary were her purported apparitions during the nineteenth and early twentieth centuries, mostly to peasant women and children. On December 17, 1830, St. Catherine Labouré claimed to have had a vision of the Immaculate Conception. Surrounding this vision were the words, "O Mary, conceived without sin, pray for us who have recourse to thee." Catherine was told to request that a medal be struck with this image. Known as the Miraculous Medal, over a million of these medals were distributed throughout the world during Catherine's lifetime, and many miracles were attributed to it.[20]

In 1846, it was reported that Mary appeared to an eleven-year-old boy, Maximim Giraud, and a fourteen-year-old girl, Melanie Calvat, at La Salette in the French Alps. Mary was weeping over sins of blasphemy and the neglect of attendance at Mass and warned against famine and catastrophe. The children were said to have received secrets, which they sent to the pope.

One of the most widely known of the apparitions of Mary are those that are said to have occurred at Lourdes in France in 1858 to a fourteen-year-old peasant girl, Bernadette Soubirous. The lady in the vision asked Bernadette to drink from an invisible fountain. When she scratched the earth, water welled up. It has been a source of healing for generations. On March 25, 1858, Bernadette asked the lady in the vision who she was and received the answer, "I am the Immaculate Conception." These appearances at Lourdes occurred after the definition of the doctrine of the Immaculate Conception by Pope Pius IX in 1854; they seemed to be a confirmation of the dogma that had recently been pronounced.

In 1917, Mary reportedly appeared to three children at Fatima in Portugal. She asked the children to pray for peace and shared some so-called secrets with them. It was not until after World War II, during the anti-Communist era, that this devotion to Mary began to flourish. Although there are other Marian apparitions of note—and some that have proven to be hoaxes—the most recent one to have attracted enormous crowds occurred in 1981 in Medjugorje, Bosnia, in the former Yugoslavia. Again, Mary is said to have requested that people repent, pray, and live good lives.

One theory for apparitions is that when ordinary people perceive that the church has become too intellectual, they seek a more emotional connection with their faith. According to John Shinners, a cultural historian, "What theologians ignore, ordinary people will provide: Lourdes and Fatimas and even Medjugorjes will probably always be with us."[21] The images of the lady in the apparitions have mostly been of a European woman, beautiful, usually of simple status. Few, if any, of these apparitions have looked like a simple Jewish peasant woman. Also noteworthy is that recipients of these visions have normally been poor, humble children who have communicated Mary's concern for ordinary people. It is perhaps no coincidence that the rise of industrialism, with its de-humanizing effects on laborers, might also explain Mary's appearances to those in the working class.

### *Defining the Immaculate Conception*

Ironically, in order to understand what led to the definition of the Immaculate Conception, one must look at the political context of the church and the states in the aftermath of the French Revolution and the Napoleonic era. The goal of both the church and the states was the restoration—a return of Europe to pre-revolutionary status. What most of the leaders failed to realize was people under the age of twenty-five had little or no recollection of what life had been like prior to the revolution! They were ripe, therefore, for the revolutions of 1830 and 1848.

Liberty, democracy, equality, separation of church and state, freedom of speech, freedom of the press, and freedom of religion were all perceived as threats to the church. The near destruction of the church during the French Revolution had confirmed the conviction that a union of church and state, with the Catholic Church as the one true church, was the only ecclesiastical/political structure that would allow the church to survive. It was clear, as riots and revolutions continued to occur from 1815 to 1871, that stability had not been restored.

Pope Gregory XVI, envisioning an ongoing struggle between the church and the modern world, promulgated the encyclical *Mirari Vos* (1832), in which he condemned separation of church and state, freedom of the press, and freedom of religion. Many Catholics believed that the only defense against liberalism was a centralized church. The result was the growth of ultramontanism, which signified going "beyond the mountains"—the Alps—to Rome to find the answers.

The movement for the political unification of Italy (the *risorgimento*) became more menacing to the church as the nineteenth century progressed. The Papal States, a theocracy in the middle of the Italian peninsula, represented the opposite of all that the republicans were striving to accomplish. Pius IX (pope from 1846 to 1878) had initially accepted some liberal ideas when he ascended the papal throne in 1846. However, the revolution of 1848 was shattering for Pius: riots in the streets; the assassination of his confidante and the premier of the Papal States, Pellegrino Rossi; Pius himself a prisoner of the revolution until he escaped into exile. The Republicans flooded into Rome and voted to end the temporal power of the pope, although the struggle continued until 1870.[22] In response to a cry for help by the pope, the French army occupied Rome in 1849. Pio Nono (as he was known, especially in Italy) was returned to his papal throne in 1850.

With its temporal power fading away, the church began to compensate by relying more on its spiritual power. In 1854, Pope Pius IX made a radical move. Although his political power had become increasingly limited, he decided unilaterally to declare a teaching of the church, the doctrine of the Immaculate Conception, to be a solemn dogma of the Catholic Church, allegedly to underscore his authority. Devotion to

Mary under the title Immaculate Conception had been long-standing, despite the theological disputes regarding Mary during the thirteenth century and after. True, Pius IX consulted with bishops from around the world, but he did not call an ecumenical council, as had always been done in the past to solemnly define theological teachings. He reserved the power of definition to himself.

On December 8, 1854, after a splendid papal procession to St. Peter's Basilica, Pius IX promulgated the constitution *Ineffabilis Deus*, proclaiming "the doctrine which holds that the blessed Virgin Mary, at the very first instant of her Conception, by a singular privilege and grace of the omnipotent God, in consideration of the merits of Jesus Christ, the Savior of mankind, was preserved free from all stain of original sin." The definition of the Immaculate Conception was a surprise to Protestants, to the Eastern Orthodox, and even to many Catholics. In addition to formalizing a doctrine about Mary, it had huge ecclesiological implications. In retrospect, some scholars have interpreted Pius's action as a test case for declaring papal infallibility.[23]

### *Papal Infallibility and Mary*

Pius IX was challenged by modern theology, liberal political theories, new scientific understandings, and the disaffection of many workers during the Industrial Revolution who were attracted to socialism. In 1864, following the lead of Gregory XVI in *Mirari Vos,* Pius IX promulgated the *Syllabus of Errors,* an enumeration of the condemnation of errors from some thirty previous papal documents. The concluding statement condemned anyone who believed that "the Roman Pontiff can, and ought, to reconcile himself, and come to terms with progress, liberalism, and modern civilization." This document once again condemned fundamental concepts especially dear to the hearts of people in the United States, such as religious liberty, separation of church and state, and freedom of the press.

Understandably, Protestants in the United States were nervous about these statements, especially with the enormous migration of Catholics to America in the nineteenth century. They feared that as the number of Catholics with a right to vote in the United States increased, the democratic/republican system of government in their nation could be reversed. In Peter D'Agostino's words, "Nativism intensified in the United States as Know-Nothings shuddered at the sight of Celtic arrivals with rosary beads overrunning the Protestant Israel."[24] This migration had huge implications for Catholics who were suffering from Nativism and who were trying to prove that they could be good Americans and still be Catholic. Exuberant devotion to Mary, frequently manifested by the new immigrant groups, only instilled further fear in Protestant hearts.

The high point of ultramontanism was Vatican Council I, which opened on the feast of the Immaculate Conception, December 8, 1869. Many of the bishops present, 80 percent of whom were Italian, thought that a declaration of papal infallibility was "inopportune" and some eighty even absented themselves from the council rather than vote against the statement. Despite the misgivings of many of the members of the council, the motion passed by a vote of 533–2. Three days before the dogma was formally proclaimed, war broke out between long-time enemies France and Prussia. Napoleon III, whose troops had been defending the Papal State, withdrew his army from Rome because of the Prussian challenge. The Italian armies immediately invaded Rome. The pope proclaimed the doctrine of papal infallibility on July 18, 1870, and the members of the council hastily departed.

The pope—now declared infallible—became "the prisoner of the Vatican." A "Law of Guarantees" was passed by the Italian government that "allowed the pope to retain his personal status as a sovereign [including] the use of the Papal palaces, offered him a substantial pension, and abandoned most of the control of the state over the Church in Italy."[25] The pope, however, refused to accept the agreement or to recognize the new regime.

Recourse to Mary to free the pope became part of an ongoing crusade of prayer through the nineteenth and early twentieth centuries. Devotion to Mary, especially under the title Immaculate Conception, seemed to go hand in hand with the infallibility of the pope. As the pope's temporal power was lost, his spiritual power was enhanced. It was not until 1929 that the Lateran Treaty with Mussolini finally established Vatican City as a sovereign state.

## MARY IN THE NEO-THOMISTIC REVIVAL: 1920–1960

New immigration laws in the United States in 1924 militated against the arrival of Catholics (as well as Jews and some Protestants) from southern and Eastern European countries. An unexpected byproduct of this discrimination was that church financial resources which had been devoted to the immigrants were now available to build the Catholic Church in the United States. The vision of a new "Catholic Christendom" in America evolved.[26] Parishes unexpectedly had funds to build new churches and schools. Coupled with this brick-and-mortar phenomenon was the Neo-Thomistic Revival, which emerged in the 1920s. It emphasized "The Thirteenth the Greatest of Centuries," a medieval era when devotion to Mary was at its height.[27] Catholic life flourished with chivalric images, litanies, May crownings, and rosary processions where thousands gathered. The Neo-Thomistic thought of Jacques Maritain and Etienne Gilson, neo-Gothic architecture, Gregorian chant, sodalities in honor of our Lady, guild programs, the liturgical renewal, thriving Catholic schools, the Catholic Worker Movement, and even the often radical radio sermons of Father Charles E. Coughlin gave Catholics in the United States a new sense of identity.

### *Three Significant Movements*

In this period when Mary was portrayed as the perfect woman whom all Catholic girls and women should emulate, three particular movements regarding Mary warrant special consideration.[28] First, the Sodality of Our Lady, a national movement led by Father Daniel A. Lord, SJ, with its magazine *The Queen's Work*, became very influential among high school and college students from the 1930s through the mid-1960s. Father Lord developed the Summer School of Catholic Action (SSCA), at which thousands of high school and college students would assemble for a week in four different locations in the United States to hear inspirational talks; socialize; and build spirit, identity, and a commitment to Catholic values.

Father Lord also composed hymns such as "Mother Beloved" and wrote dramas and musicals with Marian themes that he sometimes directed at various Catholic high schools around the country. His contagious enthusiasm had an enormous impact on Catholic young people and their commitment to Christ as king and Mary as queen. He was especially concerned about the development of morals and attitudes regarding modesty, dress, purity, and the censorship of films, for which he helped to develop the Legion of Decency. Lord was a charismatic leader who cultivated devotion to Mary among young people in the United States. For some young women, however, she appeared to be a loving but unattainable model.

Second, the novena movement exemplified by devotion to the Sorrowful Mother received an enthusiastic response. Dedicated to the Seven Sorrows of Mary, this movement was founded by a Servite priest, James R. Keane, in 1937. Within one year, seventy thousand people were attending thirty-eight services to the Sorrowful Mother in Chicago. The novena moved to other cities and countries and was translated into thirty-five languages, with cumulative attendance estimated at thirty-five million people. It was broadcast on the radio each Friday night for those who could not attend services in church. A pamphlet entitled *Novena Notes* allowed people to continue their reflections at home. During World War II this devotion proved to be a solace for many families.[29] Along with the novena to Our Lady of Perpetual Help—also popular during the Depression and World War II—it was among the most influential devotions in the United States during the pre–Vatican II era.

Third, although the apparitions at Fatima took place in 1917, devotion to Our Lady of Fatima did not evolve into its more elaborate form until the post–World War II period. Endorsed by the papacy, it reached its high point in the 1940s and 1950s because of anxiety over Communist infiltration of the United States, especially during the McCarthy era. As a result of Fatima, prayer and repentance for the conversion of Russia became major themes in Catholic piety during these years.

Many Catholics feared what they understood to be the diabolical dimensions of Communism. According to Thomas Kselman and Steven Avella, "Catholics perceived another battle raging in which Christ and Mary had sided with the United States to fight Satan and his Communist allies . . . The millions who believed in Our Lady of Fatima saw the Cold War on earth as a reflection of a war in heaven."[30] Once again, Mary had become an instrument of the political realm, far removed from her Jewish roots.

### *Reflecting on Mary as "The Reed of God"*

For centuries most writings about Mary were either theological tracts—intellectual discourses that often seemed antiseptic—or sentimental prayers and meditations with an emotional and often exaggerated piety. In both cases the "real" Mary seemed elusive. During the Neo-Thomistic revival, however, an English Catholic lay woman, a social worker named Caryll Houselander, wrote a small volume about Mary entitled *The Reed of God*. In the words of F. J. Sheed, "She wrote the plainest prose, deeply emotional, totally unsentimental, taking us to the depths in Christ and Mary and ourselves."[31]

Houselander made Mary human. In the chapter "Advent" she wrote: "For nine months Christ grew in His Mother's body. By His own will she formed Him from herself, from the simplicity of her daily life. She had nothing to give Him but herself. He asked for nothing else. She gave Him herself."[32] Influenced by the theology of the mystical body of Christ, she presented Mary as a model for each person whose mission it is to bear Christ in the world. She wrote of Mary walking the streets of Nazareth and Jerusalem as a strong and courageous woman of great simplicity. Houselander's writings resonated with Catholics, above all those committed to social justice and the liturgical revival. Women, especially those in Catholic high schools and colleges, meditated on *The Reed of God* and found hope as they searched for Mary as a human person.

### *The Proclamation of the Assumption of Mary*

The declaration of the dogma of the bodily assumption of Mary into heaven contributed even further to the image of the perfect Mary. Pius XII, who became pope in 1939, was an ardent advocate of this doctrine. He was also a zealous foe of atheistic communism. Because of popular enthusiasm regarding Marian devotion, as well as a pervasive fear of communism, defining Mary's assumption was well received by Catholics. Papal authority to make such a declaration was more readily accepted because of the definition of the Immaculate Conception in 1854 and the declaration of papal infallibility in 1870.

Although there was no biblical evidence to support Mary's bodily assumption into heaven, the feast has been celebrated by Christians since the fifth century. It was a major feast for the Greek Orthodox, who had no objection to the definition itself but were exceedingly troubled by the pope's unilateral definition of the Immaculate Conception and the claim of papal infallibility. For the Protestants, it was a setback to the hope for dialogue and unity. In 1950, in the apostolic constitution *Munificentissimus Deus*, Pius XII solemnly proclaimed the dogma of the assumption of Mary.

Richard McBrien suggests that in the aftermath of two world wars and the horrors of the death camps at Auschwitz, defining the belief in the assumption of Mary was an acknowledgment of the dignity of the human person and faith in bodily resurrection.[33] The psychologist Carl Jung surprisingly welcomed the definition and saw it as "the prototype of man's bodily resurrection."[34] Possibly this recognition of the assumption of Mary links her to her ancient Jewish heritage and to the conviction of the Pharisees regarding bodily resurrection. They had proclaimed God's incomparable power by which "at the end of time God will cause the dead to live again."[35] Mary became an exemplar of this belief.

## MARY AND VATICAN II

During the immediate pre–Vatican II period, scholars such as Yves Congar, René Laurentin, Karl Rahner, Edward Schillebeeckx, and Otto Semmelroth shed new light on understanding Mary by placing her in the context of the mystery of Christ and the church. Edward Schillebeeckx, in the second edition of *Mary, Mother of the Redemption* (1955), added a chapter entitled "The Gospel Picture of the Mother of Jesus," in which he draws attention to the Jewish Mary. He later explained that exploring the historical figure of Miriam, the Jewish mother of Jesus, addressed the question: "Is the Madonna of Catholic Mariology the same as the Jewish mother of Jesus?"[36]

In preparation for the Second Vatican Council, which convened hardly more than a decade after the definition of the assumption, and with devotion to Mary increasingly popular, many bishops wanted to continue the "Mariology from above" (an emphasis on Mary's supernatural prerogatives), articulating her titles and her privileges, a practice that had been common both doctrinally and devotionally for centuries. A separate document on Mary was drafted and presented at the first session of the council, but there was no time for it to be considered.

After Session I (October 8–December 8, 1962) many bishops found that their horizons were widened. They became more aware of biblical scholarship and theological insights that had provided new data for their consideration. Theologians such as Rahner, Congar, de Lubac, and Schillebeeckx were now *periti* at the council. A new "Christology from below" (an emphasis on the humanity of Jesus, while not denying his divinity), seemed to warrant a consideration of a "Mariology from below" as well.

At Session II (September 29–December 4, 1963), the draft of a separate document on Mary was brought back unchanged. Some of the bishops, however, who were involved in developing *Lumen Gentium (The Dogmatic Constitution on the Church)*, were convinced that incorporation of statements on Mary in that document was possible. Would that not be more theologically appropriate? George Tavard, a council *peritus*, described the situation as follows: "As soon as the suggestion was made, however, a number of suspicious bishops began to wonder if there was not a dark plot to downgrade the Virgin Mary in piety and possibly in doctrine."[37]

With tempers rising, Pope Paul VI assented to the request of the moderators and presidents to have a vote on this issue. Following a heated debate, the council fathers decided by a very narrow margin (1,114 to 1,074) to reject the first schema on Mary and to draft a new text for presentation at the next session. This significant decision eventually resulted in the decision to include a final chapter on Mary in *Lumen Gentium*. It created a highly emotional atmosphere that continued to affect the council throughout its later sessions.

The approach and tone of the statement on Mary changed considerably. *Lumen Gentium* asserts: "She is endowed with the high office and dignity of being the Mother of the Son of God, by which account she is also the beloved daughter of the Father and the temple of the Holy Spirit." However, because she belongs to "the offspring of Adam she is one with all those who are to be saved" (no. 53). Like us, Mary is among the redeemed. Anthony J. Tambasco notes that "the final text of the Council kept only fourteen of the one hundred and seventeen papal quotations of the original draft and greatly increased the biblical references."[38] Quotations from scripture and the fathers of the church substantially exceed the notes on papal decrees and encyclicals in *Lumen Gentium*.

Even the title of the chapter caused controversy. Some wanted "Mary, Mother of the Church" to be part of its heading. Others disagreed because they were convinced that wording would depict Mary as "above" and "outside" the church and should be avoided. Chapter VIII was finally titled "The Role of the Blessed Virgin Mary, Mother of God, in the Mystery of Christ and the Church."

Pope Paul VI, however, in the closing ceremony of the second session on November 21, 1963—perhaps to assuage the anger of the minority—stated, "To the glory of the Blessed Virgin and for our consolation we declare the Most Holy Mary is Mother of the Church." George Tavard commented, "Undoubtedly some among the *periti*, and possibly among the bishops, considered this introduction of a new Marian title highhanded in form, for it was widely held that the council had implicitly rejected the title."[39]

Schillebeeckx concurred. "Paul VI felt called on to satisfy the minority position in the council . . . by making Mary 'mother of the church' on his own personal, and thus non-conciliar authority."[40] Throughout the council there continued to be the "minimalists" and the "maximalists" regarding Mary. Emotions spilled over into the post–Vatican II church when traditional Marian devotionalism appeared to evaporate. However, a new appreciation of Mary eventually emerged in succeeding decades as historical studies, new scripture scholarship, theological insights, feminist theology, and interfaith dialogue intermingled to offer new opportunities for insights into the Jewish Mary.

## CONCLUSION

In Part I we examined how various images and ideas of Mary were constructed over the centuries: Mary—the icon of the empress; Mary—"the Lady" of the medieval period;

Mary—the Renaissance Madonna; Mary—the absolutist queen; Mary—the Nordic virgin. All of these are non-Jewish figures who evoked love and devotion from people of particular ages and places. Sometimes Mary became a political or ecclesiastical "football" used for individual or collective gain. Theological controversy has surrounded her through the ages and continues to this day. All of these images and understandings are part of our heritage. Yet, we keep searching for the little Jewish girl who accepted the invitation to be the mother of Jesus.

Now we will move forward toward recovering and reconstructing the Jewish Mary. Multidisciplinary approaches are available today due to advances in scripture studies and archeological discoveries. We will explore how research on the Jewish Jesus might help us to find the Jewish Mary. Lastly, we will explore how Hebrew prayer that was—or might well have been—extant in the first century can help us probe Mary's own prayer life, and possibly our own.

# PART II

# DISCOVERING THE JEWISH MARY

# Chapter 4

## Will the Real Mary Please Stand Up?

### Multidisciplinary Approaches to a New Question

After the kosher luncheon and the business items were completed at a regular Friday clergy meeting of the North Phoenix Corporate Ministry, which was being held that month at Beth El Congregation, we began our theological reflection session. We had agreed to discuss the role of Mary, the mother of Jesus, in our religious traditions. Suddenly, Catholic and Protestant clergy were arguing vociferously over Mary's place in Christian history. Finally, one of the rabbis interjected: "I don't know what you are all upset about! She was a nice little Jewish girl!"

For centuries scholars have theologized about, defined, and categorized Mary, usually according to the culture of the time. Artists sculpted and painted what they perceived to be her image. She was a major subject for an untold number of poets and musicians. Until Vatican II she was a centerpiece for devotion in the Catholic Church. After the council, however, many Catholics believed that Mary was neglected and even downgraded. The reality, however, was that study and reflection on Mary moved, for the most part, from a doctrinal and devotional emphasis to a historical one. Who was this mother of Jesus who lived, worked, prayed, and played in first-century Galilee?

In the late 1960s and early 1970s, there was a popular phrase: Will the real Jesus please stand up? There was excitement about relating Jesus to recent archeological discoveries in the Middle East, the world of the Dead Sea Scrolls, emerging socioeconomic studies on the first century, and new scripture scholarship. In the 1970s some of that scholarship began to be applied to Mary, albeit in lesser fashion. The question became: Will the real *Mary* please stand up? Scholars searching for the "real" Mary began to reexamine through a critical biblical-historical lens assumptions that contributed to the pre–Vatican II idealized Mary. From this de-constructive phase of Marian studies, a new bibliography emerged.

Five major threads in the development of Marian thought emerged in the post–Vatican II era: (1) historical studies; (2) biblical scholarship; (3) new theological interpretations; (4) feminist theology; and (5) spirituality and culture. I find myself drowning in books about Mary in all of these areas written from the middle of the twentieth century to the present! I have lined them up according to date of publication. That, itself, is instructive. The number of books increases with each decade. One realizes that approaches to studying Mary became more integrated as the twentieth century progressed. Authors no longer studied Mary from only a theological perspective. They increasingly drew on the work of colleagues across disciplinary lines. Although time and space allow for reflection on the works of only a few authors in each category to illustrate this development, what becomes clear is that a dialogue across the disciplines enriches scholarly work and allows us to develop a holistic view. The fruits of scholarship have become increasingly integrated as we search for the Jewish Mary in the twenty-first century.

## MARY IN HISTORICAL STUDIES

German scholar Hilda Graef was one of the first lay women to explore in depth and scholarly detail the history of Marian thought in doctrine and devotion from the first century to

Vatican II. Originally published in German, her two-volume study *Mary: A History of Doctrine and Devotion* provided the historical and theological background against which new approaches to Mary could be understood in the post–Vatican II period. She used French and German sources, wrote with openness and honesty, and admitted to the controversies and sometimes-exaggerated devotions to Mary over the centuries.[1]

Graef's work was revised and updated into a single volume in 2009. Thomas A. Thompson, SM, director of the Marian Library at the University of Dayton, Ohio, wrote a substantive final chapter entitled "Vatican II and Beyond." Lawrence S. Cunningham describes the volume as having "near classic status." Richard McBrien, who also affirms the volume as a classic, commends it for its "clarity, comprehensiveness and balance."[2] By placing Marian doctrine and devotion in historical context, Graef liberated the study of Mary from isolated interpretations.

Rosemary Radford Ruether's excellent work as a historical theologian of the patristic period laid the groundwork for exploring anew the role of women in the early church. In 1974 she edited *Religion and Sexism: Images of Women in the Jewish and Christian Traditions*. In her chapter, entitled "Misogynism and Virginal Feminism in the Fathers of the Church," she opened the eyes of many women to the radically dualistic teachings of revered saints and scholars whose negative attitudes toward women in the early centuries affected the church for years to come.[3] Their writings influenced the formulation of teachings on the virginity of Mary and on sexuality in general.

In a world with a dualistic perspective, and some such communities exist even today, the spiritual and the material are in opposition. Men are identified with the higher elements of life: the spiritual, the intellectual, light, and good. Women are identified with the material (the body as opposed to the spirit), emotion and will (as opposed to intellect), darkness (as opposed to light), and evil (as opposed to good). In the patristic era the only way a woman could rise above her carnal condition was to commit to a life of virginity.

Statements of Augustine, Tertullian, Jerome, and even Clement of Alexandria regarding women shocked many readers. Because Jesus had to be removed from any connection to the material/physical sphere of life, especially sexual intercourse, the perpetual virginity of Mary seemed essential to many of these theologians. Their further conclusion was that a life of virginity was a higher calling. These ideas became foundational for understanding Mary as the ethereal figure she became in the patristic period.

Ruether's slim book *Mary: The Feminine Face of the Church,* published as part of a feminist ecumenical dialogue, presented a broad historical overview of Mary.[4] Attentive to feminist issues, Ruether discusses, among other topics, Mary in the context of goddess worship, patristic and medieval approaches to Mary, the divergence of views on Mary since the Reformation, and Mary and the humanization of the church. The book was widely accepted, particularly for women's dialogue groups, in Protestant and Catholic churches. Ruether's volumes, both scholarly and popular, provided much-needed historical background and laid the groundwork for understanding Mary in ecumenical perspective and in feminist studies.

In *Sexism and God-Talk* Ruether approached Mariology in the context of liberation theology. She states: "Lucan Mariology suggests a real co-creatorship between God and humanity, or, in this case, woman. . . . Only through [Mary's] free human responsiveness to God is God enabled to become the transformer of history." Ruether concludes: "Mary's faith makes possible God's entrance into history. . . . God enters history in the person of Christ to effect a liberating revolution in human relationships." In turn, the liberating action of God in history also liberates Mary, who personifies the oppressed and subjugated persons of whom she is a part. Ruether argues, "It is women especially who represent the Church by calling others out of bondage into freedom."[5] In her writings on Mary, Ruether integrates historical theology with philosophy, feminism, and liberation theology, with attention to biblical studies.

For Marina Warner in *Alone of All Her Sex* Mary "represents a central theme in the history of western attitudes to women. She is one of the few female figures to have attained the status of myth." Warner describes Mary in art, literature, and inspiring legends, and concludes that the "myth" about Mary, which grew up in conjunction with her status as "immaculate," and "above all creatures," is responsible for the sense of inferiority inculcated in women which has been so common over the centuries. She states: "In the very celebration of the perfect human woman, both humanity and women were subtly denigrated."[6]

Warner claims that "by emptying history from the figure of Mary, all the various silks interwoven for centuries on the sensitive loom of the mind are deprived of context, of motive, of circumstance, and therefore seem to be spontaneous expressions of enduring archetypal ideas." She believes that the image of Mary as both virgin and mother, in whom opposites are reconciled, is responsible for women's frustration. "By setting up an impossible ideal, the cult of the Virgin does drive the adherent into a position of acknowledged and hopeless yearning and inferiority."[7]

Warner's critique of Catholicism's use of Mary to subjugate women, however, does not eliminate her criticism of Protestantism. She concludes: "Although Mary cannot be a model for the New Woman, a goddess is better than no goddess at all, for the somber-suited masculine world of the Protestant religion is altogether too much like a gentlemen's club to which ladies are only admitted on special days."[8] Warner's study was published in 1976, the same year that the Congregation for the Doctrine of the Faith under Pope Paul VI issued *Inter Insigniores,* stating that women could not be ordained to the Catholic priesthood, and the study evoked provocative dialogue in theological, feminist, and ecumenical circles.

Three decades after Graef's work and two decades after Warner's volume, Sally Cunneen wrote *In Search of Mary.*[9] In personal, readable, and sometimes poetic style, she reexamines Mary in history and theology for the late twentieth century generation. She challenges readers not to put Mary on a shelf, but to appreciate her in all her humanity. Cunneen accomplishes those goals by taking advantage of thirty years of additional scripture scholarship not available to Graef. In five chapters, she describes Mary in historical perspective from the second through the nineteenth centuries, highlighting Mary's influence on art, literature, and poetry.

Cunneen states: "What is startling, in a supposedly post-Christian time, is the persistence of old devotions to Mary." She describes visiting Marian shrines crowded with devout pilgrims in a variety of countries. Many of the Marian devotions, however, are being interpreted in new ways. Liberation theologians place new emphasis on social justice when honoring Our Lady of Guadalupe. Asian Christian women insist that "virgin" symbolizes Mary's autonomy, not her sexual celibacy.[10]

Cunneen then reports on interviews she conducted with contemporaries—artists, writers, and ordinary people—who describe how Mary influenced their lives. She concludes: "Contemporary artists like those we have seen in this chapter see Mary freshly. They challenge the rest of us to look more closely at traditional elements of faith we may take for granted or assume we understand." Beyond just offering introspective insight, Cunneen comments: "They ask us to see the connection between our faith and everyday life crises, pressing social problems, and even advanced scientific theories about human nature and the universe. To see, in other words, the possible eruption of the holy at any point in life, not simply in a different and higher sphere."[11] Cunneen's volume offers an avenue for integrating history and theology with a very practical spirituality.

Comprehensive volumes that broaden our perspectives on Mary, not only in Christianity but also in Judaism and

Islam, include George H. Tavard's *The Thousand Faces of Mary* (1996) and Jaroslav Pelikan's *Mary Through the Centuries: Her Place in the History of Culture* (1996). Miri Rubin's *Mother of God: A History of the Virgin Mary* (2009), explores ideas, practices, and images of Mary from the earliest times until the sixteenth century. All of these provide a tapestry background for understanding Mary through the centuries.[12]

## BIBLICAL SCHOLARSHIP REGARDING MARY

### *Ecumenical Efforts*

*Mary in the New Testament,* edited by Raymond E. Brown, Karl P. Donfried, Joseph A. Fitzmyer, and John Reumann, became a model for quality academic explorations by ecumenical teams. Interestingly, there was not a woman among the contributors.[13] Biblical scholars admit that Mary is not mentioned frequently in the Christian scriptures. Scripture scholars now believe that the infancy narratives and other descriptions of Mary are reflections of the early Christian communities on Mary's role in the life of Jesus and the early church. Still, these passages remind us that Mary was a Jewish woman of strength and courage. Brown's essay on Mary in *Biblical Reflections on Crises Facing the Church* popularized the phrase from Paul VI's 1974 papal encyclical *Marialis Cultus,* in which the pope describes Mary as "the first and most perfect of Christ's disciples."[14]

Ecumenical dialogue groups, although not limited to scriptural studies, have been exceedingly fruitful in exploring the role of Mary in the church. Among them is Le Groupe des Dombes, comprising twenty Catholic and twenty Lutheran and Reformed theologians in France, who devoted their sessions from 1991 to 1997 to discussions of Mary. Its work was published as *Mary in the Plan of God and in the Communion of Saints.*[15] The working papers of the Anglican-Roman Catholic International Commission, published in *Studying*

*Mary,* advanced the dialogue significantly.[16] *Lutherans and Catholics in Dialogue,* has been a valuable tool for ecumenical conversation.[17]

Though without official status, one of the more comprehensive ecumenical efforts is *Mary: The Complete Resource,* edited by Sarah Jane Boss. The contributors, mostly British and American, include Chris Maunder, whose valuable essay "Mary in the New Testament and the Apocrypha" is an excellent summary and critique of recent research regarding Mary in today's modern critical scholarship.[18] *Mary, Mother of God* is a compilation of the papers given at a conference of the Center for Catholic and Evangelical Theology at St. Olaf College in Northfield, Minnesota in 2002.[19] These and other anthologies have enriched discussions of Mary across denominations.

### *Scripture Scholarship and Feminist Hermeneutics*

Although not directly focusing on Mary, Elisabeth Schüssler Fiorenza's volume *In Memory of Her* is important because her biblical methodology provides for a new interpretation of women's role in the early church. In the first chapter, titled "Toward a Feminist Hermeneutic," she states clearly: "To discuss the relationship between biblical-historical interpretation and feminist reconstruction of women's history in biblical times is to enter an intellectual and emotional minefield."[20]

Schüssler Fiorenza is convinced that feminist interpretation must begin with a "hermeneutics of suspicion." Because the Hebrew and Christian scriptures were written by men, a key question becomes whether important experiences and events related to women were omitted in the majority of these documents. She uses the argument from silence to suggest that women had a more important role in a patriarchal society than is evidenced in the Gospels and epistles. Her goal is to reclaim the Bible as a feminist heritage. She argues, "A feminist reconstitution of the world requires a feminist hermeneutics that shares in the critical methods and impulses of historical scholarship on the one hand and in the theological goals of liberation theologies on the other."[21] Her scholarship was an important step in integrating biblical studies with feminist theories. Schüssler Fiorenza, like Rosemary Ruether, related her research to liberation theology.

### *Feminist Studies and Anti-Judaism*

One of the negative byproducts of some of the earlier work of Christian feminist liberation theologians was placing the blame for the patriarchal situation in the first century on Judaism. In highlighting how Jesus befriended women, there was the tendency to see him apart from the many Jewish movements of his day. As early as 1971 Leonard Swidler, in "Jesus Was a Feminist," placed Jesus in juxtaposition to what Swidler portrayed as a highly patriarchal misogynist Jewish society.[22] Latin American liberation theologian Leonardo Boff, in *The Maternal Face of God,* described women suffering discrimination in Jewish religion and society and suggested that in offering a message of liberation to women, "Jesus must be considered a feminist."[23]

Brazilian feminist theologians Ivone Gebara and Maria Clara Bingemer, in their efforts to free Mariology from patriarchal language and reflect on Mary as representative of the poor and oppressed, sometimes take a supersessionist approach which holds that the covenant with God in Jesus replaced the covenant of God with the Jewish people.[24] They seem unaware that the relations between Catholics and Jews radically changed in the post–Vatican II era with *Nostra Aetate*. Pope John Paul II spoke on more than one occasion of "the People of God of the Old Covenant, never revoked by God." In an address to Jewish leaders in Rome on March 12, 1979, the pope stated, "Our two religious communities are connected and closely related on the very level of their respective religious identities."[25]

Jewish feminist scholars such as Judith Plaskow and Susannah Heschel considered the implications of such anti-Judaic approaches and responded.[26] Heschel describes the two motifs of anti-Judaism in Christian feminist theology: "First there is a tendency to blame Judaism for the origins of patriarchy. . . . Second, is the motif that highlights the alleged positive treatment of women in early Christianity by negating first century Judaism's negative treatment of women."[27]

One of the strongest Christian responses to this anti-Judaism that was creeping into Christian feminist writings was from Elisabeth Schüssler Fiorenza. In *Jesus: Miriam's Child, Sophia's Prophet* she warned that "anti-Judaism is contrary to a Christian feminist theology of liberation because an anti-Jewish perspective does not recognize that Jesus and his followers were *Jewish wo/men*. They were *not Christian* in our sense of the word."[28]

Schüssler Fiorenza reminds us that struggles for emancipation have a long history in the Greco-Roman world and beyond, and should not be limited to Jewish patriarchy. "The emancipatory struggles of biblical wo/man must be seen within this wider context of cultural-political struggles . . . not over against Judaism, but against kyriarchal structures of domination in antiquity."[29] Schüssler Fiorenza's scholarship integrates biblical studies with attention to the sociocultural and political studies that were emerging.

### *"The Illegitimacy of Jesus" from a Feminist Perspective*

Jane Schaberg in *The Illegitimacy of Jesus* contends that there was an early tradition of belief in the illegitimacy of Jesus, possibly from rape. She takes seriously the allegation of Celsus that Jesus' father was a soldier named Pantera. She is convinced that remnants of this can be found in the Gospels in questions brought forth on the origin of Jesus.[30]

In addition to using historical-critical methodology, Schaberg's interpretation is strongly grounded in feminist hermeneutics. She believes that the illegitimacy tradition was obliterated by the patriarchal Gospel writers, who found it unacceptable. Far from it being a disgrace, however, she claims that "Mary represents the oppressed who have been liberated." She concludes:

> In this case there is subversion of the patriarchal family structures: the child conceived illegitimately is seen to have value—transcendent value—in and of himself, not in his attachment and that of his mother to a biological or legal father. Mary is a woman who has access to the sacred outside the patriarchal family and its control. The illegitimate conception turns out to be grace not disgrace, order within disorder.[31]

Barbara Reid in *Choosing the Better Part?* agrees that Schaberg's work offers a helpful insight because "Mary's story can also provide hope for women who are victims of sexual violence." She brings a note of realism to Mary's challenge. "The tendency to wrap Mary in an aura of romantic joy at the annunciation obscures the reality that in her culture, to be found with child before she comes to live with her betrothed is a horrendously shameful situation." She agrees with Schaberg that "it may be out of alarm and fright that Mary went in haste to Elizabeth (Luke 1:39), not out of eagerness to share the joy of her news."[32]

In Reid's review of Schaberg's book in the *Catholic Biblical Quarterly,* she notes that there is value in attempting to reconstruct and analyze the pre-Gospel tradition, and she believes that Schaberg offers "a balanced interpretation of all possible interpretations of the texts." Reid believes, however, that "the greatest weakness of Schaberg's study is that it is so highly speculative." Even Schaberg admits that her proposal is conjecture. Reid reflects, "There is no doubt that her interpretation is possible, but the question remains whether the texts demand such an interpretation."[33]

Among others who are skeptical of Schaberg's thesis is Princeton professor of New Testament Literature Beverly Roberts Gaventa, one of the first contemporary Protestant women biblical scholars to write a major work on Mary. She believes that Schaberg relies too much on the argument from silence.[34]

### *Jewish Silence on Mary*

In October 1986, the Sixth International Symposium on Mariology sponsored by the Pontifical Faculty at the Marianum in Rome had as its subject "Mary in Judaism and Islam." Avital Wohlmann, an Israeli professor from the Hebrew University in Jerusalem, presented the first lecture on a Jewish woman's answer to why there is silence today regarding the Jewishness of Mary.[35] She believes Christians may be disappointed, but in reality, Mary "does not arouse any particular interest or even indifference in the Jewish people, nor even any questions."[36] She accepted the challenge of offering reasons for this silence.

In her introductory remarks Wohlmann compares the Jewish people to the brother who stays home in the parable of the Prodigal Son. "The silence of the older brother, the Jewish people, means that he feels that he has already said everything by staying home, within this wall which for you [Christians] is the Law and for him, his very way of life."[37] She reviews the history of anti-Christian folklore, such as the story of Ben Pandera, but notes that modern Jewish scholars such as Joseph Klausner do not attribute historical value to such stories. She commends Jewish writer Sholem Asch, author of *Mary*,[38] for presenting a more realistic portrait of Mary as a Jewish mother.

Wohlmann observes that, in Judaism, virginity does not have the value that is placed on it by Christianity. The injunction in Genesis to "be fruitful and multiply" (1:28) is seen as an obligation to procreate. It is difficult for Jews to understand why Mary would be honored as a virgin, because virginity does not play an important role in Judaism. Second, she observes that Jews cannot comprehend how Mary can be the mother of God and also the spouse of God. For the Jew, this is incompatible. Jewish symbolism refuses to mix the images of mother and spouse. Last, Wohlmann discusses

Mary as mother of God and mediatrix. She claims that for the Jew to establish any quasi-divine intermediary with God is idolatry. For Jews, salvation can only come directly from God. Wohlmann attributes the Jewish silence about Mary to these three factors.[39]

### *Protestant Women Scholars and Mary: Beverly Roberts Gaventa*

Beverly Gaventa, in *Mary: Glimpses of the Mother of Jesus,* explores Mary in the four Gospels. After analysis of Mary's role in Matthew, Luke-Acts, and John, as well as the Protevangelium of James, she offers concluding reflections on three motifs that she sees intertwined in these narratives: (1) the *vulnerability* of Mary, not as a helpless victim but as one caught within circumstances in unexpected ways; (2) Mary's *reflection* on the events of her life, whether the warning of Simeon, or the loss of Jesus in the Temple; and (3) Mary's *witness* to Jesus even to his death on the cross. Gaventa concludes, "Mary remains a model for all Christians."[40]

Gaventa also co-edited, with Cynthia Rigby, *Blessed One: Protestant Perspectives on Mary*, an impressive assemblage of the writings of Protestant scholars discovering Mary anew.[41] In the foreword Kathleen Norris asks: "Is Mary a cultural artifact or a religious symbol? A literary device or a theological tool? A valuable resource for biblical exegesis or the matrix of extrabiblical piety that we, as Protestants, must avoid at all costs? The point about Mary is that she is all these things, and more, always more."[42]

As Protestants today raise questions in the realm of theology and feminism, ecumenism, liturgy, parenting, and religious education, Gaventa and Rigby suggest that Mary's "absence has become a presence." They conclude, "The absence of Mary not only cuts Protestants off from Catholic and Orthodox Christians; it cuts us off from the fullness of our own tradition." They therefore provide a collection of essays framed in response to three questions: Who is Mary?

How does Mary's story intersect with contemporary life? and What can Mary teach us about God? The purpose of their research is "an invitation to Mary to be present once again in Protestant faith and life."[43]

## NEW THEOLOGICAL INTERPRETATIONS

### *Paul VI and Marialis Cultus*

Whether it was church leaders arguing for Mary to be declared Theotokos at Ephesus in 431 or Pope Pius V instituting the feast of the Holy Rosary after the defeat of the Turks at Lepanto in 1571, pronouncements about Mary have been a conspicuous part of church history. Since the promulgation of the dogmas of the Immaculate Conception and the assumption in the modern era, there have continued to be devotees of Mary who expect that another more exalted title for her is just around the corner.

One need only Google "Co-Redemptrix" and "Mary" to find a variety of options on the web. One group, Vox Populi Mariae Mediatrici, is particularly active in lobbying the Vatican for the "fifth Marian dogma." Its webpage includes a link allowing one to send a message to Pope Benedict XVI (choose Dutch, English, French, Italian, Polish, or Spanish) requesting that an infallible dogma be proclaimed stating that Mary is co-redemptrix with Jesus in the salvation of the world. It is worth noting that there is no mention of that title in the chapter on Mary in *Lumen Gentium*. Many of these groups have developed because they believe that Mary has been neglected after Vatican II.

Paul VI, aware of the growing concern that Marian devotions were disappearing in the post-conciliar period, promulgated an apostolic exhortation in 1974 entitled *Marialis Cultus: For the Right Ordering and Development of Devotion to the Blessed Virgin Mary.* His goal was to rejuvenate devotion to Mary at a pivotal time when Catholics were adjusting to the liturgical reforms after the Council.

One interpretation for the so-called demise of devotionalism in general was that, once the Mass was in the vernacular, there was not the same need for devotions in the language of the people. In addition, lay Catholics were now encouraged to pray the Liturgy of the Hours (the Divine Office). The Rosary, which came into existence in the Middle Ages, had developed as a substitute for those who could not say the Divine Office, either because they were illiterate or did not know the psalms in Latin.

Throughout the centuries Catholics have appreciated the Rosary as a helpful devotion. In the later part of the twentieth century, however, the reason for the recitation of the Rosary did not seem as applicable once the Mass and the Liturgy of the Hours were no longer in Latin. This explanation did not assuage the Catholics who felt that Mary had been "demoted." It only emboldened many of them to fight for her cause.

Pope Paul VI, who was very supportive of the changes in the liturgy, believed in a "both/and" approach. He was convinced that, first and foremost, devotion to Mary should be put in the context of the liturgy. The first half of *Marialis Cultus* describes the prominent place Mary holds in the liturgical year, especially in the Advent and Christmas seasons. Her solemnities and feasts are opportunities for the faithful to venerate her. Some feasts are particularly meaningful to certain religious communities or to particular ethnic or national groups. The revised Liturgy of the Hours provides for due reverence for Mary. Indeed, in the new liturgy she holds an integral position in the official prayer of the church.

The importance of devotion to Mary developing "in harmonious subordination to the worship of Christ" is emphasized in the introduction to the document. Concern about the appropriateness of some devotions in the post–Vatican II period is addressed with candor: "Certain practices of piety that not long ago seemed suitable for expressing the religious sentiment of individuals and of Christian communities seem today inadequate or unsuitable because they are linked with social and cultural patterns of the past." The purpose of *Marialis Cultus,* stated in its introduction, is to reflect and dialogue on "the place that the Blessed Virgin occupies in the Church's worship" and to offer guidelines for implementing devotion to Mary in the post–Vatican II era.

The pope is clear that devotion to Mary must be grounded in sound trinitarian, christological, and ecclesial theology, as articulated at Vatican II. In Part II, "Renewal of Devotion to Mary," Paul VI reminds the bishops (and the faithful) that worship is an offering to God—Father, Son, and Holy Spirit. Mary, indeed, has a unique relationship to all three Persons. She was invited by the Father, empowered by the Holy Spirit, and became the mother of Jesus. In keeping with *Lumen Gentium*, however, Mary is also among the redeemed. The christological dimension is paramount: "In the Virgin Mary everything is relative to Christ and dependent upon Him" (no. 25). In turn, she has a special "mission in the mystery of the Church and . . . a preeminent role in the communion of saints" (no. 28). As Mother of the church, she is mother of the mystical body of Christ and our mother as well.

Paul VI's "Four Guidelines for Devotion to the Blessed Virgin: Biblical, Liturgical, Ecumenical, and Anthropological" is perhaps the most ground-breaking contribution of the document. These categories would have been unlikely areas for consideration in a pre–Vatican II era. The Second Vatican Council based its documents, for the most part, not on the decrees of previous councils or pronouncements of earlier popes, but on the new scripture scholarship and on the writings of the fathers of the church. The result was a new reverence for scripture, implementation of what many considered radical changes in the liturgy, the opening of doors to ecumenical relationships, and the study of anthropology—understanding human beings in their relationship to the natural and social sciences—so as to understand the church's role in the modern world.

Regarding biblical guidelines, Paul VI reminds us that "every form of worship should have a biblical imprint." This should not be a matter of proof texting, but "devotion to the

Virgin should be imbued with the great themes of the Christian message." In the era after Vatican II when Catholics were "rediscovering" the Bible, the pope refers to using "the Bible ever increasingly as the basic prayer book, and to draw from it genuine inspiration and unsurpassable examples" (no. 30). Christians should look to the scriptures for insights on Mary.

Regarding guidelines for worship, two attitudes must be avoided. Pope Paul states that those who scorn devotions of piety seem to "forget that the Council has said that devotions should harmonize with the liturgy, not be suppressed." For those who "mix practices of piety and liturgical acts in hybrid celebrations" [sometimes saying novenas or reciting the Rosary during the eucharistic celebration], pastoral leadership, exercised with sensitivity, should clarify these practices (no. 31).

Regarding the ecumenical age that blossomed in the wake of Vatican II, the Catholic Church should be more open to "our separated brethren." Although many Marian devotions are unique, "every care should be taken to avoid exaggeration which could mislead other Christian brethren about the true doctrine of the Catholic Church." In addition, "the Church desires that any manifestation of cult which is opposed to correct Catholic practice should be eliminated" (no. 32). Clearly, exaggerated forms of devotion that appear to divinize Mary are not acceptable.

Regarding the category of anthropology, which includes being attentive to advances in science, psychology, and sociology in understanding the human person, Paul VI is realistic in stating: "The picture of the Blessed Virgin presented in a certain type of devotional literature cannot easily be reconciled with today's life-style, especially the way women live today." To the surprise of some Christian feminists, he adds, "In the home, woman's equality and co-responsibility with men in the running of the family are being justly recognized by laws and the evolution of customs." He acknowledges that in politics women now hold prominent offices in many countries and are employed in many areas "getting further away every day from the restricted surroundings of the home. In the cultural field new possibilities are opening up for women in scientific research and intellectual activities" (no. 34).

The pope states that, due to this evolution, "some people are becoming disenchanted with devotions to the Blessed Virgin and finding it difficult to take as an example Mary of Nazareth because the horizons of her life, so they say, seem rather restricted in comparison with the vast sphere of activity open to mankind today" (no. 34). Paul VI believes, however, that Mary can still be a model to be imitated, but one must look beyond the sociocultural experiences of her time.

What the faithful are called upon to imitate is not her life in Nazareth but her faithfulness to God's call and her commitment to service. She heard the word of God and responded. "She is worthy of imitation because she was the first and most perfect of Christ's disciples" (no. 35). This profound statement resonated with Christians, particularly women, who were searching for the Mary to whom they could relate in a modern world. The pope notes that rather than being timid or submissive, Mary, at the visitation, proclaimed that God would take down the mighty from their thrones and exalt the humble (Lk 1:51–53). At Cana and at the cross she exhibited extraordinary strength as a woman who could be a model in the modern era.

In Part III Paul observes that the Angelus and the Rosary are exercises of piety, scripturally based, which can be fruitful, especially in building up the Christian family as the domestic church (no. 52). The pope then reminds us that Mary is one of us. "Mary, in fact, is one of our race, a true daughter of Eve—though free of that mother's sin—and truly our sister, who as a poor and humble woman fully shared our lot" (no. 56). In acknowledging Mary as sister as well as mother, Paul VI opened up the possibility for a new relationship with Mary, especially for women. Mary will always be the mother of Jesus, the Theotokos, mother of the mystical body of Christ. But describing her as "the first and most perfect of Christ's disciples" and "truly, our sister" is perhaps Paul VI's greatest contribution to women in their search for Mary in the modern era.

In retrospect, perhaps one of the reasons why *Marialis Cultus* did not have "staying power" with Catholic women, and is only recently receiving new attention, is that two years later, on October 15, 1976, the document *Inter Insigniores (Declaration Concerning the Question of Admission of Women to the Ministerial Priesthood)* was issued by the Congregation for the Doctrine of the Faith with Paul VI's approval. At a time when women were being ordained in the Protestant churches and Reform Judaism, Catholic women were dismayed. One of the reasons given for this conclusion was that women did not have a physical resemblance to Jesus. This occasioned responses, both substantive and humorous, in the national, religious, and popular press.

### *Pope John Paul II on Mary and Women*

Pope John Paul II's 1987 encyclical *Redemptoris Mater* was written in anticipation of the millennium—two thousand years since the birth of Jesus. Although the pope specified that we cannot know exactly when Mary was born, it seemed appropriate to celebrate her birth some years in advance of the birth of Jesus. Therefore, a Marian Year was proclaimed for 1988, and this letter was its introduction.

Pope John Paul's devotion to Mary is well known. He grew up in Poland under the control of the Nazis during World War II, and the Communist regime thereafter. He looked to Mary as his mother, especially after the death of his own mother at a relatively early age. He reflects, "The Marian dimension of Christian life takes on special significance in relation to women and their status." The basis is that God "in the sublime event of the Incarnation of his Son, entrusted himself to the ministry, the free and active ministry of a woman" (no. 46).

One of the most mysterious passages of the document is in the section, "The Mother of God at the Center of the Pilgrim

Church." When discussing Mary's presence among those praying in the upper room at Pentecost, John Paul II states specifically that the Holy Spirit came upon those assembled to send them forth on mission to preach the good news. However, he states: "*Mary did not directly receive this apostolic mission.* She was not among those whom Jesus sent 'to the whole world to teach all nations' when he conferred this mission on them" (no. 26, emphasis added). One wonders how he knew so clearly whom the Holy Spirit descended upon, and who was omitted—and for what tasks. Mary was in the group, praying and supporting the members of the early church. It was unthinkable for the pope that Mary might also be given the mission to teach and preach the gospel. One wonders: Does his understanding of events in the upper room reflect the pope's willingness to limit the ministry of women even at that early stage in the life of the church?

The following year John Paul II promulgated his apostolic letter *Mulieris Dignitatem*. While it is encouraging to read that "*both man and woman are human beings to an equal degree*" (no. 6), it becomes clear that the foundation for his document is a belief in the complementarity of men and women grounded in a dualistic anthropology. He states, "In the sphere of what is 'human'—of what is humanly personal—*'masculinity' and 'femininity' are distinct,* yet at the same time they *complete and explain each other*" (no. 25).

John Paul II repeats the stipulation of Paul VI that the Mass can only be performed by a man, the priest who acts "*in persona Christi*" (no. 26). He acknowledges the great contributions of women in the church, as presented in the New Testament and throughout the history of the Church. He concludes: "Holy women are an incarnation of the feminine ideal; they are also a model for all Christians . . . an example of how the Bride must respond with love to the love of the Bridegroom" (no. 27). This motif of the bridegroom and the bride are dominant in the rest of the document.

Returning to Genesis (2:18), the pope reiterates the role of woman as "a helper fit for him." Drawing on the letter to the

Ephesians—with its imagery of Christ as the Bridegroom and the church as the Bride—he asserts "*the truth about woman as bride.*" He concludes: "The Bridegroom is the one who loves. The Bride is loved: *it is she who receives love, in order to love in return*" (no. 29).

Mary is the model and fullest expression of this love. He states unambiguously, "A woman's dignity is closely connected with the love which she receives by the very reason of her femininity; it is likewise connected *with the love that she gives in return.*" Lest there be any doubt, he emphasizes, "*Woman can only find herself by giving love to others*" (no. 30). One wonders how he believes that men find themselves?

God entrusts human beings to women in a special way "precisely by reason of their femininity—and this in a particular way determines their vocation . . . Thus, the 'perfect woman' becomes an irreplaceable support and source of spiritual strength for other people, who perceive the great energies of her spirit. These 'perfect women' are owed much by their families, and sometimes by whole nations." Admitting that in this scientific age, there has often been a "*loss of sensitivity for man, that is, for what is essentially human,*" the pope claims that it is the "genius" of women to "ensure sensitivity for human beings in every circumstance: because they are human!—and because 'the greatest of these is love'" (no. 30).

Needless to say, many Catholic women, not just feminists, saw this as a regression. To understand woman only in terms of complementarity to man rather than in her own identity was, to many, both unrealistic and insulting. To some, the "perfect woman" model of the Neo-Thomistic revival appeared to be alive and well at the end of the twentieth century. Mary, as presented by John Paul II, was not the strong Jewish woman for whom some were searching.

## MARY IN RECENT CATHOLIC FEMINIST THEOLOGY

The most comprehensive and creative contemporary theological work on Mary in the new millennium is Elizabeth A.

Johnson's *Truly Our Sister.*[44] Drawing on Paul VI's description of Mary as "truly our sister," and true to her feminist insights, Johnson begins by listening to women from every continent. Her point of departure is "the global chorus of women's voices, which . . . offers critical and creative theological interpretations of the Marian tradition."[45] The insights of women from Africa, Asia, and Latin America open up new avenues for understanding Mary, who is too often depicted only in European mode. Through extensive research, Johnson presents the history of doctrine and devotion through the centuries and the various interpretations of Mary in each culture. She describes cul-de-sacs in which mostly male theologians have presented Mary as the idealized form of the feminine, including Leonardo Boff's portrayal of Mary as "the maternal face of God."[46]

A key insight of Johnson in her search for the historical Mary (underscored in her article "Galilee: A Critical Matrix for Marian Studies")[47] is that we will only recover the "real" Mary if we explore the socioeconomic, political, and religious milieu of Galilee in the first century. What was life like in Second Temple Judaism in the north? How did one live an everyday life in Nazareth and its environs? Recent archeological studies have provided remarkable artifacts that help us reconstruct life in that period. Johnson's comprehensive research allows us to imagine the family life of observant Jews in first-century Galilee.

Anchoring us in history, Johnson then proceeds with the tools of modern biblical studies and feminist hermeneutics to do a careful analysis of the passages in scripture that refer to Mary. She offers critical and fresh interpretations of these scenes, sometimes with a hermeneutics of suspicion, reconstructing the world behind the text and creating a biblical mosaic. She sees each of these biblical passages as a tessera (a small piece of marble, glass, or tile), which, when glued into the mosaic, offers us a totality. Johnson invites us to "study tesserae, then, these individual theological memories of Mary, as flashes of color that form part of the texture of the story of the living God's engagement with the flesh and matter of the world, including in our day the uprising of women into full humanity." This "dangerous memory of Mary" is a "multi-faceted, living, memory-image of Mary within the cloud of witnesses."[48] Johnson concludes by placing Mary within the Communion of Saints, naming her a "friend of God and prophet" (Wis 7:27).[49] Not queen, nor empress, nor Nordic virgin—but a Jewish woman who is "truly our sister."

## MARY IN SPIRITUALITY AND CULTURE

It was not until the 1960s that "spirituality" became a popular category for study and discussion.[50] The word is derived from the French *spiritualité,* which was used in the seventeenth century to denote a personal encounter with God and stressed the subjective and psychological dimensions of such a relationship. It was sometimes connected to emotional excesses, for example, Quietism in Catholicism, or Pietism and Spiritualism in Protestantism.

Books on living "the devout life" became popular in the seventeenth century. In Catholic texts, under the umbrella of theology, a section developed devoted to ascetical and mystical theology, which was later titled spiritual theology. By the mid-twentieth century, Catholic theology began to include elements of psychology in reflections on prayer life. Louis Bouyer's volume *The Spirituality of the New Testament and the Fathers*, published in the 1950s, used the term to mean "the study of the reactions that the objects of religious faith arouse in religious consciousness."[51]

Protestants preferred the words *piety* and *devotion* as they enjoined their members to live a devout and holy life. *Devotionalism,* so popular in the Catholic Church during the nineteenth and twentieth centuries, included elements of spirituality, often in communal settings such as the recitation of the Rosary, novenas, and adoration of the Blessed Sacrament.

Multiple definitions of *spirituality* sprang up in the 1960s. The *Westminster Dictionary of Christian Spirituality* defines it as "those attitudes, beliefs, and practices, which animate people's lives and help them to reach out toward supersensible realities."[52] Questions then arose: How does one distinguish between spirituality and religion? between spirituality and worship? Having taught spirituality over the years, I have come to understand spirituality in the broadest sense as a personal or communal encounter with the Transcendent that affects and is lived out in the attitudes, relationships, and motivations in one's life. It is usually associated with an experience that is intuitive, relying more on the inner life and emotions than on the cognitive, intellectual dimensions of theology or the specific practices of worship. Spirituality, although ultimately personal, often develops in a collective framework (for example, Jewish, Franciscan, Ignatian, Methodist, Celtic).

Publishing houses started developing series, often ecumenical and interfaith in character, devoted to the classics of spirituality. The bibliography burgeoned. In retail super-stores and smaller Christian bookstores, the sale of books on spirituality multiplied. Sometimes these were intermingled with books with psychological themes or those related to Eastern religions.

Jean Leclerq claims that what is distinctive about American Catholic spirituality, however, is that it is *popular, committed,* and *pluralistic.*[53] From his European background, Leclerq observes that there is a pragmatic approach that infuses spirituality in the United States. It is not only individualistic but is often inspired by a commitment to live one's spirituality in the context of social justice.

The greatest challenge appears to be integrating spirituality with social justice. This effort began in the 1930s, when Dorothy Day, co-founder of the Catholic Worker Movement, dialogued with Virgil Michel, OSB, who was the leader of the Liturgical Revival in the United States. Many of their ideas were articulated in the documents of Vatican II, but the effort at integration is ongoing. Recently I taught a course at Loyola University Chicago titled "Mystics and Social Activists:

Abraham Joshua Heschel, Thomas Merton, Dorothy Day, and Martin Luther King, Jr." Students were eager to explore how these four individuals integrated their spirituality with their commitment to social justice. We might ask: How might Mary have been challenged to integrate her spirituality into a life of social justice?

### *Reflecting on Mary's Prayer*

In 1949, before the explosion of spiritual writings about Mary in the post–Vatican II period, a Jewish author, Sholem Asch, wrote what might be described as a historical novel simply entitled *Mary.*[54] In a reverent manner he describes Mary's life of Jewish prayer in the context of her family, her marriage, and the life of her remarkable son. This volume might be seen as a precursor, of sorts, to future works that reflect on how Mary and Jesus may have prayed.

The new emphasis on spirituality in the later twentieth century motivated Christian writers to reflect on Mary's possible prayer life. A trilogy of books by Ann Johnson, beginning in the 1980s, offers a framework for how we might understand Mary's spirituality. In the first volume, *Miryam of Nazareth,* she explores Jewish heroines who would have been exemplars for Mary and how the Magnificat can model other prayers of Mary in her lifetime. In *Miryam of Judah* Johnson focuses on the Kaddish prayer and the way Miryam would have celebrated the Sabbath. In *Miryam of Jerusalem* she conjectures about the post-resurrection Mary and her role in teaching the early church. Throughout these volumes she offers poetic renditions of how Mary might have prayed and invites the reader to reflect on Mary in that context.[55]

Among other sources reflecting on Mary in meditation and prayer is *Mary's Song*. Mary Catherine Nolan discusses Mary's great prayer, the Magnificat, building her meditation on a strong biblical foundation, interspersed with personal reflections. The chapters, one on each of the phrases of the Magnificat, conclude with questions for reflection and a prayer.[56]

*Blessed Among All Women,* a book of stories and reflections about extraordinary women throughout history by Robert Ellsberg, is structured around the Beatitudes. Leading the first section, "Blessed are the poor in spirit" is Mary, mother of Jesus. In her simplicity she becomes something of a beacon for those who follow. Ellsberg concludes: "In the darkness of faith, she offered her consent to the mysterious plan of God. In the light of grace she responded with her extraordinary song."[57] That song, of course, is the Magnificat, which incorporates the cry for spirituality and justice. These are only a few examples of authors who have accepted the challenge of trying to understand how Mary might have prayed and the possible effects on how she lived her life.

### *Symposia, Art, and Film*

Exploring Mary as peacemaker, liberator, and a symbol of justice and freedom became topics for events such as the Mary Festival at Mundelein College in Chicago in 1983, with the papers later published as *Mary According to Women.*[58] The lectures from a symposium at Saint Mary's College, Notre Dame, Indiana, were published as *Mary, Woman of Nazareth.*[59] It was not uncommon to have a "Mary Day" celebration on May 1 at many Catholic women's schools as a substitute for a May Crowning. These events often included music, art, and dance related to a Mary theme, and they opened up new vistas in the post–Vatican II understanding of Mary, especially for women in Catholic high schools and colleges of that era.

Although not specifically about Mary, Dutch artist Rien Poortvliet produced an artistic volume in 1974 titled *He Was One of Us.*[60] He tells the Jesus story by letting faces and hands "do the talking." He sketches Jesus, Mary, and Joseph in a very Jewish community and in very human situations. One sees an exhilarated pregnant Elizabeth welcoming her pregnant cousin Mary. Later, a very pregnant Mary on the donkey is being led by Joseph to Bethlehem. Mary is depicted scolding an adolescent Jesus (who is wearing his *kepah*) after they finally find him in Jerusalem. Poortvliet captures the joy, humor, pain, and suffering of Mary and does so in the historical context of the land of Israel in the first century.

Images of the Jewish Jesus and Mary appeared in 1977 in Franco Zeffirelli's television mini-series "Jesus of Nazareth," which offered an impressionistic version of the annunciation and was attentive to the details of Jewish life. Other television specials include "Jesus of Nazareth" (1996) and "Mary of Nazareth" (1997), in which I was privileged to have a part. The NBC special "Mary, Mother of Jesus" (1999) also placed Jesus and Mary in historical context. Despite the criticism of Mel Gibson's "The Passion of the Christ" (2004) for its anti-Semitic overtones, the role of Mary as a Jewish mother, played by Maia Morgenstern, was applauded by the critics.[61] Slowly, an appreciation of the Jewish Mary has been making its way into the culture.

## CONCLUSION

Prior to the middle of the twentieth century, many scholars functioned within the confines of their own sometimes-narrow discipline. Historians dialogued with historians; biblical scholars spoke mostly with other biblical scholars; and theologians related largely with other theologians. Although there have always been exceptions to this approach, the advances in communication after World War II allowed the conversations to expand. Discovery of the Dead Sea Scrolls and the Nag Hammadi documents not only was exciting for biblical scholars but had huge implications for studying the history of the inter-testamental period. In turn, theological statements and beliefs were influenced by the new insights gained by scripture scholars and historians.

The work in historical studies of Hilda Graef, Rosemary Ruether, Marina Warner, Sally Cunneen, and others reached far beyond the factual history, or even the consequences of the facts and events, to encompass the study of philosophy, art, literature, psychology, and devotionalism.

Biblical scholars, instead of doing exegesis in a narrow framework, followed the lead of Raymond Brown and encouraged ecumenical conversations and publications. Elizabeth Schüssler Fiorenza expanded the field of biblical interpretation to include a "hermeneutics of suspicion." She, and Rosemary Ruether, saw that dialoguing about women's roles in the early church could be enhanced by connecting the topic to liberation theology. Interaction with Jewish scholars, regarding the perceived anti-Judaism in the writings of some Christian feminists, allowed for more in-depth appreciation of the sociocultural context of the period. Protestant women scripture scholars, such as Beverly Roberts Gaventa, came together with other Christians and feminists for conversations about Mary.

Although many would see him as an unlikely candidate, Pope Paul VI, with his remarkable document *Marialis Cultus,* provided new opportunities for Catholics to reconfigure Mary as "truly our sister" and "the first and most perfect of Christ's disciples." The approach of Pope John Paul II regarding woman as "the bride" and as "the perfect woman" was discouraging, but Elizabeth Johnson, drawing on Pope Paul's meaningful phrase for the title of her creative and comprehensive volume on Mary, *Truly Our Sister,* forged a new path for men and women not only in scripture studies and theology but in spirituality as well.

A multidisciplinary approach to Mary emerged, not only in the scholarly world, but also on the grass-roots level in art, film, conferences, parish programs, and dialogue groups. Now, Christians (and some Jews) are enjoying the fruits of this interdisciplinary approach to Mary. As a result, there is interest in how she lived as a Jewish woman, and in how her life of Jewish prayer might influence our own.

# Chapter 5

# Searching for the Jewish Jesus to Find the Jewish Mary

## INTRODUCTION

"If Jesus came to Phoenix, Arizona, he would not go to any of your churches," announced Rabbi Albert Plotkin at a Friday clergy meeting. "He would come to my synagogue! He was a good Reform rabbi." After a hearty laugh, all the Jewish and Christian clergy and other professionals present agreed with him. Until recent years most Christian congregants would have been more than a little surprised by such a statement. In one Catholic church where a Star of David was displayed during Advent, an elderly parishioner questioned the pastor about it. The priest explained that Jesus was a Jew. The irate woman replied, "He was not! He was a Roman Catholic!" Certainly if she believed Jesus was a Roman Catholic, she would have thought the same about his mother! Prior to Vatican II many Christians would probably not have identified either Jesus or Mary as Jews.

The New Testament demonstrates beyond question that Jesus was born, raised, lived, and died a Jew. How then is it possible that Christianity over the centuries came to develop a case of pernicious amnesia about the Jewishness of Jesus? How has this amnesia affected our memory of his mother? How might a recovered understanding of the particular form of Judaism that most influenced Jesus help us to recover the Jewish Mary? These are the questions we explore in this chapter.

Before we begin, it bears noting that there is a dearth of material about Mary in the New Testament, and a near absence of information about her in any other literature of the early centuries CE. Therefore, an indirect approach to reconstructing the life and spirituality of the Jewish Mary must be taken. Since Jewish children often learned their first prayers and home rituals from their mothers, it is not unrealistic to presume that Mary would have taught Jesus his earliest prayers and instructed him in simple Jewish rituals. We can also accept, based on the Pentecost account in Acts of the Apostles (1:14) and church teaching about Mary, that Mary was a disciple of her son. By learning more about Jesus as an observant Jewish man, we will be taking a vital step toward learning how Mary might have lived as an observant Jewish woman, what she might have believed, and how she might have prayed.

Any exploration of the Jewishness of Jesus and Mary must presuppose that first-century Judaism was a complex, pluralistic religion. In fact, many scholars have observed that it is more accurate to speak of Judaisms in the Second Temple period in which Jesus lived. New research on the Pharisees indicates that Jesus shared many ideas and rituals in common with them. In this chapter we compare the primary characteristics of first-century Pharisaic Judaism with the life and teachings of Jesus. We also consider the role of women in Pharisaic Judaism as another resource for reflection on the Jewish life and spirituality of his mother, Mary.

## THE SUPPRESSION OF THE JEWISH JESUS

### *It's in the Bible*

It is always curious to read that the author of the Gospel of John writes about "the Jews" who killed Jesus, and yet realize that Jesus, Mary, Joseph, Peter, Paul, Mary Magdalene, James, and John were all Jews. The earliest followers of Jesus considered themselves to be faithful Jews, even as they were gradually carving out a new identity as Jewish-Christians (or Christian-Jews). The Gospel of John, considered by some to be the most anti-Jewish of the Gospels, is now widely understood to have been written by and for a community of Jewish followers of Jesus who were living in the midst of intra-Jewish tensions.[1]

Scholars such as Raymond Brown have contended that during the Jewish war against the Romans in the late 60s CE, Christian-Jews in Judea were informed that if they were not willing to fight with the Jews against the Romans they could no longer consider themselves Jews. This was very likely a traumatic event for them. The Gospel of John suggests it was equivalent to being expelled from the synagogue. There was pain and anguish, a kind of rejection by one's "mother." Much of the angry, hostile language in John's Gospel against the Jews, therefore, is representative of the attitude of many in the Christian community in the later first century rather than from words that would have been spoken at the time of Jesus. Brown points out that many of the angry sections in John's Gospel are often interpreted today as expressions of Christian triumphalism. They were really written at a time of pain, however, when Christians were going through a kind of "adolescent identity crisis" and Jews were struggling to survive the final destruction of their Temple.[2]

Recent scholarship suggests that the parting of the ways—when Christianity launched off on its own from what we now call Judaism—was not solidified in the first century. It took place over an extended period, particularly in various parts of the East. There is evidence that Christians attended synagogue services up through the fourth century and later. The recent volume of essays, *The Ways That Never Parted*[3] provides evidence that although separation occurred in some places, it would be simplistic to assume that it was finalized in the first century.

Modern biblical scholarship has taught us to interpret John's Gospel in light of the specific context in which it was written. Additionally, in recent years the Catholic Church has made efforts in its official teaching to encourage awareness of and sensitivity to the intra-Jewish tensions reflected in John's Gospel, so as to contain anti-Jewish hostility within its time. As early as 1974 the Commission for Religious Relations with the Jews published "Guidelines and Suggestions for Implementing the Conciliar Declaration 'Nostra Aetate' (n. 4)," in which the commission urged caution and stated: "Thus the formula 'the Jews,' in St. John, sometimes according to the context means 'the leaders of the Jews,' or 'the adversaries of Jesus,' terms which express better the thought of the evangelist and avoid appearing to arraign the Jewish people as such."[4] In the 1985 document "Notes on the Correct Way to Present Jews and Judaism in Preaching and Catechesis," the same commission states: "Some references hostile to or less favorable to the Jews have their historical context in conflicts between the nascent Church and the Jewish community. Certain controversies reflect Christian-Jewish relations long after the time of Jesus." Unfortunately, official statements such as these are often read only by scholars and are not preached from the pulpit in many Christian churches.

Often passages from the Hebrew Scriptures are quoted in the Gospels and the epistles. Members of the early Jewish-Christian communities would have recognized them as quotations from the Hebrew scriptures, but those in the pews today are sometimes unaware of their origin. In more than one homily I have heard a priest or minister state: "The God of the Old Testament is a God of anger and wrath—*but* Jesus said you should love the Lord your God with your whole heart and soul and mind and strength—and love your neighbor as yourself!" I have wanted to raise my hand and respond: "But Jesus did not make that up! He is quoting from Deuteronomy (6:5) and Leviticus (19:18), parts of the *Hebrew* scriptures."

The Hebrew scriptures were the only scriptures that Jesus and Mary ever knew. This is not always clear to Christians today. Paul's earliest epistle, 1 Thessalonians, was written some time around 50 CE—two decades after the crucifixion—and the earliest Gospel, Mark, was not written until sometime around 70 CE. The New Testament, as we know it, consists of a collection of books and letters that were not officially recognized as the authoritative canon of scripture until the late fourth century.[5]

In the second century the church rejected as heretical the Marcionite teaching that the God of the Hebrew scriptures had nothing to do with the God of Jesus Christ. This formal recognition of the Hebrew scriptures by the early church underscores their importance both historically and theologically for our understanding of Christianity. We demean these scriptures by not recognizing them as God's revelation and how they were valued by Jesus and the early Christians. This point is wonderfully expressed by Raymond Brown at the time of the death of Rabbi Abraham Joshua Heschel, who once said, "The Old Testament would still be God's revelation if Jesus Christ had never come." Brown reflects: "This is not blasphemy but a truth that the Christian must ponder. And even when Jesus has come, the Old Testament reflects insights into God's dealing with men that cannot be found in the New."[6]

### *Anti-Judaism Through the Ages*

The *Adversos Judaeos* (against the Jews) tradition developed in the Patristic Era, exemplified by the sermons of fathers of the church such as Saint John Chrysostom, prominent bishop and theologian known as "the golden-mouthed orator." Scholars believe that his vitriolic words against the Jews from the pulpit of the church in Antioch during the High Holy Days 386–87 are evidence that Christians were still attending synagogue, especially on special occasions. Chrysostom was trying to dissuade them from this practice. Whatever the motive, it is painful to read such words from a saint and theologian of the church.[7]

Unfortunately, the responsibility for Jesus' death was ascribed to the Jews by the populace, if not by the popes.

Rejection of Jews by Christians flourished in the Middle Ages. Because of superstition, ignorance, and fanaticism, myths about Jews included blood libel, well poisoning, and sorcery. Jews were massacred by Crusaders in the Rhineland en route to the Holy Land. Jews were relegated to the ghetto, and prescriptions about Jews from Roman law were incorporated into church law, including "the marking of Jewish clothes with a badge" (Fourth Lateran Council, 1215).

In the art and architecture of the later medieval period the figures of two women—Ecclesia (representing the church), and Synagogua (representing the synagogue)—were sometimes sculpted on either side of the crucified Jesus on the portals of cathedrals. Ecclesia was portrayed receiving the blood of the crucified savior in a cup; Synagogua was usually blindfolded, sometimes with the broken tablets of the Ten Commandments in her hands. These architectural portraits communicated a theology of the rejection of the Jews even to the unlettered masses of people during the period.[8] That Jesus and Mary were themselves Jews did not seem to enter the consciousness of those who were rejecting Jews at this time. One wonders if some people identified Mary with the figure of Ecclesia, as she has sometimes been described as mother of the church.

During the Inquisition there was a great effort to convert Jews or to persecute them if they did not convert. They were regularly expelled from various nations depending on the whim of the rulers. The Renaissance provoked some scholarly interchange between Christians and Jews. Some scripture scholars wanted to explore Hebrew sources. Some artists reflected anew on Jesus from a humanistic perspective. Rembrandt used a Sephardic Jew in Amsterdam as a model for one of his portraits of Jesus. With Martin Luther's horrendous tract *On the Jews and Their Lies* (1546), however, further persecution of the Jews was encouraged.[9]

The nineteenth-century conviction of the superiority of the Nordic people flowing from a pseudo-science sparked by Darwinian thought also produced a movement for the "aryanization" of Jesus. Johann Gottlieb Fichte (1762–1814) claimed that Jesus was not a Jew, basing his contention on the Gospel of John, which does not provide a genealogy for Jesus and offers a more mystical interpretation of his life. In his "romantic quest for a German racial identity," Fichte questioned, "How, then, could Jesus have been Jewish, when his religion was so un-Jewish, in fact so *German*?"[10]

This gradual process of the aryanization of Jesus was continued by Ernest Renan and Paul de Lagarde. Traditionally, the word *Semitic* had been accepted as a description within the family of languages. Christian Lassen, however, extended the linguistic understanding of this term to the ethnic and psychological areas, an idea upon which Renan and Lagarde elaborated. The latter, in particular, denied that Jesus was a Jew and instead described him as a religious genius. Why else, Lagarde asks, did he always refer to himself as the "Son of Man"?[11]

Perhaps the most radical racist approach to the aryanization of Jesus was that of Houston Stewart Chamberlain. He claimed that Jesus was a Galilean and, therefore, an Aryan and not a Jew. He stated, "The probability that Christ was no Jew, that he had not a drop of genuinely Jewish blood in his veins is so great that it is almost equivalent to a certainty."[12] He believed that Jesus' life and teaching could be understood only as a negation and rejection of Judaism.

This emphasis on Nordic superiority produced both an Aryan Jesus and an Aryan Mary in art. One need only look at the paintings of Jesus and Mary with blond hair and blue eyes that were popular in the nineteenth and twentieth centuries in both churches and homes to understand this claim. Jesus and Mary were often portrayed as more German than Jew.[13] In *Jesus Through the Centuries* Jaroslav Pelikan offers a fascinating reflection:

> Would there have been such anti-Semitism, would there have been so many pogroms, would there have been an Auschwitz, if every Christian church and every Christian

> home had focused its devotion on icons of Mary not only as Mother of God and Queen of Heaven but as the Jewish maiden and the new Miriam, and on icons of Christ not only as Pantocrator but as *Rabbi Jeshua bar-Joseph*, Rabbi Jesus of Nazareth, the Son of David, in the context of the history of a suffering Israel and a suffering humanity?[14]

## CHRISTIAN QUESTS FOR THE HISTORICAL JESUS

The first quest for the historical Jesus, one of the results of the Enlightenment, was initiated mostly by liberal Protestant scholars in the nineteenth century. Ironically, in their search for the historical Jesus, they further obliterated the Jewish Jesus, and along with him, the Jewish Mary. According to Anglican biblical theologian N. T. Wright, "Nineteenth century historians ignored the Jewishness of Jesus, trying as hard as they could to universalize him, to make him the timeless teacher of eternal verities. This strand of their work . . . served the interests of their romantic-idealist interpretation of Jesus."[15] This incompatible coupling of modern historical-critical methods with an idealizing christological tendency created an intellectual dilemma that was finally resolved when scholars began to make a distinction between "the Jesus of history" and "the Christ of faith."[16]

At the end of the nineteenth century a German scholar named Martin Kähler published *The So-Called Historical Jesus and the Historic, Biblical Christ.*[17] Kähler claimed that the Gospels could not be sources for the "Jesus of history" because the Gospels were not historical accounts but, rather, post-Easter confessionals. He believed that the "Christ of faith" revealed in the Gospels ought to be the major concern of Christians.

The first quest for the historical Jesus reached its definitive moment and final stage with the publication of Albert Schweitzer's (1875–1965) *Quest of the Historical Jesus.*[18] Schweitzer pointed out that rather than discovering the "original" Jesus, liberal scholars presented the portrait of Jesus most congenial to them and to the times in which they were writing—images of Jesus that looked more like themselves and their culture than like Jesus. Schweitzer believed that any effort to understand the historical Jesus must first allow him—and the scholars investigating him—to fit into first-century Jewish life and culture. He concluded that no quest could ever be historical enough and that ultimately Christians must be content to accept the Christ of faith. With interest firmly focused on "Jesus as the Christ," the "Jewish Jesus" or the "Jewish Mary" were of little concern.

The Christian quest for the Jewish Jesus was further hampered by a popular technique called the "criterion of dissimilarity." First offered in 1921 by Rudolph Bultmann in his *History of the Synoptic Tradition*,[19] this approach was based on the presumption that what Jesus shared with any form of first-century Judaism would not disclose his uniqueness. Therefore, any of the Judaisms with which Jesus may have agreed were automatically ruled out as a source of insight about him. The same would apply to Mary. Anything she had in common with the Judaism of her time would not identify her as unique, so it could be (and was) discarded.

Bultmann's method dominated scholars for many years. It was embraced by Norman Perrin as late as 1967. In *Rediscovering the Teaching of Jesus* Perrin stated: "By definition it the criterion of dissimilarity] will exclude all teaching in which Jesus may have been at one with Judaism or the early church at one with him."[20] Fortunately, the criterion of dissimilarity has fallen into disfavor due to a new appreciation of historical consciousness that has developed in our era. Sociologists and psychologists affirm we cannot be unrelated to the world in which we live. We are shaped in large part by family and culture. To understand Jesus, therefore, we must set him in his environment of first-century Judaism. As N. T. Wright puts it, "Texts matter, but contexts matter even more."[21]

The so-called new quest for the historical Jesus found its catalysts in a famous lecture by Ernst Kasemann in 1953, and in Gunther Bornkamm's remarkable attempt to synthesize what can be known about the historical Jesus in his volume *Jesus of Nazareth*, published in German in 1956. Other scholars who challenged Bultmann and made outstanding contributions were Joachim Jeremias, C. H. Dodd, H. Conzelmann, Oscar Cullmann, and Jewish scholar David Flusser.

Catholic biblical scholarship, finally liberated by Pius XII in 1943, blossomed after Vatican II in the writings of Raymond Brown, SS, Joseph Fitzmyer, SJ, Roland Murphy, OCarm, and other scripture scholars. Theologians—Protestant and Catholic—such as Karl Rahner, SJ, Edward Schillebeeckx, OP, Wolfhart Pannenberg, Jürgen Moltmann, and Walter Kasper explored the christological dimensions of the new research.

A "renewed New Quest" was born in the 1980s with the founding of the much-publicized "Jesus Seminar," with Burton L. Mack and John Dominic Crossan as two of the leading scholars.[22] This search widened the circle of documentary sources and included, among other works, the Gospel of Thomas in addition to the canonical Gospels. A major emphasis has been the attempt to discern which of the sayings of Jesus are authentic. The Jesus Seminar has been criticized for failing to consider the Jewish context of Jesus' sayings among the criteria for discerning their authenticity.[23]

More recently, a group of Christian and Jewish scholars has emerged that has been dubbed the Third Quest. Among them are E. P. Sanders, James Charlesworth, John P. Meier, Bernard Lohfink, and the Jewish scholar Geza Vermes. They believe that non-canonical and extra-biblical sources need to be taken seriously, as well as the complexity of first-century Judaism.[24] Serious historical method has finally made a comeback, and so has the Jewish Jesus. Recent archeological findings, the retrieval of ancient manuscripts, and insights owing to increased collaboration among Jewish and Christian scholars now indicate that there is more that can be known about the historical Jesus than previously thought.

## THE JEWISH SEARCH FOR JESUS

During the Enlightenment some Jewish scholars began to study Jesus. Matthew Hoffman's recent volume, *From Rebel to Rabbi: Reclaiming Jesus and the Making of Modern Jewish Culture* agrees in part with Schweitzer. Hoffman believes that "Jewish writings on Jesus tell us more about Jews than about Jesus."[25] Throughout the centuries when Jews were persecuted by Christians, they had little that was good to say about Jesus, whom they portrayed as a heretic or worse.

During the Jewish Enlightenment *(Haskalah)*, Moses Mendelssohn (1729–86) and others made efforts to ameliorate Christian attitudes toward Jews. Mendelssohn believed that Jesus was an observant rabbinic Jew. Hoffman notes that although Jesus could not be accepted by Jews as the messiah, he could be "embraced by Jews of the Enlightenment as proof to their Christian contemporaries that even as practicing Jews they maintained no inherent enmity toward Jesus or Christianity, and thus they should not be barred from full participation in Christian society."[26]

The separation of the historical Jesus from the Christian dogma of Christ by Protestant scholars in the nineteenth century opened up the possibility for Jewish scholars to explore Jesus from a less threatening perspective.[27] Samuel Sandmel suggests that because Protestant research had sought to discover the historical Jesus, "some Jews feel compelled to give serious attention to him, and, indeed, there arose in some of them the tendency which has properly been called 'a Jewish reclamation' of Jesus."[28]

With the establishment of the *Wissenschaft des Judentums* (science of Judaism) movement in 1819, pioneer studies of Jesus on the part of Jewish scholars took on new momentum. Two major figures of nineteenth century German Jewry—Abraham Geiger (1810–74) and Heinrich Graetz (1817–91)—applied the ideas of the *Wissenschaft* in differing ways.[29] Susannah Heschel credits Geiger as "the first Jew to subject Christian texts to detailed historical analysis from an explicitly Jewish perspective."[30]

Joseph Klausner published *Yeshu ha-Notsri,* the first modern full-length history of Jesus in Hebrew, in 1922. Following the approach of Geiger and Graetz, Jesus is presented as an observant Jew. The English translation, *Jesus of Nazareth: His Life, Times, and Teachings,*[31] which appeared in 1925, received both substantial criticism and commendation from Jews and Christians. In the final paragraph Klausner states: "In his [Jesus'] ethical code there is a sublimity, distinctiveness and originality in form unparalleled in any other Hebrew ethical code; neither is there any parallel to the remarkable art of his parables."[32]

Rabbi Stephen S. Wise enthusiastically endorsed Klausner's work in a lecture at Carnegie Hall in New York City in 1925. He stated emphatically that it marked a first chapter in a new literature—Jews writing about Jesus. He concluded: "Thank God the time has come when men are allowed to be frank, sincere, and truthful in their beliefs."[33] Liberal Christians and liberal Jews were beginning to find possibilities for conversation. Just as Jesus had seemed to be "de-christologized" by some Christians, some liberal Jews were convinced that the Torah had to be de-legalized. A de-christologized Jesus became a proto-Reform Jew—a good Reform rabbi! There was great optimism that a new universal age was about to appear in America. Little did Jews in America or around the world realize how their lives would change with World War II and the *Shoah* (Holocaust).

Jewish scholarly interest in researching Jesus has increased since World War II. More recently a new generation of Jewish scholars with proficiency in New Testament studies has emerged. Leaders in this field include Rabbi Michael J. Cook, who wrote a valuable volume entitled *Modern Jews Engage the New Testament*, and Amy-Jill Levine, author of *The Misunderstood Jew*.[34]

Anthologies on the Jewishness of Jesus by Christian and Jewish scholars have also multiplied. They include *Jesus*

*Through Jewish Eyes*, edited by Beatrice Bruteau; *The Jewish Jesus*, edited by Zev Garber; and *Christ Jesus and the Jewish People Today*, edited by Philip Cunningham et al. Perhaps the crowning achievement is *The Jewish Annotated New Testament* edited by Amy-Jill Levine and Marc Zvi Brettler. In addition to a commentary on each of the books of the New Testament by a Jewish scholar, the volume contains valuable essays on multiple topics of importance for understanding Judaism in the first century.[35]

That Jesus and Mary were Jews in first-century Palestine is not disputed today. Every culture in every century has tried to understand this rabbi and his mother in multiple ways. Whereas Jews might accept him only as a rabbi, Christians believe Jesus to be the messiah and Son of God. Is it possible to know in greater depth how he worshiped and prayed, and how his prayer, his human relationships, and his commitment to justice were integrated in his life? Might these insights offer us clues as to how his mother would have lived and prayed? Learning more about the particular form of Judaism that most influenced the Jesus of history could help us to answer these questions. A closer look at the Pharisees—and Jesus' relationship to them—provides us with yet another opportunity to continue the quest for the Jewish Jesus and, particularly for this study, for the Jewish Mary.

## JESUS AND THE PHARISEES

When I arrived at church to celebrate Eucharist one Lenten Tuesday, I had forgotten that the Gospel for the day was about the Pharisees (Mt 23:1–12). When the young priest began his homily, he stated with great gusto: "Let's face it—Jesus was furious with the Pharisees! The reason was—for want of a better word—their hypocrisy!" He preached at length on the topic. After the liturgy was over, I could not resist encouraging my priest-friend to check out some of the new research on the Pharisees. I told him that he might be surprised with his discovery.

A dictionary definition of *Pharisee* (uppercase) is "a member of a Jewish sect of the intertestamental period noted for strict observance of rites and ceremonies of the written law, and for insistence on the validity of their own oral tradition." The meaning of *pharisaical* (lowercase), however, has become over time less flattering: "hypocritical censorious self-righteousness."[36] Unfortunately, many Christians imagine a Pharisee to be like the self-righteous religious leader who encounters a publican at prayer (Lk 18:10–13). Or they may remember Jesus' denunciation of Pharisees as "whited sepulchers!" (Mt 23:27–28). Certainly these are not role models for human beings at any time in history.

Just as there was the quest for the historical Jesus, so too there has been a search for the historical Pharisees. Initially, this was the work of Jewish scholars. In the early nineteenth century, Talmudists set out to prove that Christian scholars, who were mostly ignorant of or ignored rabbinic teaching, had an anti-Judaic agenda. According to Jacob Neusner, many Jewish scholars were themselves polemical toward Christian portrayals and/or uncritical of Talmudic material. Their goal was to prove that the Pharisees were the opposite of those portrayed in the Gospels.

In the post–World War II period, ground-breaking work performed by Jacob Neusner and Ellis Rivkin provided Jewish and Christian scholars with comprehensive new understandings of the Pharisees. Neusner's 1970 three-volume work, *The Rabbinic Tradition About the Pharisees Before 70* was made more accessible in his work entitled *From Politics to Piety.* Rivkin's study, *A Hidden Revolution,* offered fresh insights in 1978.[37]

Christian scholars such as Eugene J. Fisher, John Pawlikowski, and Clark Williamson expanded this research and made the new approach to the Pharisees available to the Christian community. E. P. Sanders's work *Jesus and Judaism*, and John P. Meier's monumental study *A Marginal Jew* have enriched recent literature by integrating their discussion of Jesus and his relationship to Judaism into larger studies. Anthony J. Saldarini's volume, *Pharisees, Scribes, and Sadducees in Palestinian Society,* approaches the topic from the perspective of sociological and literary analyses. All of these studies and others have challenged us to broaden our vision of the Pharisees as understood in both Jewish and Christian traditions.[38]

As a consequence of these contributions, many scholars have concluded that Jesus had more in common with the Pharisees than he did with any of the other groups within Judaism at that time. Some scholars have even asked—was Jesus a Pharisee? True, he had disagreements with them, but according to the Gospels, Pharisees such as Nicodemus and Joseph of Arimathea were his friends. Gamaliel, who encouraged the Sanhedrin not to punish the new Christian movement, is described as a Pharisee (Acts 5:35–42). As with most religious and political parties today, there are groups antagonistic to certain stances within the larger body. Sometimes when members of a group are fighting among themselves their arguments are more vehement than when they are fighting against obvious opponents. In the words of Edward Kessler, these arguments between Jesus and his adversaries were more of "an intense family feud, an internal Jewish argument."[39]

Rabbi Harvey Falk, who authored *Jesus the Pharisee*, believes that Jesus was indeed a Pharisee and belonged to the School of Hillel.[40] Most scholars, however, are slow to identify Jesus as such, but they would agree that he was more at home with the Pharisees than with any other group in the complex Judaism of his time. More common would be the statement of Lawrence H. Schiffman: "In regard to social matters, he [Jesus] can be placed in the camp closest to the Pharisees and furthest from such sectarians as those who left us the Dead Sea Scrolls."[41] The Vatican document "Notes on the Correct Way to Present Jews and Judaism in Preaching and Catechesis" agrees that Jesus was closer to the Pharisees than to any of the other Jewish groups in the first century.[42]

***Who Were the Pharisees?***

A significant challenge faced by scholars investigating the Pharisees has been that primary sources by and about them are meager. As a group, the Pharisees are explicitly mentioned in (a) the writings of the Jewish historian Josephus; (b) the New Testament; and (c) the Tannaitic (early rabbinic) literature. Some scholars also see an indirect reference to the Pharisees in the Dead Sea Scrolls literature.[43]

The etymology of the word *Pharisee*" is disputed. John Bowker states: "The Greek language sources (Josephus and the N.T.) refer to a group known as the *pharisaioi;* the Semitic language sources [particularly the rabbinic sources] refer to unidentifiable groups of people known as *perushim.* Both can legitimately, but loosely, be transliterated as 'Pharisees.'"[44] According to Anthony Saldarini, "The name seems to come from the Hebrew and Aramaic root *prs* which means 'separate' and 'interpret.'" He describes them as "people who separated themselves from normal Jewish society or from gentile society in order to observe Jewish law [purity, tithing] rigorously."[45] Although they began as a religious social movement in mid-second century BCE, they became immersed in the political scene during the Maccabean period (c. 175–135 BCE). Their fortunes rose and fell, as did the various leaders of the ruling class to whom they related—a web of relationships too complicated to discuss here.

Perhaps the best known Pharisee of the first century is the sage Hillel. Scholars admit that what we know about the historical Hillel (c. 60 BCE–c. 20 CE) is from material written hundreds of years after his death. He is credited with establishing the basic rules of hermeneutics for interpreting the Hebrew scriptures. He introduced the method of *midrash*—an exposition and interpretation that not only cited tradition but, with logical reasoning, allowed a passage of scripture to be applied to the needs of the day. According to Edward Kessler, *midrash* is the Hebrew word for "asking, searching, inquiring and interpreting."[46] Nahum Glatzer states: "Torah was now looked upon as the perennial record of wisdom and instruction, ever ready to offer an answer to a question at hand provided the proper logical principles were applied to the text. Both historic continuity and freedom of reasoning were safeguarded by this concept of Torah."[47]

The parable is a form of *midrash* found in the collection of rabbinic teaching known as the Talmud.[48] One wonders how Jesus became so adept at teaching in parables. Although there is no proof, some authors have suggested that Jesus could have been a pupil of Hillel as a boy. David Flusser has even suggested that Hillel might have been one of the sages whom Jesus questioned during his visit to the Temple at age twelve, as recounted in Luke 2:46–47.[49] We will never know if the young Jesus met Hillel, or if Hillel met Mary and Joseph when they finally found their wayward son in Jerusalem. However, there are similarities in the teaching methods of Hillel and Jesus.

### *Two Schools: Beit Hillel and Beit Shammai*

Many Christians are unaware that there were different Schools within the Pharisees; the best known were the School *(Beit)* of Hillel and the School of Shammai. Beit Hillel tended to be more open and liberal, while Beit Shammai was more strict and conservative. It appears that Jesus sided with Hillel more often than not. A famous and oft-repeated *midrash* found in the Talmud is a good illustration:

> A heathen came to Rabbi Shammai and said: "I will become a convert on condition that you teach me the whole Law while standing on one foot." Shammai drove him away with a measuring rod he held in his hand. Then the man went to Rabbi Hillel with the same challenge. Hillel said, "What is hateful to you, do not do to your fellow. That is the whole Law. All the rest is commentary. Go and learn." (Shabbath 31A)[50]

Both Hillel and Jesus echoed the biblical proverb, "Do to no one what you would not want done to yourself" (Tobit 4:15). Jesus states this adage, which is also found in other religions, in the positive form: "Do to others whatever you would have them do to you. This is the law and the prophets" (Mt 7:12; cf. Lk 6:31).

Eugene Fisher notes that the guiding spirit of the rabbinic approach to the Law that grew out of the school of Hillel can be fairly summed up in the saying, "The Sabbath is given to you; but you are not surrendered to the Sabbath" (Mekhilta 31:13). Jesus' saying shows how close he was to the followers of Hillel: "The sabbath was made for humankind, not humankind for the sabbath" (Mk 2:27, NRSV). The context in Mark is also revealing; here Jesus' disciples are being censured by some of the Pharisees for plucking ears of corn to eat on the Sabbath (Mt 12:1–8). Although there is no evidence, Fisher suggests that these Pharisees could have been followers of Shammai.[51]

The Hillel-influenced Pharisees prescribed *kavanah*—spiritual concentration.[52] One should have the proper intention and not resort to mere externalism. One should live the *spirit* and not just the letter of the law. The spirit of the law can only be discerned by opening the heart to God. They argued: "It matters not whether you do much or little as long as your heart is directed to heaven" (Ber 17a). And again: "The Torah that is practiced and studied for its own sake is a law of love; the law followed not for its own sake is a law without love" (Suk 49b).

## THE PHARISEES, JESUS, AND THE EARLY CHRISTIANS

According to Fisher, Jesus' teachings and those of the Pharisees were similar and in some cases appear identical. The sayings of Jesus are not radically different from what was being taught in the complex Judaisms of the first century.[53] This similarity does not diminish Jesus' uniqueness but sets him in the context of his time, a time in which the Pharisees brought extensive changes and adaptations into Judaism. To what degree did these influence Jesus and the Jewish followers of Jesus who came to be known as Christians? Drawing once again on Ellis Rivkin, Jacob Neusner, John Pawlikowski, Eugene Fisher, and others, I discuss seven major areas in which basic ideas of the Pharisees are compatible with and very likely influenced both Jesus and the emerging Christian movement: (1) the Oral Torah; (2) the concept of *mitzvah* (pl. *mitzvot*); (3) the developing role of the rabbi; (4) the synagogue as a center for study and prayer; (5) table fellowship; (6) interiority of covenant; and (7) the resurrection of the body. Although elements of these concepts, such as *mitzvah*, were a part of the Hebrew religion from earlier years, a new emphasis was given them by the Pharisees.

Foundational to all of these is what Pawlikowski describes as "the theological underpinnings of Pharisaism." Relying on Ellis Rivkin, he describes "a fundamentally new perception of the God-human person relationship" based, in part, on belief in the resurrection of the body.[54] A brief reflection on these seven elements that Jesus shared with the Pharisees will hopefully give us insights into Jesus, Mary, and the early Christian movement. Five areas where Jesus differed from the Pharisees are also discussed.

### *Similarities*

#### *1. Oral Torah*

Jews believed that the Written Torah, consisting of the first five books of the Hebrew Bible, was given by God to Moses on Mount Sinai. The Sadducees, members of the Temple elite, believed that the exposition and interpretation of the Written Torah was the exclusive prerogative of the priestly class. The Pharisees, however, believed that the Oral Torah, a process of rabbinical interpretation of the Written Torah, also originated at Sinai and that Oral Torah was authoritative as well. The

Sadducees were bitterly opposed to that concept, but since the Sadducees disappeared after the fall of the Second Temple in 70 CE, the Pharisaic interpretation prevailed. The Oral Torah eventually "came to mean the sum totality of Jewish law and guidance as imparted to Israel by divine revelation."[55]

By the turn of the second century the School of Hillel recognized that survival of the Jewish tradition required that the Oral Torah be written down. The Talmud, the written record of the Oral Torah, was born. The Talmud consists of two main components. The foundational document, the Mishnah (Hebrew for "teaching by oral repetition"), is a topical collection of interpretations of the biblical Torah. The Gemara (Aramaic for "teaching") is an elaboration and commentary on the Mishnah.

How did the Oral Torah function in daily life? One example among Hillel's rules of interpretation *(middoth)* is referred to as the rule of "light and heavy." Fisher states, "Under it, a principle that applies in a lesser case can be applied as well to a weightier one or more important matter." The phrase "How much more?" is often used to indicate that a rabbi is making use of this principle. Fisher illustrates this by quoting Matthew 7:11, in which Jesus states, "If you, with all your sins, know how to give your children what is good, *how much more* will your heavenly Father give good things to anyone who asks him?" Again, in Luke 12:28, "If God clothes in such splendor the grass of the field, which grows today and is thrown on the fire tomorrow, *how much more* will he provide for you?" Jesus was using a rabbinic method of interpretation not unlike that of the Pharisees influenced by Hillel.[56]

### *2. Mitzvah—Living the Commandments*

The Pharisees believed all 613 commandments had to be restudied continually in light of human need and the situation of the day. They believed the commandments were an opportunity to sanctify everyday life. The word *mitzvah* means "commandment." The various rituals that were prescribed were rituals of interpersonal behavior, not just the fulfilling of an obligation. The offering of prayers of blessing *(bracha)* for *everything* in Jewish life highlights the relationship of people to one another and to God. Oral Torah emphasizes this relationship between the Law and a good and loving deed. I am reminded of an experience I had in Israel when I helped an elderly lady off of a bus. Smiling, she said to me, "That's your *mitzvah* for the day!" It isn't enough to believe the Law; one has to live it as the loving deed in one's life.

The relationship of the Law to the doing of *mitzvot* is also related to the question of justice. In the Hebrew scriptures, *tzedek* (justice) is sometimes translated as "righteousness" or "charity." It does not refer to legal justice, which is usually translated as *mishpat*. I recall a rabbi friend preaching passionately on the eve of Yom Kippur on *tzedakah*—repeating it many times. After the service I asked him if he was referring to justice. He replied, "Oh, no! It means charity! I was telling the people that they should live out the Torah by acts of charity!" At first I was puzzled. Then I understood that charity is not philanthropy, giving out of our largesse. It is also justice. According to biblical scholar Luis Alonso Schökel, SJ, *tzedakah* means redressing the imbalances in society.[57]

The connection between charity and justice was highlighted for me the following year when I received a phone call during the High Holy Days from one of the Jewish board members of the North Phoenix Corporate Ministry (NPCM). During the ten-day period between Rosh Hashanah and Yom Kippur, Jews examine their lives and ask how they might atone for sins of the past year and prepare to live a better life in the year ahead. He told me that he would like to donate $1,000 to the St. Mary's Food Bank—a project which our group supported—but that he would like the gift to be anonymous. Could he please send the check to me, and would I donate it from the NPCM? I told him that I would be happy to do so. It was a powerful example of the Gospel verse: "When you do some act of charity, do not let your left hand know what your right is doing; your good deed must be secret, and your Father who sees what is done in secret will reward you" (Mt 6:3–4). His *mitzvah* made Jesus' description of doing the good deed without advertising it a reality for me. It seemed to me that this donor's anonymous generosity was an example of living out *tzedakah*—his effort to redress the imbalances in society.

Reading the Gospels we become aware that Jesus did his share of *mitzvot.* Certainly healing Peter's mother-in-law, the leper, the man born blind, the son of the centurion, and the daughter of the synagogue official are only a few examples. The multiplication of the loaves and fishes nourished the bodies and spirits of many hungry people. A life of *mitzvot* is not just doing good deeds. It is living the commandments in the sanctification of daily life. "Give us this day our daily bread," "Consider the lilies of the fields"—Jesus' whole life was a *bracha*, a blessing, in which he lived out his covenant with God.

One might also reflect on Mary's life and ask how she lived a life of *mitzvot.* According to Luke, Mary, after learning that she would be the mother of Jesus, went immediately to help Elizabeth, her elderly cousin who was pregnant (Lk 1:39–56). This would have been a *mitzvah,* as was her concern for the young bride and groom who were running short of wine at their wedding at Cana (Jn 2:1–11). Mary lived the commandments in her daily life and did so with love. How else would Jesus have learned that lesson so well?

### *3. The Role of the Rabbi*

A rabbi was/is not a priest or a prophet but primarily a teacher. With the new emphasis on the Oral Torah there was need for interpreters of the Law within this broader framework. According to Pawlikowski, the rabbi had a "two-fold function: interpreting Torah and . . . specifying its generalized commandments found in the Pentateuch and the Prophets into concrete duties that would answer the needs of Jewish society in any given period of history."[58] The rabbi also had the responsibility of living out the message of the Torah and promoting the way it should be lived so as to fulfill the social responsibility of the time.

Jesus is addressed as rabbi five times in the Gospel of John. This most likely reflects the era of the writing of the text and not the period when Jesus lived, since the term *rabbi* was not used in Jesus' time. It was and is a term of respect for a teacher. An unexpected experience allowed me to learn what it means to be a rabbi. I was invited to preach at the Shabbat service at Temple Israel in Minneapolis one spring night in 1991. Among those who came up to congratulate me after the service was an elderly Jewish couple. The gentleman said with a smile, "You would make a wonderful rabbi!" Next in line was Father Rick Banker, a young priest who was one of my former students. He interrupted them and stated with positive glee, "Oh, but she is!" The rabbi is, indeed, the teacher.

Jesus very likely found joy in teaching those who were hungering for God's word, such as the Samaritan woman at the well or the crowds who came to him seeking wisdom. Sometimes his teaching was in parables. At other times he spoke mysteriously regarding the future, for example, "Destroy this temple and in three days I will build it up again." He was a conduit for expressing the knowledge and love of God to those who were hungry and thirsty for truth and life.

Where did Jesus learn some of the homespun examples that he used to describe God's love? Could it have been from his mother? Perhaps stories she told him of the neighbor who lost a coin? Or how she reflected when she baked bread and waited for the yeast to cause the dough to rise? One can suspect that Mary was a good teacher, and Jesus might have learned insights into human nature and what might touch people's hearts from his mother.

### *4. The Synagogue*

My good friend Rabbi Moshe Tutnauer was fond of saying to me: "The synagogue was good enough for Jesus and Mary.

It should be good enough for you!" This led me to inquire as to the origin of the synagogue. The Hebrew word *kehillah* (community) comes from the word *kahal* (assembly). In the Hebrew scriptures the *kahal Yahweh* was the assembly of the people of God. It is sometimes described as "the gathered together of God."

Until the year 70 CE the Pharisees continued to worship in the Temple when possible. In places distant from Jerusalem, however, the focus was increasingly on the synagogue—a gathering place for a variety of activities including prayer and worship. Lee I. Levine, in *The Ancient Synagogue,* states that although some scholars have opted for a date as early as the ninth century BCE, and others from the time of the sixth century BCE Babylonian Exile, there is no hard evidence for the existence of a synagogue until third-century-BCE Egypt. "It is not until the first century CE that the synagogue emerges into the full light of history as the central communal institution of Jewish communities throughout Judaea and the Diaspora." He claims: "Major cities such as Jerusalem, Alexandria, Rome and probably Antioch, boasted a number of such institutions, not to speak of villages, towns and cities throughout the Roman Empire."[59]

Ironically, archeologists have not found the remains of many synagogues in Galilee, but it is important to remember that, like the early church, the synagogue was not necessarily an official building, but rather the assembly of the people.[60] Sometimes the "synagogue" was a space under a tree or adjacent to a building in the center of the village, or in the home of one of the members of the community. It was a designated area with multiple purposes—what we might call today a community center. Jewish men and boys—and perhaps some women, as recent research suggests—would gather there to engage in Torah study and discussion. The community would assemble there to listen to the Torah being read and to participate in the accompanying prayers on Shabbat.

It is not unlikely that Joseph, Mary, Jesus, and members of their extended family would gather there for Sabbaths and feasts to pray and to worship the God of Abraham and Sarah, Isaac, Rebecca, Jacob, and Rachel. The rabbis would explain the concrete demands of the Oral Torah and emphasize the relationship between worship and ethical service. Although disputed by some scholars today, Ellis Rivkin believes that "the synagogue emerged spontaneously in the course of the Pharisaic revolution."[61] Participating in Jewish life at home and synagogue would have been a regular part of Jesus' life, a life that Mary shared.

When Jesus and his disciples traveled, they prayed in synagogues and sometimes preached there. It was probably the first place they went when they moved to new territory. In Capernaum they were greeted warmly, and people were eager to hear the new "rabbi," who taught and healed. In his hometown of Nazareth, however, he was not so fortunate. Could this have been because the Nazarenes were jealous of a local who became famous in other places? Not unlike other Jewish prophets, Jesus was not welcomed in his hometown, as we read in Luke 4:24, "Amen, I say to you, no prophet is accepted in his own native place."

After the destruction of the Temple the synagogue expanded in its communal function. In addition to being a place of assembly for study and prayer, it was the site of the courts of the Law, and a locus for the schools. The poor and the needy would come there for assistance and to find a haven. In time, the synagogue included a whole web of relationships. It became crucial as the place for Jews to connect in the Diaspora. The synagogue community became a unique institution and, in many ways, is the mother of the Christian Church. The house churches of the early Christians were not dissimilar to the synagogues that met in Jewish homes.

### Women in the Synagogue

Perhaps one of the most startling excursions into research since the enormous archeological discoveries of the mid-twentieth century is a remarkable book by Bernadette J. Brooten, *Women*

*Leaders in Ancient Synagogues*. It is a carefully tuned study of nineteen Greek and Latin inscriptions from synagogue excavations dating from 27 BCE to approximately the sixth century CE. On these inscriptions from Italy, Asia Minor, Egypt, and Palestine, "women bear the titles 'head of the synagogue,' 'leader,' 'elder,' 'mother of the synagogue,' and 'priestess.'" Several of these inscriptions had been known to scholars from earlier years, but Brooten offers a new interpretation.[62]

The presupposition of earlier scholarship was that women would not have been allowed to hold positions of leadership in the synagogue, so the conclusion was that these titles were only honorific. Earlier writers believed leadership titles were awarded because the woman's husband was the head of the synagogue. In more recent years some scholars began to question this assertion. Brooten concludes that only by examining each title and inscription individually is it possible to discern and interpret this phenomenon. She offers a variety of examples from inscriptions where it seems evident that women exercised authority in their own right.[63]

Brooten has also explored whether there were separate seating areas for women, such as an upstairs gallery or a sectioned-off room. She believes that although some such spaces may have existed, there is no indication in either archeological or literary evidence that these spaces were for the purpose of segregating women.[64] Brooten offers examples from the Gospels and Acts of the Apostles. In Luke 13:10–17 Jesus heals the crippled woman *in the synagogue* on the Sabbath. The Gospel writer describes the leader of the synagogue as indignant, not because a woman was in the congregation, but because Jesus healed on the Sabbath. Women were a part of the synagogue community.

Too often we forget that the women disciples of Jesus and Paul were indeed *Jewish* women who often took initiative, provided resources, and offered hospitality in a Jewish context to a charismatic rabbi who won their allegiance. We can, I believe, reasonably presume that Jesus' mother, Mary, Martha and Mary, Mary Magdalene, and other women who believed in Jesus and his mission would have attended synagogue and could have been actively involved there.

### *5. Table Fellowship*

Because the Pharisees were convinced that priestly activity was not necessarily reserved to the priestly class, the laws of ritual purity were to be kept at home and at the table as well as in the Temple. Anthony Saldarini describes the Pharisaic belief in extending the holiness of the Temple and its priesthood to the people by underscoring the necessity of living the laws in everyday life. Opportunities to participate in priestly activity included "observing biblical rules of ritual purity at home. Food was to be prepared and eaten in ritual purity. . . . Sabbath was to be rigorously observed, and the laws and traditions of Israel were lovingly studied and interpreted."[65]

According to Jacob Neusner, the Pharisees hoped to alter the power structure in Jewish life. He states:

> Therefore one must eat secular food (ordinary, everyday meals) in a state of ritual purity *as if one were a Temple priest*. The Pharisees thus arrogated to themselves—and to all Jews equally—the status of the Temple priests, and performed actions restricted to priests because of their status. The table of every Jew in his home was seen as being like the table of the Lord in the Jerusalem Temple. The commandment, "You shall be a kingdom of priests, and a holy people," was taken literally. Everyone is a priest, everyone stands in the same relationship to God, and everyone must keep the priestly laws.[66]

The shift away from the Temple and its priests to the ordinary people created a new sense of equality. Christians have sometimes characterized the minute prescriptions and laws that the Jews seemed to require as legalism. To do so is to fail to understand that the extension of the complicated laws of priestly purity to every Jew in his or her home was embraced, not as a new burden, but as a new privilege. The Pharisaic emphasis on what Christians might call "the priesthood of all believers" gave new power to the people. According to Rivkin, the Pharisees were a revolution within the religious tradition of Judaism—a successful and a radical revolution.[67]

After the destruction of the Temple, this Pharisaic emphasis on the all-pervasive presence of God in the home enabled the Jewish community to survive and prosper at a time when extreme demoralization could have brought about the disintegration of the community. In the post-70 CE period, laws became a way for the Jews to retain their communal sense of themselves as a people. The belief that the Law, should be experienced in the home by living out every prescription in table fellowship (all meals, but especially dinner on Shabbat and the Passover Seder) allowed Jews to retain their identity in a period of crisis.

Table fellowship was also a priority for Jesus in terms of relationships. He invited himself to the home of Zacchaeus for dinner. In Luke 7:36 we read: "One of the Pharisees invited him to dinner; he went to the Pharisee's home and took his place at table." He appears quite at home enjoying dinner with Martha, Mary, and Lazarus. After he cured Peter's mother-in-law, she fixed dinner for Jesus and his disciples. He seemed to relish the opportunity to eat, teach, pray, and enjoy companionship in table fellowship—an experience not atypical for a Pharisaic lifestyle. Prior to his last Passover with his apostles, Jesus gave specific directions for locating a place and making preparations. His example of washing their feet and praying at his last meal with them in John 13—17 offers us an intimate glimpse of Jesus' life with his friends. It should be noted that Jesus' table fellowship was radically inclusive. Sometimes he ate with people whom the Pharisees would have excluded.

### *6. Interiority of Covenant/Abba*

The theological foundation for the Pharisaic perspective on life was a fundamentally new perception of the God-human person relationship sometimes referred to as "interiority of covenant." This perspective evolved in the period just before the time of Jesus. The Pharisees proclaimed that the God of revelation was the heavenly Father of each individual person. There was an awakening to a new sense of intimacy, (or sensitivity, as some prefer to call it) between God and the human individual.[68]

Rivkin states that Josephus, who claimed to have been a Pharisee at one point in his life, "gave eloquent testimony to the enduring achievement of the Pharisaic Revolution: *a system of internalized laws mapping the road to salvation*."[69] Josephus stated, in the conclusion to *Against Apion,* that Jews must "be convinced that everything in the whole universe is under the eye and direction of God" (II: 288–95).[70] In the final chapter of *A Hidden Revolution*, titled "God So Loved the Individual," Ellis Rivkin summarized this phenomenon:

> When we ask ourselves the source of this generative power, we find it in the relationship the Pharisees established between the One God and the singular individual. The Father God cared about *you*; He was concerned about *you*. He watched over *you*; He loved *you*, and loved *you* so much that He wished *your* unique self to live forever. One's earthly father was here today and gone tomorrow; but the one Father-God was here forever. . . . The heavenly Father was ever present. One could talk to Him, plead with Him, cry out to Him, pray to Him, person-to-Person, individual-to-Individual, heart-to-Heart, soul-to-Soul. It was the establishment of this personal relationship, an inner experience, that accounts for the manifest power of Pharisaism to live on. . . . Internalization is the only road to salvation.[71]

With this understanding of God's relationship to the human person the rabbis developed new names for God. They relied on some of the older biblical terms when directly citing the scriptures but felt the need for new ways to address God in light of this new development. Pawlikowski calls attention to the following: "Among their principal names for God, in addition to the fundamental one of Father, were *Makom*, 'the All-Present;' *Shekhinah*, 'the divine presence;' *Ha-Kadosh Baruch Hu*, 'the Holy One, blessed be He;' and *Mi She-Amar Ve-Hayah Ha-Olam*, 'He who spoke and the world came into being.'"[72] All of these are indicative of a warmer and more intimate God-human person relationship. Notably, *Shekhinah* is a feminine term for God that has been given renewed emphasis by many Jewish and Christian feminists today.[73]

For Christians, the most familiar name of God is "Our Father Who art in heaven" (in Hebrew, *Avinu She-Bashamayim*). Eugene Fisher offers examples of how the Our Father can be paralleled in Jewish literature. For example, "Hallowed be Thy name" in Matthew 6:9 is almost identical to the *Kaddish*, "Let thy great name be magnified and hallowed." In Matthew 6:10, "Thy will be done on earth as it is in heaven," reads in the Mishnah (Ber T3.7), "Do Thy will in the heavens above and give tranquility of spirit to those who fear Thee on earth." And from the *Alenu* we read, "Lead us not into temptation, but keep us far from all evil" (Ber 16b). There are many areas in which the teachings of Jesus have significant similarities and parallels with the teachings of the Talmud.[74] One of the most beautiful prayers sung in the synagogue on Yom Kippur each year is the *Avinu Malkinu* (Our Father, our king), which might resonate with Christians praying the Our Father.

For many years Christians have believed that Jesus' unique prayer life centered in the fact that he called God Abba. This Aramaic word was wrongly translated by Joachim Jeremias as "Daddy" or "Papa, a translation he retracted in later years. Abba is not an expression associated only with little children but is a personal, some might say intimate, form of address.[75] My first experience of appreciating the meaning of Abba was on one occasion when I was in Israel. I was sitting near a swimming pool where a group of families had gathered. A little boy, possibly four years old, wearing his *kepah,* ran up to his father and said: "Abba, I want an ice cream cone!" With a smile, his father set aside what he was doing, took his son by the hand, and they went to find some ice cream. The tenderness of the scene exemplified for me the intimacy of Jesus referring to God as his Abba. I have also heard adult Jews speak to their fathers as Abba. Although Christians believe that Jesus had an altogether unique relationship with God as his Father, this manner of speaking of God as Abba was part of the Pharisaic tradition that Jesus made his own.

Each of these titles and prayers describes the sense of intimacy with God that seems to have crept into Jewish prayer and life in the first century CE, and even before. Pawlikowski suggests that this important "drift" in human history regarding the personalization of God and the sense of interiority is the milieu out of which Jesus' Abba-experience grew.[76] Even on the cross Jesus prayed, "Abba, forgive them, they know not what they do" (Lk 23:34).

One might even speculate whether this same sense of intimacy with God allowed Mary to be open to God's invitation to her to be the mother of his Son. In our concluding meditations we reflect on Mary in terms of her intimacy with God.

### *7. Resurrection of the Dead*

Many Christians, and indeed many Jews, are unaware of the fact that the concept of the resurrection of the body has been a part of Jewish as well as Christian belief. It was a distinctly Pharisaic idea, rejected by Sadducees in Jesus' time. Jon D. Levenson and Kevin J. Madigan in their recent volume *Resurrection: The Power of God for Christians and Jews* explore the resurrection of the dead as "central to both of our traditions: the teaching that at the end of time God will cause the dead to live again." They distinguish resurrection from immortality, that is, life after death in which the soul lives on without the body. Resurrection refers to the return of the whole person, not just the soul. They add, "It is a *transformed* body. But it is still a body. N. T. Wright has helpfully used the term 'transphysical' to describe Jesus' resurrected body." The same would be true for all resurrected bodies.[77]

References to the resurrection of the body are meager in the Hebrew scriptures. Enoch (Gn 5:24) and the prophet Elijah (2 Kgs 2:1–15) were taken by God from the earth in mysterious ways as a reward for their goodness. There is the poetic rendition of the "dry bones" in Ezekiel 37:1–14. The book of Daniel states: "Many of those who sleep in the dust of the earth shall awake; some shall live forever" (Dn 12:2). There are also references in 2 Maccabees 7. All of these attest to a conviction that God's incomparable power can revive the dead.

The New Testament describes major quarrels between the Sadducees and the Pharisees over the resurrection of the body in Matthew 22:23, Mark 12:18, Luke 20:27, and Acts 23:8. This belief bitterly divided the Pharisees, who strongly asserted resurrection of the body, from the Sadducees, who vehemently denied it. Jewish scholars such as Rivkin believe that this key doctrinal evolution of the Pharisees was a direct consequence of the perceived change in the God-human relationship referred to above. John Pawlikowski reflects: "The integrity and uniqueness of each individual were deemed so precious in the eyes of God that they would not be extinguished by death."[78] Jesus was clearly in agreement with the Pharisees. Rivkin goes so far as to say: "The Pharisaic revolution thus seeded the Christian revolution." He notes that one reason Paul, who claimed to be a Pharisee, proclaimed the resurrection of Christ with such vehemence was that his spiritual life had been rooted in the certainty of the resurrection.[79]

Madigan and Levenson state clearly, "A highly liturgical religion, whose forms of worship are regulated by religious law, rabbinic Judaism early on gave the doctrine of resurrection a central place in its daily worship."[80] Because the core doctrine of Christianity is Jesus' resurrection, Jewish belief in resurrection was later downplayed and some prayers regarding it were retranslated and diluted, especially after the Enlightenment. Even today, however, observant Jews pray three times each weekday, four times on Shabbat and festivals, and five times on Yom Kippur a version of the following prayer in the second benediction:

> You, O Lord, are mighty forever,
> You revive the dead,
> You have the power to save.
> You sustain the living with loving kindnesses,
> You revive the dead with great mercy,
> You support the falling, heal the sick, set free the bound and keep faith with those who sleep in the dust.
> Who is like You, O doer of mighty acts?
> Who resembles You, a king who puts to death and restores to life, and causes salvation to flourish?
> And You are certain to revive the dead.
> Blessed are You, O Lord, who revives the dead.[81]

Reform and Conservative rabbis today agree that many Jews in their congregations would be surprised to learn that belief in the resurrection of the body is a part of Jewish prayer. Rabbi David Sandmel has suggested a helpful distinction: for Christians, resurrection is a belief that ranks highest on their scale of convictions; for Jews, it is lower on the ladder. Many Jews would be amazed to know that it is a Jewish belief at all.

Would belief in the resurrection of the body, a conviction of the Pharisees that might have been known to Mary, have given her hope in the aftermath of Jesus' crucifixion? Would that hope have sustained her in the darkest hours of the crucifixion?

### *Differences*

Lest we think there are nothing but similarities between Jesus and the Pharisees, some clear differences need to be stated. Pawlikowski gives an extended description of nine dissimilarities.[82] I briefly discuss only five that I think deserve particular attention.

First of all, Christians believe that the divine-human relationship that Jesus experienced with his Father is a kind of intimacy that goes beyond any relationship the Pharisees might have understood possible for a human to have with God. Jesus' profound language (as in the discourse at the Last Supper in John 14—17) ignores the sense of proper distance that Jews would presuppose in relationship to the Deity.

Second, Pawlikowski claims that Jesus emphasized the individual person, whereas the Pharisees tended to focus on the community. This may have been because the Pharisees were concerned that Jewish communal survival might be jeopardized by absorption into another culture if the individual took center stage.

Third, regarding the love of one's enemy, Jesus urged love even for those who harm us. Jewish scholar David Flusser agrees that "according to the teachings of Jesus you have to love the sinners, while according to Judaism you have not to hate the wicked." The uncompromising nature of love in Jesus' message seemed to go beyond what was required of a Jew. It extended even to one's enemy. In Judaism, hatred is forbidden, but love of enemy was not necessarily prescribed.[83]

Fourth, the Pharisees believed God alone possessed the power and authority to forgive sins. Jesus not only claimed power to forgive sins but transferred the power to forgive sins to certain disciples. This was clearly revolutionary. The Pharisees would never have gone so far as to suggest that a human being (and that is how they understood Jesus) could forgive sins or give others the power to do so.

Fifth, as the ways parted over the centuries, the foundational difference was that Christians came to accept Jesus as

Messiah. The Hebrew word *messiah* means "the anointed one" and was translated into the Greek as "Christos," which did not necessarily include divinity. In the Hebrew scriptures kings were messiahs, the anointed. The understanding and development of the idea of Jesus as Messiah for Christians came only after the resurrection. Combining the idea of messiah and the divine was an exalted notion far beyond the wildest of Pharisaic dreams, but it became the core of Christian belief.

### The Pharisees and Women

How does Jesus' affinity with the Pharisees relate to our understanding of Mary as a Jewish woman? Is it possible that Mary could have been familiar with some of the Pharisaic ideas that her son and his followers might have accepted? If so, how might that have affected the way she lived and prayed in Galilee in the first century? Let us now consider the relationship of the Pharisees to women of Mary's time.

Recent research by Tal Ilan, in *Integrating Women into Second Temple History,* breaks new ground on Beit Hillel, Beit Shammai, and the role of women in relation to the Pharisees.[84] Ilan contends that women in ancient patriarchal societies have often been attracted to sects where they had the opportunity for leadership. They sometimes used their money and influence to support groups opposed by their husbands. The Pharisees were one such sect. She offers examples of influential women, such as Queen Shelamzion Alexandra, who ruled by herself during the Hasmonean period until her death c. 58 BCE at age seventy-three. The queen, who was a promoter of the Pharisees, was admired by many of her subjects and ruled successfully for nine years, as attested to by Josephus.

Other wealthy Jewish women were also able to support the Pharisees and often acted independently of their husbands. Ilan states: "It appears that women followers were an accepted phenomenon on the Pharisee scene before the destruction of the Temple. I propose a sociological model which explains this within the framework of the attraction of women to marginal opposition groups. This model allows further discussion of two other Second Temple sects, Early Christianity and the Dead Sea Sect."[85]

Ilan believes that although Beit Hillel did not interpret laws favorably toward women in the pre-70 CE period, its followers did not do anything to discourage participation of women because they found their support useful. After the destruction of the Temple, however, the Pharisee movement at Yavneh went through an evolution whereby it transformed itself from a sect to a religion, one which was eventually recognized by the Roman authorities as rabbinic Judaism. During the years that the Pharisees were only a sect, both schools had a special relationship to women, but when the Hillelites became the major authority in Judaism, they rejected "Beit Shammai's ideology, together with its decidedly favorable attitude toward women's economic independence and personhood."[86]

Ross Shepard Kraemer states "that intensification of prescriptions against women is often a response to the increased autonomy and authority of women." Perhaps statements curtailing women's activities "reflect some rabbinic opposition to the power and prestige of women in Jewish communities previously outside the influence and authority of rabbinic traditions."[87] In other words, curtailment of rights often occurs where the degree of freedom previously enjoyed was great enough to pose a threat to those in positions of authority. A striking example of this phenomenon is discussed by Tal Ilan. She points out that some teachings that had been favorable to women's rights were removed from the Mishnah and relegated to the Tosefta, an early third-century "supplement" to the Mishnah. Unlike the Mishnah, the Tosefta is generally not considered to be "authoritative" rabbinic law.[88] The diminishment of women's status among the rabbinic successors to the Pharisees begs the question: Were women ever full members of the Pharisees whose presence had become a threat to authority? Similar arguments have been advanced to explain the apparently diminished status of women in some early Christian communities.[89]

Until recently, Tal Ilan accepted the conclusion of Elisabeth Schüssler Fiorenza that "we do not know for sure whether the Pharisees admitted women to their ranks, and especially to their table communities of the *havuroth*." In a 2004 festschrift in honor of Schüssler Fiorenza, however, Ilan states that there is evidence that women might well have been members of the Pharisee sect.[90] Although this book does not allow space for a detailed presentation of Ilan's thesis, I believe it is an interesting prism through which to view Jewish women, including Jewish women in the early Christian movement such as Mary and others who followed and supported Jesus.

To support her thesis, Ilan examines portions of rabbinic literature not previously discussed by feminist scholars. Ilan asserts, as she had done in earlier writing, that the Pharisees were a sect and not the dominant group in Judaism in the Second Temple period. She then quotes from *Tosefta Demai*, Chapter 2, and distinguishes between the names attributed to the members of Jewish society: the *am-haaretz* (the people of the land), and the *haverim* (companions or members). *Haver* (plural *haverim*) belong to a fellowship group known as a *havura* (pl. *havourot*).

Ilan believes that *havura* was the name the Pharisees gave to themselves. The word we often associate with the Pharisees is *perushim* (separatists), but it was used largely by their opponents as derogatory. Citing *T. Shabbat* 1:15 as an example, Ilan concludes, "There is some textual evidence that they chose to call themselves *haverim*."[91] If *Pharisees* was a word used by their opponents, there could be interesting ramifications for interpreting the references to the Pharisees in the Gospels.

Ilan then asks if women were included in the *havura*. Despite the fact of male-generic language in much of the document, she finds in *Tosefta Demai*, chapter 2, verses 16–17, evidence that supports the fact that women did not become members as a result of marriage. They had to go through an initiation process themselves to become members. If their husband died or they were divorced, their membership continued, even if they subsequently married an *am-haaretz*. She states that if a sectarian male was married to a non-sectarian wife, the woman "would become a member only if she accepted the practical (and probably ideological) requirement that went with membership." Therefore, Ilan concludes, "women must have been full and independent members of the *havura*. If the *havura* is synonymous with the Pharisees . . . women were full members of the Pharisee sect."[92]

If, indeed, women were members of the Pharisees and participated in the *havura,* they would have enjoyed the distinguishing features of Pharisee life mentioned above. If Jesus shared at least seven of these similarities with the Pharisees, as I have suggested, then it is likely that women and men who followed Jesus would have been familiar with and possibly participated in these rituals, practices, and prayers.

We know from the Gospels that Jesus welcomed women to the community. Although the Gospel writers tell us of Mary's presence with Jesus on only a few occasions in his public ministry, and her presence with the early Christian community at Pentecost, we can ask—would it be possible that she was indeed herself part of a *havura?* We don't know. However, if Jesus was closer to the Pharisees than he was to any other group in Judaism at that time, and if women who were followers of Jesus participated in or were influenced by the prayers and rituals of that sect, our quest for the Jewish Mary takes a significant step forward. In the Acts of the Apostles we read that the first community of the followers of Jesus in Jerusalem went to the upper room and "devoted themselves with one accord to prayer, together with some women, and Mary the mother of Jesus, and his brothers" (Acts 1:14). Mary gathered with the disciples of Jesus on the Jewish festival of Pentecost, also known as *Shavu'ot*, the celebration of the giving of the Torah.[93] Perhaps they had gathered that Pentecost night as a *havura,* as they had in the past when Jesus was with them, this time receiving the gift of the Holy Spirit he had promised.

## CONCLUSION

I am not suggesting that Jesus, James, John, Mary, Mary Magdalene, Martha, Mary, or other friends and followers of Jesus and Paul were "card-carrying members" of the Pharisee sect. However, I believe that if Jesus accepted many of the tenets of Pharisaism and the milieu in which he and his followers lived was permeated by ideas and rituals of a Pharisaic sort, it seems very likely that such an atmosphere would have influenced their perspective on life, motivations, daily living, and prayer. I believe it would have been part of the context of Mary's life as well.

One could reasonably imagine that Mary would have been aware of and likely knew some of the women who were friends of Jesus and active in the Pharisee-influenced early Christian movement. What might Mary have thought about Jesus' willingness to teach women? How might she have responded to her son's confidence in women? Would she have been supportive of them in their active participation in Jesus' ministry? Might Mary have actively participated in the ministry of Jesus or held a position of leadership herself, especially after his death? Scripture offers no answers to these questions. However, recent scholarship about Jesus, the Pharisees, and the role of women among them justifiably provokes our asking these and other new questions that might take our reflection about the spirituality of the Jewish Mary in a more multidimensional direction. In doing so, we open new windows for reflecting on Mary and her life of Hebrew prayer.

# Chapter 6

# Jewish Spirituality and Hebrew Prayer

## Praying as Mary Prayed

Some kids collect baseball cards. Some Catholic kids in the old days collected holy cards—small pictures of Jesus, Mary, or the saints that are sometimes copies of the great masters but often the work of an imaginative artist. They were meant to remind us of the virtues we should practice or the devotions that should be a part of our lives. I recall seeing an old holy card depicting a scene of the annunciation in which Mary is bowed in submission. To my amazement, as she awaited the arrival of the angel Gabriel, she was praying the Rosary! Apparently the painter believed that Mary herself had been a participant in this devotion which did not come into existence until the medieval era. One wonders if the artist understood that Mary would be praying to herself!

Too often Christians have forgotten that Mary was a faithful, prayerful, observant *Jewish* woman. We rarely ask: How did she really live as a religious person? How might she have prayed? In this final chapter, we briefly describe how one might define Jewish prayer and spirituality. We then reflect on some of the prayers and rituals that we can presume that Mary would have known in the first century. We discuss some of the elements of Ignatian spirituality as a methodology for connecting more deeply with how Mary might have prayed as a first-century Jewish woman. Last, meditations are presented as illustrations of how a richer understanding of Hebrew prayers, which might well have been extant in the first century, can give us an entree into Mary's possible prayer life.

## JEWISH SPIRITUALITY

Jewish scholar and rabbi Arthur Green offers the following definition of Jewish spirituality: "Life in the presence of God—or the cultivation of a life in the ordinary world bearing the holiness once associated with sacred space and time, with Temple and with holy days—is perhaps as close as one can come to a definition of 'spirituality' that is native to the Jewish tradition and indeed faithful to its Semitic roots." He adds that "seeking the face of God, striving to live in His presence and to fashion the life of holiness appropriate to God's presence—these have ever been the core of that religious civilization known to the world as Judaism, the collective religious expression of the people Israel."[1]

The ancient psalms of the Hebrew scriptures, many composed about the year 1000 BCE, are powerful expressions of Jewish prayer. They articulate cries of joy, triumph, anguish, and despair not only of the Hebrew people but of humankind. They describe—sometimes as a community, sometimes personally—almost every emotion, including pain, anger, happiness, and hope. They have become an integral part of prayer books in both Jewish and Christian traditions.

Throughout the centuries traditional forms gradually developed for communal Hebrew prayer. Initially, such prayer was associated with covenant, law, and sacrifice. The First Temple in Jerusalem, built by Solomon (968–961 BCE), resulted in the centralization of sacrificial worship in Jerusalem. The Temple was seen as a place of the divine Presence *(Shekhinah)*—"the earthly equivalent of God's heavenly home."[2] Destruction of the Temple by Nebuchadnezzar (605–562 BCE) in 587 BCE was traumatic for the Jews who were exiled to Babylon.

While in exile, according to many scholars, Jews gathered on Shabbat to listen to the Torah and pray the psalms—an early version of synagogue prayer. In doing so, an alternative non-sacrificial form of worship appears to have emerged. When the Second Temple was built (537–515 BCE), sacrificial worship resumed, but the synagogue as an institution apparently continued, especially in areas distant from Jerusalem. The study of Torah, prayer, and works of charity were intertwined in Jewish life, and the locus for these became the synagogue.

Although official prayer in the Temple and in the synagogue was communal in language and form, we know from the Hebrew scriptures that extemporaneous individual prayer had developed over the years as exemplified by prayers of Moses, Jeremiah, Hannah, Esther, and by the psalms. The following *midrash* from *Pesikta d'Rab Kahana* in the Rabbinic period offers practical advice for personal prayer: "God says to Israel, 'I bade thee read thy prayers unto Me in thy *synagogues*, but if thou canst not, pray in thy *home*; and if thou art unable to do this, pray when thou art in the *field*; and if this be inconvenient to thee, pray on thy *bed*; and if thou canst not do even this, think of Me in thy *heart*.'" (emphasis added).[3] Personal prayer was very likely part of Mary's life.

## MARY AND JEWISH PRAYER

Although Mary was possibly illiterate, she undoubtedly knew some of the Torah, psalms, and other Hebrew prayers by heart. We can presume, I believe, that Mary would have known the central affirmation of the Jewish faith, *Shema Israel Adonai Eloheinu Adonai echad* (Hear, O Israel, the Lord our God, the Lord is one) (Dt 6:4). For probably twenty-five hundred years the *Shema* has been recited in its longer form (Dt 6:4–9; 11:13–21; Nm 15:37–41) each morning and evening and on special occasions by observant Jews. Mary would have begun each meal with a blessing similar to that which Jews recite today: *Baruch atah Adonai Eloheinu melech ha olam, ha motzi lechem min ha aretz* (Blessed are You, Lord our God, Ruler of the Universe, who has given us the bread from the earth).

Mary and Joseph would have participated in rites of Jewish ritual purification; witness them presenting Jesus in the Temple according to Jewish Law (Lk 2:22–35). Mary would go to the *mikvah* (ritual bath) with the other women for the monthly purification. We cannot know specifics, but Joseph and Jesus (when he was of age) would have fasted and prayed all day on Yom Kippur, according to Leviticus 16:29–31. Women fasted on Yom Kippur, unless they were pregnant, breastfeeding, or ill. It would have been the responsibility of Mary, as a Jewish woman, to keep a kosher home.

Whether or not women attended services, depending on the need to care for their children and other necessities, they certainly prayed privately. Ritual blessings and private prayer would have been part of the life of a Jewish woman, including Mary. It appears that women attended synagogue worship on Shabbat and festivals.

Is it possible that Mary was aware of the prayers of the great women of the Hebrew scriptures: Ruth, Judith, Hannah, Esther, and the mother of the Maccabees?[4] Would she have found inspiration in these strong women when she encountered struggles in her own life? A Jewish view of life is holistic. In Judaism there is a blessing for *everything*. How could Mary have lived otherwise? The challenge to the Jew has always been to "choose life!" (Dt 30:19), a challenge Mary accepted.

Could it be that it was only after the resurrection that Mary finally came to understand the meaning of the day that the angel came to her to tell her that she was to be the mother of the one whose name means "savior," the reasons for God's ongoing challenges to her through the years, and the significance of the life of her remarkable son?[5] According to Jewish scholar David Flusser, "Mary is a certain link between Jesus and the Jewish people."[6]

## IGNATIAN CONTEMPLATION

Spiritual writers have used the word *contemplation* over the centuries with various meanings and nuance. Often it has been defined as a state of mystical awareness. For Ignatius of Loyola, however, contemplation involved the use of imagination and stories rather than abstract theology. He was a man of Renaissance humanism who lived in an age of exploration, war, explosion of creativity in art and literature, corruption in the church, intense religious conflict, and religious reformation. His conversion was based on his own experience, which he translated into a method of spiritual reflection in his famous *Spiritual Exercises*.[7] Studying at the University of Paris not too long after Erasmus and John Calvin, Ignatius was very likely aware of the new approaches to scripture. His emphasis on the Gospels in the *Exercises* was a central focus for him in contemplation.

Ignatius's goal in the *Spiritual Exercises* was to present a roadmap for conversion whereby the person making the retreat could follow a particular psychological dynamic and, according to John O'Malley, SJ, "respond in a new way to an inner call for intimacy with the divine." Ignatius's genius was his sense of "psychological organization." The purpose of the *Exercises,* O'Malley believes, "is promoted less by logic than by an activation of the affections, especially through the key meditations and considerations."[8]

The *Exercises* are organized into four "weeks"—each an undetermined amount of time. The first week begins with the "The First Principle and Foundation." We reflect on the purpose of our creation—to praise, reverence, and serve God on this earth and, by this means, to save our souls. We then realize with gratitude that all of the things on the face of the earth are given to us by God. We should use those things that help us to reach God, and set aside those which do not.

We also reflect in the first week on how we have failed to use things well and have sinned. We meditate on the realities of sin, death, judgment, and hell. Ignatius invites the participant to "see" the fires of hell, to "hear" the wailings of those who are suffering, and to "smell" the smoke emanating from the fire. Imagination and a sensory approach to understanding are key elements for Ignatius.

In the second week we are challenged to hear "The Call of the King," after which we reflect on various scenes from the life of Christ. Ignatius's language then moves from meditation to contemplation. He follows a specific method—a *preparatory prayer* and three *preludes*: (1) reflect on the historicity of an event; (2) establish the composition of place; and (3) request a particular grace. Generally there are three *points* for our contemplation, usually drawn from the Gospels. We are encouraged to insert ourselves in the particular scene we are contemplating. By using our senses, we become at home in a setting, and acquire an inside understanding of Jesus, Mary or the others present. We conclude with a colloquy—a heart-to-heart conversation in which we speak with Jesus and Mary and ask for the grace to follow them with love.

After meditating on the life of Jesus, the second week continues with contemplations that lead to the challenge of making an "election." We are invited to put on the mind of Christ (Christ's standard rather than the World's standard); to have the same openness toward doing God's will as Christ (three classes of persons); and to love the way Christ loves (three degrees of humility). In this call to "intimacy with the Divine," we are to choose how we might better serve God. In making an election, we specifically commit or recommit ourselves to God in Christ in a more intimate way.

Throughout the third week we contemplate the passion and death of Jesus as further motivation for intimacy with the Divine. Once again, in contemplating the sufferings of Jesus through scripture and imagination, we express our gratitude for all he has done and is doing, and we choose to be at one with Christ poor, rejected, and suffering. We seek the gift of compassion.

In the fourth week we contemplate the joy of the resurrection and reflect on the scripture passages of the appearances of the risen Jesus. We seek intimacy with the Divine in the joy of triumphing over sin and death. The culmination is the *contemplatio*—the "contemplation for obtaining divine love." Ignatius invites us to immerse ourselves in the beauty of nature, humanity, and "finding God in all things." Our response is: "Take, O Lord, and receive all . . . that I am and I have. . . . Give me only your love and your grace." In all of these contemplations, by identifying sometimes with Jesus and sometimes with Mary, we are growing in intimacy with the Divine. Ignatius asks us to "see, watch, notice," and to imbibe God's love as we experience the Gospel message in our own hearts.

Ignatius continually invites us to develop, embellish, and elaborate on Gospel passages so that we can come to know more intimately God's love and live it in our daily lives. These contemplations could be described as *midrash* on the Christian scriptures. In the words of Jewish scholar Jacob Neusner: "For the task of all scriptural study is to make sense of eternity for the here and now, the moment in which we [in the language of Judaism] receive the Torah ourselves." He adds, "In Midrash we see how the sages, living in challenging times, reread Scriptures so as to learn what God wanted of them that day, that hour. This acutely contemporary response to Scripture provides us with models for our own approach to the Hebrew scriptures."[9]

Ignatius, I believe, would agree! It is interesting to note that recent studies reveal that many of the early followers of Ignatius, indeed some in his inner circle, were *conversos*—Spanish Jews who had converted, or who were from families who had converted, to Christianity, often under duress, in the late Middle Ages.[10] Would Ignatius have been familiar with *midrash*? Could these relationships with *conversos* have influenced his approach to prayer? Ignatius's method, akin to *midrash*, can enhance our contemplation of the scriptures, all for the greater glory of God. In using this method, we may discover more clearly how Mary might have prayed.

## CONTEMPLATIONS

About a dozen years ago I made a thirty-six day retreat based on the *Spiritual Exercises* of St. Ignatius at El Retiro, the Jesuit Retreat House in California.[11] It was a remarkable opportunity to meditate in silence on God; the purpose of one's life; Jesus' life, death, and resurrection; Mary's role in the Gospels; and how we might live our lives for God's greater honor and glory. It was enhanced by a semester I taught in the Holy Land that allowed me more easily to visualize some of the places where scriptural events probably took place.

What I discovered, following Ignatius's methodology, was that it freed me to reflect on Mary in a new way. I very naturally found myself using Hebrew prayers that I had come to know and love, and that might have been prayers Mary would have said during special events in her life. The following are some of my experiences of modified Ignatian contemplations regarding Mary, with the accompanying Hebrew scripture passages and prayers.

In keeping with the focus on the gift and purpose of life in week one of the *Spiritual Exercises*, I share with you my contemplation on the annunciation and the visitation to Elizabeth. My contemplations on the birth of Jesus and on his early public ministry follow the focus of week two and on the person and ministry of Christ. The fourth and final contemplation follows the emphasis of weeks three and four on the passion, crucifixion, and resurrection of Jesus.

In each of the contemplations that follow, I place myself in the role of Mary and speak in her voice. How might Mary have experienced those pivotal events in her life? What were her fears, hopes, dreams, and realities? Would she have remembered prayers and experiences of some of her Hebrew ancestors in the faith? Did recollections of the Hebrew scriptures allow her insights as to how she could grow in her relationship with God in the midst of challenges? Might these prayers and scriptures also serve to inspire us as we search to better understand what might have been her prayer life—and help us to see how we, too, may grow in intimacy with God?

Notably, rabbinic prayers and customs were not put into writing until after the destruction of the Second Temple in 70 CE. Although it cannot be proven historically that some of the prayers and rituals in the following meditations were pre–70 CE, it is a possibility, perhaps even a likelihood, that they were part of an earlier oral tradition that was finally articulated in the Mishnah and other documents beginning in the second century CE. My explanation for the use of certain sections of the book of Esther, the Passover ritual, and other prayers and texts are explained in the notes at the end of the book.

## ANNUNCIATION AND THE VISITATION

*When I was about fourteen years old I was living with my extended family in the small village of Nazareth in the Galilee during the Roman occupation. That was a very difficult time for Jews in Palestine. Finances were tight due to taxation. Many of the men held jobs in the nearby city of Sepphoris, so the women often had to take on extra responsibilities. I was grateful to be with extended family and friendly neighbors, and I kept busy carrying out household tasks, taking care of the garden, and tending some animals. I was betrothed to a wonderful young man named Joseph, a carpenter with additional special skills. Joseph was a good person, eager to prepare a home for us. He was close to God and glad that I was too. It promised to be a happy marriage.*

*One day I encountered a very powerful invitation from a mysterious figure. I must have looked frightened—and I was afraid! This extraordinary being who was enshrined in light appeared to be from heaven and said: "Do not be afraid, Mary!" (Lk 1:30). I realize now that it is very human to be frightened in such a situation. Eventually I remembered the words of the prophet Isaiah, "Say to those who are frightened: Be strong, fear not! Here is your God! He comes to save you!" (Is 35:1–10). The apparition seemed very gentle, kind, and comforting. I came to believe it was of God.*

*Then I heard an extraordinary statement: "Behold, you will conceive in your womb and bear a son and you shall name him Jesus" (Lk 1:31). I could hardly believe it. I had not had sexual relations with Joseph, so how could it be? So I did a very Jewish thing—I asked questions. I was young, but I was not naive. Sometimes it is important to ask questions. I remembered that my ancestors in the faith were not afraid to ask questions. Moses had been very straightforward with God: "Who am I that I should go to Pharaoh, and bring the Israelites out of Egypt?" God responded, not with a specific answer, but with very reassuring words: "I will be with you" (Ex 3:11–12). Remembering that gave me a sense of peace that God would be with me even though I might not get all the answers.*

*I asked the heavenly creature: "How can this be, since I have no relations with a man?" (Lk 1:34). The apparition replied, "The Holy Spirit will come upon you, and the power of the Most High will overshadow you; therefore the child to be born will be holy; he will be called Son of God" (Lk 1: 35). I felt a little like Jeremiah. I wanted to complain to God that I was "too young"—only "a child" (Jer 1:6). How could I take on such responsibility? But at the same time I felt overwhelmed by love! Somehow, deep inside, I felt engulfed in a call so strong that I could not turn away, could not not say yes. It was as if I had a new inner knowledge of God in the intimacy of my heart. I knew that God was "calling" me—inviting me to belong to him in a way I could never have imagined. How could I not say yes?*

*The only clue I received from the heavenly creature that seemed grounded in this world was about my dear cousin Elizabeth. She was much older than I and sad that she had never had a child, but she was also pregnant and in her sixth month "because nothing is impossible with God" (Lk 1:37). She must have been overjoyed, and I was so happy for her. Suddenly I realized that my unexplainable pregnancy could be part of a larger plan. Although I was concerned as to how Joseph would understand all of this, I wanted to be "the servant of the Lord" and to trust always in God's love. I accepted God's invitation to be the mother of "the Son of God" (Lk 1:35).*

*Elizabeth had always been a special person in my life, especially during the time I spent in Jerusalem. I knew she would need me. I also knew that I could share my concerns, my fears, and my hopes with her, and that she would be supportive. Besides, with this special "gift" I was now carrying, I needed to reach out to those in need. I convinced my family and Joseph that I should go to her. I could join a caravan from Galilee to Jerusalem. Zachariah could meet me there and take me to their hillside village of Ein Karem to help Elizabeth prepare for the coming of her baby. Finally, they agreed.*

*At first I was lonely on the trip. I recalled that Esther, who was a great leader of our people, had been frightened and lonely too. She had prayed: "My Lord, our King, you alone are God. Help me who am alone and have no help but you, for I am taking my life in my hand." Later she prayed: "Save us by your power, and help me, who am alone and have no one but you, O Lord" (Est 4C:14–15, 25).*[12] *I, too, felt that I was alone and had only God as I moved ahead on my journey.*

*As I traveled along I came to realize that my willingness to say yes to God's plan was grounded in my deep conviction of the faithfulness of God. I have prayed the Shema twice each day and sometimes more since I was old enough to do so: Shema Israel Adonai Eloheinu Adonai echad (Hear, O Israel, the Lord our God, the Lord is one). I always continued with the scripture passage I love so well—V'ahavta et Adonai Elohecha . . . " (You shall love the Lord your God with all your heart, with all your soul, and with all your might. Take to heart these words with which I charge you this day. You shall teach them diligently to your children and recite them when you stay at home and when you are away.) As I recited the words on my journey, I knew I would indeed teach those very words to my son.*

*How grateful I am that God made a covenant with my people. When the Torah is read on Shabbat and I hear the words from Deuteronomy that I love, I feel in my very bones that God will always be faithful. "Understand, then, that the Lord, your God, is God indeed, the faithful God who keeps his merciful covenant to the thousandth generation toward those who love him and keep his commandments"(Dt 7:8–9). I know in my heart that God's love will be with me no matter what happens. A child is growing within me—and it is all very mysterious, but I want to share that love with the whole world. For some unexplainable reason I have been chosen by God for a special mission, and I know I can trust him to the end.*

*To see Zachariah waiting for me in Jerusalem was reassuring, but I felt sorry for him. He had recently become mute as a result of some inexplicable experience in the Temple. He took me up the hillside, burgeoning with spring flowers, to Elizabeth in Ein Karem. When I saw her radiant face and her open arms I ran to her, buried my head in her warm bosom, and wept. There has been so much joy and fear pent up together inside of me these last weeks! She was almost like a mother-God who enfolded me in her arms. Elizabeth—now six months pregnant—experienced the child in her womb leaping for joy! It was as if our two children were speaking to each other! Then Elizabeth said, "Blessed is the fruit of your womb!"(Lk 1:42) It was the confirmation I needed to realize that this child I would bring into the world was indeed a holy one of God.*

*How does one spill out the joy and the gratitude that is in one's heart with such an extraordinary realization? I remembered Hannah, who in a moment of joy poured forth her kaddish. "My heart exalts in the Lord; my strength is exalted in my God"(1 Sm 2:1). My prayer was similar: "My soul magnifies the Lord, and my spirit rejoices in God my savior"(Lk 1:46b–47). I wanted to praise and bless God for all his goodness, express my joy, and—with a Jewish view of justice—ask God to remove the powerful from their thrones and lift up the lowly, fill the hungry with good things and send the rich away empty (cf. 1 Sm 2:5; Lk 1:53).*

*The kaddish sometimes concludes with a prayer for peace: O-seh shalom bim-ro-mav, Hu ya'a-she shalom aleinu. v'al kol yisrael, v-im-ru. Amen. (May the Lord give strength to his people. May the Lord bless his people with peace). I asked God for peace for my people, and for the whole world. I asked God for peace in my heart as well. In the months ahead, that prayer-song echoed in my heart.*

In the second week of the *Spiritual Exercises* we are asked to contemplate the birth of Jesus. Ignatius is very specific. The contemplation on the nativity of Jesus begins with three preludes: (1) *historicity*: how Mary, nine months pregnant, goes forth from Nazareth, seated on a donkey, accompanied by Joseph and a servant girl, to go to Bethlehem to pay the tribute to Caesar that he has imposed on them; (2) *composition of place:* "see with the sight of the imagination the road from Nazareth to Bethlehem; considering the length and the breadth, and whether the road is level or through valleys or over hills; likewise looking at the place or cave of the Nativity"; and (3) *ask for what I want:* pray for an interior knowledge of Jesus, who became human for me, that I may love and follow him.[13]

In the three points for contemplation that follow, based on the infancy narratives in Luke and Matthew, we are invited to join the little company. We are encouraged to use all of our senses to realize the very human dimension of what is happening. Ignatius states: "Making myself into a poor and unworthy little servant, I watch them, and *contemplate* them, and as if I were present, serve them in their needs with all possible respect and reverence; then I will reflect within myself to draw profit."[14]

We should "see, watch, notice," not as an onlooker, but as someone intimately involved in the scene. After an hour of reflection we move to a *colloquy* in which we are encouraged to talk with, or possibly just "be with" Jesus, Mary and Joseph, allowing our feelings to surface. What does it mean that Jesus would become human for me? The period concludes with spontaneous prayer and an Our Father.[15]

Among the prayers I have learned in Hebrew over the years, I think one of my favorites is what is known as the *She-he-chee-ya-nu.* At weddings, bar and bat mitzvahs, birthdays, festivals, or any celebratory Jewish event when one wants to bless and thank God, someone will say: "Do you think we should say a *She-he-chee-ya-nu*?" Together those present will recite with joy:

| | |
|---|---|
| *Ba-ruch a-tah A-don-ai* | Blessed are You, O Lord our |
| *E-lo-hei-nu, me-lech ha-o-lam,* | God, Ruler of the Universe, |
| *She-he-chee-ya-nu ve-ki-ye-ma-nu* | who has given us life, |
| *ve-hi-gi-a-nu- la-ze-man ha-zeh.* | and sustained us, |
| | and brought us to this very special moment. |

## THE BIRTH OF JESUS

*I had made the journey from Nazareth to Jerusalem many times—usually for Passover. But to make the trip when I was nine months pregnant was something I would never have imagined. The Roman governor was demanding that all males register, and Joseph, because he was of the house and family of David, had to go to Bethlehem—just a short distance from Jerusalem. Such a long and hilly road from Galilee! I was grateful to have the donkey to ride, and Joseph guided it carefully over the rocky road. It took us a little more than four days, and with each day I was sure the baby would be born at any moment.*

*Joseph had urged me to stay in Nazareth where I would be more comfortable. We had made our preparations for the baby there. But I would not let him go alone, and I did not want to be at a distance from him at such a special time. Besides, I knew he really wanted me to come so that we could be together when the baby was born. We had been through so much together. He had been so loyal and good despite his inability to understand the great mystery. His faithfulness was almost like the faithfulness of God. "I thank you for your faithfulness and love which excel all we ever knew of you. On the day I called, you answered; you increased the strength of my soul" (Ps 138:2–3). Joseph loved and cared for me when he could so easily have left. How can I ever love and appreciate him enough?*

*It was late at night when we arrived in Bethlehem, and the little town was filled to overflowing. We tried so hard to find a place to stay. If I were not expecting the baby at any moment we could have been satisfied with any place—even spread out some blankets in a field. But we needed some privacy for the delivery. Finally, an innkeeper named Jacob was sympathetic when he saw I was so very pregnant. Although they had no room, he called his wife, Sarah. She realized I was ready to give birth at any moment and hastened me around to a stable behind the inn where they kept the animals at night.*

*It was a clean place, and the animals looked peaceful. Sarah immediately made preparations for the birth—brought water and cloths. I don't know what I would have done without her. I am sure she must have assisted others in the past. She knew all the right things to do. It all happened so quickly. By the time Joseph arrived at the stable after having made arrangements with Jacob, the innkeeper, he could hear the crying baby—and he was so overjoyed! It was a beautiful healthy child—a boy, just as I had been told. We breathed a sigh of relief. Sarah cut the umbilical cord, washed the baby, wrapped him in swaddling clothes and put him in my arms. They wanted to know his name, and we said "Jesus." Jacob and Sarah looked on smiling, almost as if he was their grandchild.*

*They brought us food, but I was too exhausted and excited to eat. Some shepherds nearby must have heard Jesus crying, because they asked if they could come in and see the baby. They were people of the land—the am ha-aaretz—simple and joyful. We could hear music nearby as well—although we could not tell if it was from the inn or from travelers going by. It was a very joyful song—with a sense of shalom—heartfelt music that almost brought tears to my eyes. It was peaceful, yet exhilarating, and I was so grateful.*

*In time, the shepherds left, and the musicians moved on. Sarah and Jacob made excuses that they needed to go in and tend to their guests, but I think they knew we wanted to savor the moment by ourselves. What would we ever have done without them? I was physically and emotionally exhausted but too excited to sleep.*

*Finally, Joseph and I were alone with this beautiful child. We snuggled down into the straw with the new baby between us. We were both awed by this remarkable gift of life. What can one say at such an ecstatic moment when the heart is so full of joy and gratitude? Suddenly I found myself smiling, and I knew what was in my heart. I said softly, "Joseph, do you think we should say a She-he-chee-ya-nu?" He nodded and smiled, and we prayed together,*

| | |
|---|---|
| *Ba-ruch a-tah A-don-ai* | Blessed are You, O Lord our |
| *E-lo-hei-nu, me-lech ha-o-lam,* | God, Ruler of the Universe, |
| *She-he-chee-ya-nu ve-ki-ye-ma-nu* | who has given us life, |
| *ve-hi-gi-a-nu- la-ze-man ha-zeh.* | and sustained us, |
| | and brought us to this very special moment. |

I can't say for sure that the *She-he-chee-ya-nu* would have been said in the first century, but it is very old. The prayer is referenced in the Mishnah. I would not be surprised if, just maybe, that was the prayer that Mary and Joseph said on that very special night.

## JESUS' EARLY PUBLIC MINISTRY AND CANA

*It was such a joy to have Jesus near me for so many years, especially after my dear Joseph died. Jesus missed his abba. When I think of Joseph, these words come to my mind and heart: "For great is his steadfast love toward us, and the faithfulness of the Lord endures forever" (Ps 117:2). Without his strong arms and loving heart, how would I have lived through such complicated times? I will always be grateful for his love and fidelity.*

*It was a joy to be Jesus' mother—his ema—to care for him, to teach him, and to offer him advice. I was often amazed at his wisdom. Especially after Joseph died, he took such good care of me. He seemed to have no desire to marry and settle down with a family as many of his friends were doing. He loved children and often played with them in the village. I knew there must be a plan, but that continued to be as mysterious to me as the day the apparition came to me to tell me I would be his mother.*

*At one point in his later twenties Jesus became restless. He had been hearing stories about his cousin John in the Judean desert near the Jordan River. John and Jesus had played together as children and always had a strong bond from that day I went to visit Elizabeth before they were born. In recent years, however, they had not seen each other. After the death of Zachariah and Elizabeth, John—a good man—developed a somewhat radical streak. He seems to have been influenced by some of the groups that live down by the Dead Sea. He became quite a popular and controversial preacher, and many followed him. I encouraged Jesus to move on with his life, but I was a little apprehensive of his getting involved with those who might stir up the authorities.*

*When Jesus spoke to me one evening about his desire to go to see John, my heart sank at the thought of his leaving—but I knew the time had come. I finished a special tunic I had been sewing for him and polished up his sandals. I had a wonderful sack that belonged to Joseph, which I knew he would like, so I mended it and strengthened it so he could take some essentials with him. The morning he left, I was tearful, but I tried not to show it. I blessed him with the blessing that Joseph would have offered had he been with us:* Ye-va-re-khe-kha Adonai ve-yish-me-re-kha . . . *(The Lord bless you and keep you; the Lord make his face to shine upon you, and be gracious to you; the Lord lift up his countenance upon you and give you peace) (Nm 6:24–26). He put his strong arms around me to let me know that he would always love me, and then took off down the road. One last wave as he rounded the corner. Suddenly I felt very lonely. After all, he was my firstborn son. The rest of the family and neighbors in our compound could not have been more kind to me, but I missed him very much.*

*Some of the cousins went to Jerusalem shortly thereafter. They decided to search out John to see what this prophet was like. When they came back they told me that John was baptizing large crowds of people, and even Jesus was baptized by him (Jn 1:24–34). When they went to search for Jesus afterward, however, they were told that he went off quietly after his baptism in the direction of the wilderness and was not heard from for many days. That worried me. What would he eat in the wilderness? Would he be cold at night? His tunic and cloak would hardly be enough to keep him warm in that mountainous desert region. It is good that I did not know about it until later.*

*From what I heard, after his time in the wilderness he seemed more at peace. I prayed that he would find his direction in life and have a sense of shalom. I was excited when I learned that he was returning to Galilee with some new friends. A group of fishermen and others was gathering around him in Capernaum and seemed to be becoming his followers. I sent word to him in Capernaum that there would be a wedding in the family soon. Joseph's cousin Rebecca and her husband, Samuel, had a handsome son, Joshua, whom Jesus knew fairly well. Joshua was betrothed to a lovely young woman, Rachel, and they were to be married in Cana in a few weeks. We were invited. I so hoped that he would be able to come. Yes, of course, he could bring his new friends. I would love to meet them.*

*Cana is about nine miles from Nazareth. It would be a day's trip. I decided to go early with some of the relatives and friends so as to be there in time to be helpful with the preparations. The journey was a pleasant one—mostly women and children. The men had to work, so they would come the next morning. Joshua and Rachel's betrothal (kiddushin—sanctification) over a year ago had been a wonderful event. They had made their covenant in a lovely ceremony: the benedictions, the signing of the ketubah (marriage declaration), and then the feast. I could not help but recall my betrothal to Joseph. It, too, had been a joyous event. Oh, Joseph! How I wish you were here to see how Jesus has grown to be such a fine man. I also wish you could be with me in these sometimes difficult days. But you lived so well and died in peace.*

*We were happy to arrive in Cana, get a good night's sleep, and help with final details before the celebration. When the other guests started to arrive in the afternoon, I looked everywhere for Jesus. When he and his friends appeared, there were shouts of welcome, especially from the cousins. He looked lean and tan and happy. His arm around my shoulder and his smile were warming to my heart.*

*Eventually we gathered and walked to Rachel's home. She was standing in front with her parents, looking radiant in her new gown and veil. We were now ready for the nisuin, the wedding ceremony, to begin. The air was alive with music and excitement as we walked the short distance to Joshua's. Samuel and Rebecca were waiting for us near the beautiful canopy—the chupah—symbolic of their new home and life together. Our wonderful old sage Daniel began singing "Serve the Lord with joy! Come before him with exalting!" (Ps 100:2). Joshua invited Rachel under the chupah.*

*After a prayer Daniel began reading the ketubah to remind the bride and groom of their covenant with each other and of the agreements that were made. They affirmed the ketubah, and Joshua proudly announced that they were wedded "according to the Law of Moses and of Israel." The Seven Benedictions were sung, concluding with the blessing over the wine: Barauch atah Adonai Eloheinu melach ha olam borei p'ri ha-gafen (Blessed are you, O Lord our God, Ruler of the Universe, who has given us the fruit of the vine). Joshua and Rachel sipped from the cup of blessed wine. I especially love the final benediction from the prophet Jeremiah (3:10–11): "Yet again there shall be heard . . . in the city of Judah and in the streets of Jerusalem . . . the voice of joy and the voice of gladness, the voice of the bridegroom and the voice of the bride."*[16] *Joy abounded at this kiddushin –the "making holy" of their marriage.*

*At the feast, food was plentiful, wine flowed freely, song and dance abounded. It would be a day that Rachel and Joshua would never forget. Jesus and his friends were having a wonderful time. Cephas, the somewhat older fisherman, seemed to thrive on telling stories. He had some rough edges, but it was clear he would throw his heart and soul into whatever he would do. One of the younger men, John, was shy, but he shared some of his story with me. He was gentle, kind, and considerate. They all looked to Jesus as their leader.*

*Suddenly Rebecca came to me with a troubled look on her face. The wine was all gone, and there were many hours of celebration ahead. She had no idea what they would do. I wondered—could they buy more wine? I was concerned that perhaps Jesus and his friends had drunk more than their share. Jesus seemed to be solving people's problems these days, so I went to him and said: "They have no wine." He said to me, "Woman, what concern is that to you and to me? My hour has not yet come" (Jn 2:1–4). It was a puzzling response and reminded me of the day Joseph and I found him in the Temple when he was twelve. He sometimes offered mysterious comments. What did he mean by "my hour has not yet come"? Was he so sure? He had gone to Jerusalem, had been baptized by John, had retreated to the wilderness to discover his mission, and had gathered these lively and committed people around him. It seemed to me that maybe his time had come. Maybe he just needed a little encouragement?*

*I smiled, nodded, and turned to the servants, saying, "Do whatever he tells you." Then I moved into the crowd. I overheard him telling them to fill the stone jars that were empty after the ritual purification with water (Jn 2:6). Then Jesus motioned to the servants to take a sample to the chief wine steward. They were hesitant. Would the steward think they were making fun of him if they gave him water? When the steward tasted it, he smiled broadly! Clearly it was the best wine he had ever enjoyed (Jn 2:5–10). Suddenly, the servants were all talking excitedly among themselves in the corner. They knew it had only been water! How could it now be wine? They looked at Jesus with a kind of awe. I saw the chief steward tell Joshua that this was very special wine that had been saved for the last. Jesus looked over to me and smiled. I guess he realized that his time had come. Thinking back to that day, I really was not sure what he would do, but I was so grateful that he saved the beautiful bride and groom from embarrassment! He would do many more mitzvot in the years ahead.*

*I knew that Jesus would not be coming back to Nazareth except to visit occasionally. He was making Capernaum his new home. He loved Lake Kinneret—the Sea of Galilee—which was so close. The day after the wedding he asked me to come to Capernaum with him and his disciples. I was delighted. It was not a short distance, but I wanted to see where he would be living and doing his new work. It was a joyous trip and an opportunity to come to know his new friends. I knew it would only be for a few days, because Jesus planned to go to Jerusalem for Passover (John 2:12–13).*

*I had never been to Capernaum before. It was lovely to see this new area and have the sea nearby. Some fishermen whom Jesus had met there decided to join the group. I was especially happy to see the synagogue. I suspected that the day would come when Jesus would preach there. The return trip to Nazareth was longer and more challenging, but it was well worth the adventure. I was grateful that I could now picture where Jesus would be—at least part of the time.*

*Once back at Nazareth, I realized that his hour had come, and it was time to let him go. The men and women who were gathering around him were forming a new community. He was always such a caring person. He would preach and teach and heal those in need in the years to come. I was somewhat anxious, however. Knowing how John was always at odds with the authorities, I feared for Jesus' safety. I hoped he would be sensible and not get himself into dangerous situations. I sighed. One never knows what a grown child will be about.*

*But I knew that God would be faithful to him as he was to me—"even to the thousandth generation" (Dt 7:8–9). Every day in my heart I prayed for Jesus: Ye-va-re-khe-kha Adonai ve-yish-me-re-kha . . . (The Lord bless you and keep you; the Lord make his face shine upon you, and be gracious to you; the Lord lift upon his countenance upon you and give you peace) (Nm 6:24–26). God had given him to me in a very special way. Now I must, with love, allow him to be free and trust that his mission—whatever that would be—would be blessed.*

Time lines in the Gospels vary with respect to the last supper and the crucifixion. In Matthew, Mark, and Luke, the last supper is a Passover meal. In the Gospel of John, the last supper takes place on the night before the Passover meal. In that year, according to John, Passover fell on the Sabbath (Jn 19:14, 42). In the following meditation, I follow John's chronology.

## CRUCIFIXION AND RESURRECTION

*I could not believe how exhausted I was. If it were not for Mary Magdalene and the other women, I might have collapsed along the way. They practically carried me to Golgotha along the cobblestone streets. I had stayed at the foot of the cross with John, my sister, and Mary Magdalene—but shortly before Jesus died, the soldiers hurried us up the hill. We only saw from afar when they pierced his side. It was as if my heart were pierced, too.*

*We watched as they took Jesus' body down from the cross. It had all been so brutal! I was very grateful to John for being there to the end. Joseph of Arimathea had arranged with Pilate to remove the body and bury it. Nicodemus helped Joseph by bringing burial cloths as well as myrrh and aloes, according to custom. They were able to lay Jesus in a garden tomb nearby (Jn 20:38–42). It had to be hastily done before sundown, when Passover and Shabbat would begin.*

*After they removed Jesus' body, we walked slowly to the upper room where we would celebrate Shabbat and Passover. They don't often fall on the same day. Mary Magdalene was in tears, but I leaned on her the whole way. They let me rest while the final preparations for Passover were completed. Everything seemed so somber. There was no joy this year. They asked me to bless the candles, which had to be lit before sunset.*

*Before creation there was darkness, so after lighting the candles, I covered my eyes and beckoned the warmth of the Shabbat with my hands while saying the prayer: Ba-ruch a-ta A do-nai E-lo-hei-nu, me-lach ha o-lom, a-sher ki-de-sha-nu be-mitz-vo-tav ve-tsi va-nu le-had-lik neir shel Shab-bat ve-shelYom tov (Blessed are you, O Lord our God, Ruler of the Universe, who has sanctified our lives through your commandments, commanding us to kindle the Shabbat and the festival lights). Even from before the time of the Maccabees, our people have lit lights on Shabbat. To illumine a Jewish home with lights on Shabbat represents creation as well as a foretaste of the ineffable bliss of life eternal.*[17] *This night more than any other, I prayed that my dear son, Jesus, would taste such bliss.*

*Here I was in Jerusalem for Passover, as I had been with Joseph and Jesus and so many family members over the years. I remember so well the time Jesus got lost when he was only twelve and gave us a scare. It was such a relief to find him in the Temple where he was asking questions of the great sage Hillel and some of the other sages who seemed to admire the wisdom of our young son. But I never understood Jesus' answer to me: "Did you not know I must be in my Father's house?" (Lk 2:49). Many things he said over the years were so simple and full of truth; others were so mysterious. Yet, he was obedient to us, and grew in wisdom, age, and divine favor. Hard to believe that was almost twenty years ago.*

*The meal was subdued—and I was tired. Some of the men had brought home the lamb, which had been sacrificed that afternoon in the*

*Temple. As we ate, we recounted the story of the Exodus, how God had freed us from Egypt, allowed us to escape through the Red Sea, fed us manna in the desert. It was always a time of zikaron. Somehow, in the telling of the story and doing the ritual, the past becomes present in our lives. We were slaves in Egypt and now we are free. So, too, Jesus is now free.*

*Another favorite song of mine is the Dayeinu (It would have been enough).*[18] *Any of these gifts that God had given us "would have been enough!" Yet, God continued to bless us and shower us with gifts. How could we repay him? Even in our sorrow we sang, sometimes through our tears, Dayeinu!—It would have been enough!*

> Had God brought us out of Egypt and not divided the sea for us, *Dayeinu!*
> Had God divided the sea for us and not permitted us to cross the dry land, *Dayeinu!*
> Had God permitted us to cross the sea on dry land and not sustained us for forty years in the desert, *Dayeinu!*
> Had God sustained us . . . in the desert and not fed us with manna, *Dayeinu!*
> Had God fed us with manna and not given us the Sabbath, *Dayeinu!*
> Had God given us the Sabbath but not brought us to Mount Sinai, *Dayeinu!*
> Had God brought us to Mount Sinai but not given us the Torah, *Dayeinu!*
> Had God given us the Torah and not led us to the land of Israel, *Dayeinu!*
> Had God led us to the land of Israel and not built for us the Temple, *Dayeinu!*
> Had God built for us the Temple but not sent us the prophets of truth, *Dayeinu!*
> Had God sent us the prophets of truth and not made us a holy people, *Dayeinu!*[19]

*Somehow, on this special night, I could not stop there. In my heart I continued to sing:*

> Had God given me such a beautiful baby but not let us escape to Egypt, *it would have been enough!*
> Had God let us escape to Egypt, but not find our way back to Galilee, *it would have been enough!*
> Had God let us come back to Galilee, but not let us find him in the Temple, *it would have been enough!*
> Had God let us find him in the Temple, but not allow him to return with us to Nazareth, *it would have been enough!*
> Had God let him return with us to Nazareth, but not let him begin his ministry of preaching, *it would have been enough!*
> Had God let him begin his ministry of preaching, but not heal the sick and feed the hungry, *it would have been enough!*
> Had God allowed him to heal the sick and feed the hungry, but not let him give his life for us, *it would have been enough!*

*How could I ever thank God for the gift of Jesus? Even holding him in my arms that first night would have been enough. Yet God gave him to me for a lifetime—too short a life, but a blessed life! I knew from the beginning that it was a mystery. I also believed in God's faithful love—and that God's love would be there to the end. I needed to continue to trust. The Sabbath lights are still lit—and they are a foretaste of Life Eternal!*

*Finally, the tiredness descended upon everyone, and people started to leave. John, Peter, James, and the others all came to comfort me. I knew I had to be strong for them. They were so heartbroken, and some of them, like Peter, felt so guilty. I fear he believed he could never do enough repentance—t'shuvah. He cried through the whole meal. I told them to try to sleep—we needed a Shabbat of rest and a time to reflect. After Shabbat we would come together again and look to the future.*

*That Passover/Shabbat day was very quiet. Although we could hear others celebrating, we had no desire to go anywhere. I was very grateful to have a small room in the home of a friend of Mary Magdalene's who was generous enough to let us stay with her. Mary was so attentive to me and yet anguished herself. She loved Jesus so much. But I really needed to be alone.*

*At the end of the Shabbat we all gathered again for Havdalah—when we can finally see three stars in the sky. Jesus used to love Havdalah! He used to run outside with the other children when he was little and count the stars. The prayers of this wonderful ancient service which marks the outgoing of the Sabbath, spoke to us all: "Behold, God is my salvation; I will trust and will not be afraid."That psalm begins:"God is our refuge and strength, a very present help in trouble. Therefore we will not fear, though the earth be moved, and though the mountains be carried into the midst of the seas."*[20] *Although our world had turned upside down, God would be our refuge and our strength.*

*The cup of wine was raised and we said Baruch a-tah A-don-ai, Eloheinu mel-ach ha-olam, bor-ay p'ree ha-gafen (Blessed are you, O Lord our God, Ruler of the Universe, who has given us the fruit of the vine). After all said Amen, we each had a sip. Then the spice box was raised to remind us of the sweetness of the Sabbath, and we said,"Blessed are you, O Lord our God, Ruler of the Universe, who creates different kinds of spices." And after an Amen, we passed the beautiful box of spices around for all to sniff—to carry some of the sweetness of the Sabbath into the week ahead. I was probably not the only one who thought instead of the spices that would be brought to the tomb tomorrow to give my Jesus a proper burial.*

*Last, now that Shabbat was over we could kindle lights again—the special braided Havdalah candle with the two wicks. We prayed, "Blessed are you, O Lord our God, Ruler of the Universe, who created the lights of the fire!" We put our hands forward so we could make use of the fire. Light was the first thing created by God, and God also gave us fire to warm ourselves. On this painful night we needed light and warmth. The final benediction reminded us of the distinction between the Sabbath and the six days ahead. We needed God to help us survive the pain and sorrow of these days. What would they bring?*

*Once again, the group dispersed. The women started to busy themselves preparing spices and oil to take to the tomb in the morning. I went back to my little room, grateful for the solitude. I prayed wordlessly—remembering the joy of his smile and his laugh. It seemed so unreal that he was gone. I knew that there would be a resurrection of the body and that we would be together in the end times, but I just never thought he would leave us so young.*

*As I sat there with my eyes closed, I felt a gentle hand on my shoulder. That was something Jesus often did when he came in from the workshop—when I was engrossed in thought and prayer as I was sewing. I must be imaging it—remembering how he would thoughtfully bring me a cup of water and gently touch my hand. Then I heard him say, "Ema—mother." I opened my eyes and turned. He was there with a certain radiant glow! It was almost as it had been those many years ago when the mysterious figure appeared to tell me I would be his mother! But I was not afraid this time. He helped me stand up. Was I dreaming? I buried my head in his shoulder, and my tears overflowed. It was almost as it had been when I ran to Elizabeth and wept with pent up pain and joy—but this time it was joy overflowing with a depth of gratitude I could never have imagined. It was a joy born out of pain.*

*He held me gently and spoke softly. Somehow he had to suffer in order to enter into his glory. That's what Simeon had meant that day in the Temple so long ago. His mission would become clear in the days ahead. For tonight, all I knew was joy and gratitude. I recalled the night that he was born, and I could still think of no better prayer to offer with an overflowing heart to a loving and faithful God. I paused for moment and said, "Jesus, do you think we should say a She-he-chee-ya-nu?" He nodded and smiled, and together we prayed:*

*Ba-ruch a-tah A-don-ai*
*E-lo-hei-nu, me-lech ha-o-lam,*
*She-he-chee-ya-nu ve-ki-ye-ma-nu*
*ve-hi-gi-a-nu- la-ze-man ha-zeh.*

Blessed are You, O Lord our God, Ruler of the Universe,
who has given us life,
and sustained us,
and brought us to this very special moment.

# Epilogue

It has now been many years since I preached my first sermon in the synagogue on that hot summer night in Phoenix, Arizona. As I stated in the Prologue, listening to the cantor chant in Hebrew and the rabbi read from the Torah, I realized that—despite the changes through the centuries—this was how Jesus and Mary had prayed. On that occasion, however, I was only listening, absorbing the beauty, and letting it permeate my heart.

What ultimately changed my spirituality forever was when I began to sing and pray in Hebrew. I recall Barbara Herring, the wife of Rabbi Chuck Herring, teaching me the *motzi*—the blessing over the bread—and after that, the blessing over the wine. She is also the reason I learned the *bracha* over the Shabbat candles. Chuck invited me to join Barbara in the blessing of the candles one Friday night as the Shabbat service began. I also remember the weeks I spent in Israel with Rabbi Moshe and Margie Tutnauer and people from our two synagogues—Moshe and Margie tutoring me along the way.

I have never really learned Hebrew properly, but singing and praying it at services has touched a part of my heart that I cannot fully explain. On Yom Kippur I want to sing over and over again *V'al kulam Elo-ah selicot, selah lanu, melah lanu, kapper lanu* (For all these sins, forgiving God, forgive us, pardon us, grant us atonement). And—I want it to be the melody I learned and sang for the many years I fasted and prayed all day on Yom Kippur in one of "my" synagogues in Phoenix." (I recall being very disappointed when I attended services on Yom Kippur at other synagogues in other cities where the melodies were different!)

This existential experience, the opportunity to see, watch, hear, and notice, as Ignatius enjoined (I would add sing, pray, and participate), allowed for an interior absorption of what Hebrew prayer is and was. Somehow it got into my bones and affected my spirit deeply. On a lighter note, at the end of one Yom Kippur at Beth El Congregation, after fasting and praying for more than twenty-four hours (we had to wait for that third star in the sky), we all greeted each other with *L'Shanah Tovah* after the blowing of the shofar and final prayers. I had been sitting (and standing!) most of the day with one of the families with whom I was going to go home and break the fast. An older Jewish woman who was a few seats over had been eying me throughout the day. She knew who I was and appeared skeptical. At the conclusion, however, as people were beginning to file out, she came over to me, took my arm, and said with a heavy accent and a smile: "You do better than the Jewish girls!" A wonderful compliment! With beaming gratitude I responded "L'Shanah Tovah!"—and "Todah robah!"

Some years later I began to realize that these Hebrew prayers were creeping into my meditation. I knew something deeper was occurring. The experience was enhanced by the semester I taught in Israel and later by the extended time of retreat. I began to connect the prayers I had learned and loved in the synagogue to the ones that Mary might have prayed. This insight challenged me to delve more deeply into which Hebrew prayers might have been extant in the first century. With a few exceptions we will probably never know with certitude, but we do know that the oral tradition is very strong in Israel to this day. It is likely that some of the prayers in the rabbinic writings were part of the oral tradition of the first century. Following Ignatius's method which invites us to set the historical stage and then use our imagination, I have found in Hebrew prayer a way of connecting to Jesus and Mary that has warmed my heart.

No doubt the Gospels provide us with the basics and allow us to build a foundation for a deeper understanding of Mary. We must begin there if we are to discover, however inadequately, this Jewish Mary. What can we know about her from the Gospels?

*Mary was not afraid to ask questions.* When the angel approached Mary to tell her that she was to conceive and bear a child, she did not automatically respond but asked the question: "How can this be?" (Lk 1:34).

*Mary was a person of generosity and joy.* Her visit to Elizabeth at Ein Karem exhibits her initiative in traveling to help an elderly relative and her exhilaration at their meeting (Lk 1:39–56).

*Mary chose to be a refugee rather than stay in a dangerous situation.* When Herod was searching to destroy her child, Mary fled with Joseph to Egypt to protect her son (Mt 2:13–15)

*Mary had clear expectations of Jesus.* When Jesus stayed behind in the Temple, she was not afraid to challenge him: "Where have you been? Your father and I have sought you sorrowing" (Lk 1:42–51). She could agonize with a parent who loses a child.

*Mary understood the importance of hospitality.* At the marriage feast at Cana, Mary wanted to save a bride and groom from embarrassment. Jesus' first response to Mary's request was not positive. However, she was persistent and told the waiters: "Do whatever he tells you" (Jn 2:1–11). He acquiesced and saved the day.

*Mary was Jesus' first disciple.* The woman from the crowd called out: "Blessed is the womb that bore you and the breasts that nursed you," but Jesus replied, "Rather, blessed are those who hear the word of God and keep it" (Lk 11:27–28). As wonderful as physical birth is, Mary's fidelity to God's word is what really made her great.

*Mary was a woman of faith.* She was with Jesus at the foot of the cross (Jn 19:25). Today we might think of a mother walking with her son to the death chamber. Mary was faithful to Jesus in life and death.

*Mary was a woman of hope and love.* After the resurrection Mary was with the apostles in the upper room as they awaited the Holy Spirit at Pentecost (Acts 1:14)—that same Spirit with which she had been gifted in Nazareth so many years before.

What my quest has taught me, in addition to studying the Gospels and tradition, is that too often we have transferred our prayer patterns to Mary instead of inquiring how she might have prayed. Mary is not a figurine in a Christmas creche or a picture on a holiday card. She is a woman who experienced joy and pain, discouragement and hope, a woman whose courage and insight—born out of her own Jewish religious tradition—were a source of strength and encouragement for the disciples in the early church. She would have expressed that throughout her life in both communal and personal prayer. We can discover Mary's Jewishness, I believe, by exploring more intimately her life of Hebrew prayer.

With great gratitude to my Jewish sisters and brothers, I believe that if we Christians are willing to open our minds and hearts to Hebrew prayer, we can find an avenue that allows us to discover part of what might have been in Mary's mind and heart as she led her ordinary yet very extraordinary life. Although the quest for the Jewish Mary will continue for years to come, sharing in her life of Hebrew prayer may give us a deeper insight into this remarkable Jewish woman so dear to God, to Christians—and sometimes even to Jews?—throughout the centuries.

# Notes

### *Prologue*

1. Among other published works see Mary Christine Athans, *The Coughlin-Fahey Connection: Father Charles E. Coughlin, Father Denis Fahey, C.S.Sp., and Religious Anti-Semitism in the United States 1938–1954* (New York: Peter Lang, 1991); "Antisemitism? Or Anti-Judaism?" in *Introduction to Jewish-Christian Relations*, ed. Michael Shermis and Arthur E. Zannoni, 118–44 (New York: Paulist Press, 1991); "Judaism and Catholic Prayer: A New Horizon for the Liturgy," *New Theology Review* (November 2008): 48–58; "The Jewishness of Mary," *New Theology Review* (August 2009): 80–83; and "Courtesy, Confrontation, Cooperation: Jewish-Christian/Catholic Relations in the United States to Vatican II," *U. S. Catholic Historian* 28, no. 2 (Summer 2010): 107–34.

### *Introduction*

1. Elisabeth Schüssler Fiorenza, *Jesus: Miriam's Child, Sophia's Prophet: Critical Issues in Feminist Christology* (New York: Continuum, 1995), 163.

2. Elisabeth Schüssler Fiorenza, *Bread Not Stone: The Challenge of Feminist Biblical Interpretation* (Boston: Beacon Press, 1984), 9–20, 108–15.

3. Bernadette J. Brooten, *Women Leaders in the Ancient Synagogue*, Brown Judaic Studies 36 (Chico, CA: Scholars Press, 1982), 1.

4. Tal Ilan, "Paul and the Pharisee Women," in *On the Cutting Edge: The Study of Women in Biblical Worlds*, ed. Jane Schaberg, Alice Bach, and Esther Fuchs, 82–101 (New York: Continuum, 2004).

5. Elizabeth A. Johnson, *Truly Our Sister: A Theology of Mary in the Communion of Saints* (New York: Continuum, 2003), 137–206; Miri Rubin, *Mother of God: A History of the Virgin Mary* (New Haven, CT: Yale University Press, 2009); Edward Kessler, "Mary—The Jewish Mother," *Irish Theological Quarterly* 76, no. 3 (2011); Avital Wohlmann, "Pourquoi le Silence de 'Hébraísme D'Aujourd'hui au Sujet de Marie de Nazareth'? Une Femme Juive Répond," *Maria Nell'Ebraismo e Nell'Islam Oggi* (Rome: Marianum, 1987), 9–38.

6. Edward Kessler, "Midrash," in *A Dictionary of Jewish-Christian Relations,* ed. Edward Kessler and Neil Wenborn (Cambridge: Cambridge University Press, 2005), 293.

7. Cecil Roth, ed., *The Concise Jewish Encyclopedia* (New York: New American Library, 1980), 369.

8. Sally Cunneen, *In Search of Mary: The Woman and the Symbol* (New York: Ballantine Books, 1996), xxi.

### *1. Initiating the Search*

1. Carol Frances Jegen, "Mary Immaculate: Woman of Freedom, Patroness of the United States," in *Mary According to Women*, ed. Carol Frances Jegen (Kansas City, MO: Leaven Press, 1985), 156.

2. Portions of this section were published earlier in "Mary in the American Catholic Church," *U.S. Catholic Historian* 8, no. 4 (Fall 1989): 103–16.

3. Leon Suenens, *The Nun in the World* (Westminster, MD: Newman Press, 1963), 15.

4. Elisabeth Schüssler Fiorenza, *Jesus: Miriam's Child, Sophia's Prophet: Critical Issues in Feminist Christology* (New York: Continuum, 1995), 163.

5. Joseph P. Chinnici to author, May 24, 1988.

6. Anne E. Carr, "Mary in the Mystery of the Church: Vatican Council II," in Jegen, *Mary According to Women,* 27.

7. Elizabeth A. Johnson, *Truly Our Sister: A Theology of Mary in the Communion of Saints* (New York: Continuum, 2003), 97.

8. Ranya Idilby, Suzanne Oliver, and Priscilla Warner, *The Faith Club: A Muslim, a Christian, a Jew: Three Women Search for Understanding* (New York: Free Press, 2006).

## *2. Mary in History, Doctrine, and Devotionalism*

1. For a discussion of the origin of the document, see Beverly Roberts Gaventa, *Mary: Glimpses of the Mother of Jesus* (Minneapolis: Fortress Press, 1999), 106–7. The entire text is in the Appendix, 133–45.

2. Protevangelium, 7:2–3, in Gaventa, *Mary: Glimpses of the Mother of Jesus,* 136.

3. Protevangelium, 19:1—20:3, in ibid., 141–43.

4. Origen, *Contra Celsum*, trans. Henry Chadwick (London: Cambridge University Press, 1980), 28, 31.

5. Jane Schaberg, *The Illegitimacy of Jesus: A Feminist Interpretation of the Infancy Narratives* (New York: Harper and Row, 1987).

6. Tony Burke, trans., "The Childhood of the Saviour (Infancy Gospel of Thomas): A New Translation," *Pedagogical and Scholarly Resources for the Study of the New Testament*, n.d., available on the www.tonyburke.ca website.

7. Ibid.

8. Ron Cameron, *The Other Gospels: Non-Canonical Gospel Texts* (Philadelphia: Westminster Press, 1982), 123.

9. Robert J. Miller, *The Complete Gospels: Annotated Scholars Version* (Santa Rosa, CA: Polebridge Press, 1992), 370.

10. George Tavard, *The Thousand Faces of Mary* (Collegeville, MN: Liturgical Press, 1996).

11. Mary Ann Donovan, *One Right Reading? A Guide to Irenaeus* (Collegeville, MN: Liturgical Press, 1997), 88.

12. Raymond E. Brown, *The Virginal Conception and Bodily Resurrection of Jesus* (New York: Paulist Press, 1973).

13. Tina Beattie, "Mary in Patristic Theology," in *Mary: The Complete Resource*, ed. Sara Jane Boss, 75–105 (Oxford: Oxford University Press, 2007).

14. Tavard, *The Thousand Faces of Mary,* 65.

15. Richard Price, "Theotokos: The Title and Its Significance in Doctrine and Devotion," in Boss, *Mary: The Complete Resource*, 57.

16. Rubin, *Mother of God*, 25–26.

17. Geri Parlby, "The Origins of Marian Art in the Catacombs and the Problems of Identification," in *The Origins of the Cult of the Virgin Mary*, ed. Chris Maunder (London: Burns and Oates, 2008), 41–56.

18. Ibid., 44.

19. Ibid., 51–52.

20. Rubin, *Mother of God,* 41–42.

21. John McGuckin, "The Early Cult of Mary and Inter-Religious Contexts in the Fifth-Century Church," in Maunder, *Origins of the Cult of the Virgin Mary*, 14. McGuckin relies in this approach on the work of R. E. Witt, *Isis in the Graeco-Roman World* (Ithaca, NY: Cornell University Press, 1971), 151.

22. McGuckin, "The Early Cult of Mary and Inter-Religious Contexts in the Fifth-Century Church," 17–18.

23. Price, "Theotokos," 56. Price cites the John Rylands Papyrus 470 restoration by Giambernardini 1975: 72–74.

24. Marina Warner, *Alone of All Her Sex: The Myth and Cult of the Virgin Mary* (New York: Vintage, 1983).

25. Stephen J. Shoemaker, "Marian Liturgies and Devotions in Early Christianity," in Boss, *Mary: The Complete Resource*, 132.

26. Heinrich Denziger and John F. Clarkson, eds., *The Church Teaches: Documents of the Church in English Translation* (St. Louis: B. Herder, 1955), 1–2.

27. Rubin, *Mother of God,* 47–48.

28. Price, "Theotokos," 93.

29. Hilda Graef, *Mary: A History of Doctrine and Devotion* (Notre Dame, IN: Ave Maria Press, 2009).

30. Tavard, *The Thousand Faces of the Virgin Mary*, 60.

31. Kyriaki Karidoyanes Fitzgerald, "Mary the Theotokos and the Call to Holiness," in *Mary, Mother of God*, ed. Carl E. Braaten and Robert W. Jenson, 80–99 (Grand Rapids, MI: Eerdmans, 2004).

32. Warner, *Alone of All Her Sex*, 211.

33. Jacopone de Todi, as quoted in ibid., 213.

34. Kathleen Kulp-Hill, trans., *Songs of Holy Mary of Alfonso X, the Wise: A Translation of the Cantigas De Santa Maria* (Tempe, AZ:

Arizona Center for Medieval and Renaissance Studies, 2000). I am grateful to Dwayne Carpenter for this reference.

35. Arthur Green, "Shekhinah, the Virgin Mary, and the Song of Songs: Reflections on a Kabbalistic Symbol in Its Historical Context," *American Jewish Studies Review* 26, no. 1 (2002): 52. I am grateful to Arthur Green, a former teacher, for sharing this valuable article with me.

36. Ibid., 1.

37. Ibid., 13–14, 1 (emphasis in original).

38. Tavard, *The Thousand Faces of Mary*, 90–91.

39. Cunneen, *In Search of Mary,* 152.

40. Tavard, *The Thousand Faces of Mary*, 91–92.

41. Graef, *Mary: A History of Doctrine and Devotion*, 222–23.

42. Martin Luther, *Works of Martin Luther*, trans. A. T. W. Steinhaeuser (Philadelphia: Holman, 1930), 139.

43. Martin Luther, "Sermon on the Afternoon of Christmas Day, 1530," in *Martin Luther's Basic Theological Writings*, 3d ed., ed. Timothy F. Lull and William R. Russell (Minneapolis: Fortress Press, 2012), 174.

44. Cunneen, *In Search of Mary,* 201.

45. Jean Calvin, "Commentarius in Harmonium Evangelicam," in *Corpus Reformatum*, 101 vols. (Braunschweig: Brunsvigae, 1901), vol. 45, col. 348, as quoted in Tavard, *The Thousand Faces of Mary*, 120–21.

46. Jean Calvin, *La Nativité* 7, no. 28 (Paris: Revue Réformée, 1956), 23–24, as quoted in Tavard, *The Thousand Faces of Mary*, 123.

47. Tavard, *The Thousand Faces of Mary,* 127–28.

48. Cunneen, *In Search of Mary,* 206.

49. Graef, *Mary: A History of Doctrine and Devotion*, 279.

50. Ibid., 279–80.

51. Luis Becerra Tanco, "The Felicity of Mexico in the Wonderful Apparition of the Virgin Mary, Our Lady of Guadalupe (1648)," in *Dark Virgin: The Book of Our Lady of Guadalupe*, ed. Donald Demarest and Coley Taylor (Freeport, ME: Coley Taylor, 1956), 101.

52. George E. Ganss, ed., *Ignatius of Loyola: The Spiritual Exercises and Selected Works* (New York: Paulist Press, 1991), 26.

53. Ibid., 29–30.

54. Ignatius of Loyola, "Autobiography," in *Ignatius of Loyola: The Spiritual Exercises and Selected Works*, ed. George Ganss (Mahwah, NJ: Paulist Press, 1991), 109.

55. Heinrich Denziger and John F. Clarkson, eds., *The Church Teaches: Documents of the Church in English Translation* (St. Louis: B. Herder, 1955), 160–61.

56. Richard P. McBrien, *Catholicism*, 2 vols., rev. ed. (San Francisco: HarperSanFrancisco, 1994).

57. Trevor Johnson, "Mary in Early Modern Europe," in Boss, *Mary: The Complete Resource*, 368.

### *3. Mary in History, Doctrine, and Devotionalism*

1. Raymond E. Brown, *The Virginal Conception and Bodily Resurrection of Jesus* (New York: Paulist Press, 1973), 67.

2. Trevor Johnson, "Mary in Early Modern Europe," in *Mary: The Complete Resource*, ed. Sara Jane Boss (Oxford: Oxford University Press, 2007), 363–84.

3. Ibid., 365.

4. Ibid., 368–69.

5. Sally Cunneen, *In Search of Mary: The Woman and the Symbol* (New York: Ballantine Books, 1996), 228–30.

6. Johnson, "Mary in Early Modern Europe," 381.

7. See Carl L. Becker, *The Heavenly City of the Eighteenth Century Philosophers* (New Haven, CT: Yale University Press, 1932).

8. Richard P. McBrien, *Catholicism*, 2 vols., rev. ed. (San Francisco: HarperSanFrancisco, 1994).

9. Cunneen, *In Search of Mary*, 230–31.

10. Mary Christine Athans, "Mary in the American Catholic Church," *U.S. Catholic Historian* 8, no. 4 (Fall 1989): 108.

11. Elizabeth Cady Stanton, in *Elizabeth Cady Stanton, Feminist as Thinker: A Reader in Documents and Essays*, ed. Carol DuBois and Richard Cándida-Smith (New York: New York University Press, 2007), 351.

12. Cunneen, *In Search of Mary,* 262.

13. Harriet Beecher Stowe, *Sunny Memories of Foreign Lands*, 2 vols. (Boston: Sampson, 1854), 2:350.

14. Martin John Spalding, "Introduction," *Ave Maria* 1, no. 1 (1865): 1.

15. Gerard Manley Hopkins, "The Blessed Mother Compared to the Air We Breathe," *Poems and Prose of Gerard Manley Hopkins* (London: Penguin Classics, 1985), 56.

16. Cunneen, *In Search of Mary,* 256.

17. John Henry Newman, *The New Eve* (Oxford: Newman Bookshop, 1952), 77–78.

18. Edward Schillebeeckx, *Mary, Mother of the Redemption*, trans. N. D. Smith (New York: Sheed and Ward, 1964), 197ff.

19. Ibid.

20. McBrien, *Catholicism,* 2:879; Cunneen, *In Search of Mary,* 232–33.

21. John Shinners, Jr., "Mary and the People: The Cult of Mary and Popular Belief," in *Mary, Woman of Nazareth*, ed. Doris Donnelly (New York: Paulist Press, 1989), 181.

22. J. Derek Holmes and Bradford W. Bickers, *A Short History of the Catholic Church* (New York: Paulist Press, 1984), 237–38.

23. James J. Hennesey, "A Prelude to Vatican II: American Bishops and the Definition of the Immaculate Conception," *Theological Studies* 25, no. 3 (1964): 409–19.

24. Peter R. D'Agostino, *Rome in America: Transnational Catholic Ideology from the Risorgimento to Fascism* (Chapel Hill: University of North Carolina Press, 2004), 32.

25. Josef L. Altholz, *The Churches in the Nineteenth Century* (New York: Bobbs-Merrill, 1967), 85.

26. See William H. Halsey, *The Survival of American Innocence: Catholicism in an Era of Disillusionment 1920–1940* (Notre Dame, IN: University of Notre Dame Press, 1980).

27. James J. Walsh, *The Thirteenth: The Greatest of Centuries* (New York: Fordham University Press, 1943), 6.

28. Portions of this section were previously published in Athans, "Mary in the American Catholic Church."

29. Thomas A. Kselman and Stevan Avella, "Marian Piety and the Cold War in the United States," *Catholic Historical Review* 72, no. 3 (July 1986): 403–24.

30. Ibid., 419.

31. F. J. Sheed, back cover comment, in Caryll Houselander, *The Reed of God* (Westminster, MD: Christian Classics, 1944, 1985).

32. Houselander, *The Reed of God,* 28.

33. McBrien, *Catholicism,* 2:881.

34. C. G. Jung, *Answer to Job*, trans. R. F. C. Hull, vol. 2 in *The Collected Works of C. G. Jung*, Bollingen Series, anniv. ed. (Princeton, NJ: Princeton University Press, 2002), 36.

35. Kevin J. Madigan and Jon D. Levenson, *Resurrection: The Power of God for Christians and Jews* (New Haven, CT: Yale University Press, 2008), xi.

36. Edward Schillebeeckx and Catharina Halkes, *Mary: Yesterday, Today, Tomorrow*, trans. John Bowden (New York: Crossroad, 1993), 18.

37. Tavard, *The Thousand Faces of the Virgin Mary,* 203.

38. Anthony J. Tambasco, *What Are They Saying About Mary?* (New York: Paulist Press, 1984), 9.

39. Tavard, *The Thousand Faces of the Virgin Mary,* 205.

40. Schillebeeckx and Halkes, *Mary: Yesterday, Today, Tomorrow*, 15.

## 4. Will the Real Mary Please Stand Up?

1. Hilda Graef, *Mary: A History of Doctrine and Devotion,* 2 vols., *From the Beginnings to the Eve of the Reformation* and *From the Reformation to the Present Day* (New York: Sheed and Ward, 1963, 1965).

2. Hilda Graef, *Mary: A History of Doctrine and Devotion*, combined ed. (Notre Dame, IN: Ave Maria Press, 2009), front matter.

3. Rosemary Radford Ruether, "Misogynism and Virginal Feminism in the Fathers of the Church," in *Religion and Sexism: Images of Women in Jewish and Christian Traditions*, ed. Rosemary Radford Ruether, 150–83 (New York: Simon and Schuster, 1974).

4. Rosemary Radford Ruether, *Mary: The Feminine Face of the Church* (Philadelphia: Westminster John Knox, 1977).

5. Rosemary Radford Ruether, *Sexism and God-Talk: Toward a Feminist Theology* (Boston: Beacon, 1993), 154–55, 158.

6. Marina Warner, *Alone of All Her Sex: The Myth and Cult of the Virgin Mary* (New York: Vintage, 1983; originally published in 1976), xxv.

7. Warner, 335, 337.

8. Ibid., 338.

9. Sally Cunneen, *In Search of Mary: The Woman and the Symbol* (New York: Ballantine, 1996).

10. Ibid., 271, 281.

11. Ibid., 334.

12. George Tavard, *The Thousand Faces of Mary* (Collegeville, MN: Liturgical Press, 1996); Jaroslav Pelikan, *Mary Through the Centuries: Her Place in the History of Culture* (New Haven, CT: Yale University Press, 1996); Miri Rubin, *Mother of God: A History of the Virgin Mary* (New Haven, CT: Yale University Press, 2009).

13. Raymond E. Brown et al., eds., *Mary in the New Testament* (Philadelphia: Fortress Press, 1978).

14. Raymond E. Brown, "The Meaning of Modern New Testament Studies for an Ecumenical Understanding of Mary," in *Biblical Reflections on Crises Facing the Church* (New York: Paulist Press, 1975), 108.

15. Alain Bancy, Maurice Jourjon, and the Dombes Group, *Mary in the Plan of God and in the Communion of Saints* (New York: Paulist Press, 1999).

16. Adelbert Denaux and Nicholas Sagovsky, eds., *Studying Mary: Reflections on the Virgin Mary in Anglican and Roman Catholic Theology and Devotion*, ARCIC Working Papers (London: T & T Clark, 2007).

17. H. George Anderson, J. Francis Stafford, and Joseph A. Burgess, eds., *The One Mediator, the Saints, and Mary: Lutherans and Catholics in Dialogue VIII* (Minneapolis: Augsburg, 1992).

18. Chris Maunder, "Mary in the New Testament and the Apocrypha," in *Mary: The Complete Resource*, ed. Sarah Jane Boss, 11–46 (Oxford: Oxford University Press, 2007).

19. Carl E. Braaten and Robert W. Jenson, eds., *Mary, Mother of God* (Grand Rapids, MI: Eerdmans, 2004).

20. Elisabeth Schüssler Fiorenza, *In Memory of Her: A Feminist Theological Reconstruction of Christian Origins* (New York: Crossroad, 1983), 3.

21. Ibid., 29.

22. Leonard Swidler, "Jesus Was a Feminist," *The Catholic World* 212 (January 1971): 177–83.

23. Leonardo Boff, *The Maternal Face of God* (San Francisco: Harper and Row, 1987), 65.

24. Ivone Gebara and Maria Clara Bingemer, *Mary, Mother of God, Mother of the Poor*, trans. Phillip Berryman (Maryknoll, NY: Orbis Books, 1987), see chap. 3, esp. pp. 46–54. Relying on dated scripture scholarship such as that by Gerhard Kittel, a German Nazi sympathizer, may help to explain the anti-Judaism that crept into part of their work.

25. John Paul II, *Pope John Paul II on Jews and Judaism: 1979–1986*, ed. Eugene J. Fisher and Leon Klenicki (Washington, DC: U.S. Catholic Conference, 1987), 35, 24.

26. Judith Plaskow, "Christian Feminism and Anti-Judaism," *Cross Currents* 28, no. 3 (Fall 1978): 306–9; Susannah Heschel, "Feminism in Jewish-Christian Dialogue," in *Introduction to Jewish-Christian Relations*, ed. Michael Shermis and Arthur E. Zannoni, 232–40 (Mahwah, NJ: Paulist Press, 1991).

27. Heschel, "Feminism in Jewish-Christian Dialogue," 232–33.

28. Elisabeth Schüssler Fiorenza, *Jesus: Miriam's Child, Sophia's Prophet: Critical Issues in Feminist Christology* (New York: Continuum, 1995), 89–90.

29. Ibid., 91.

30. Jane Schaberg, *The Illegitimacy of Jesus: A Feminist Theological Interpretation of the Infancy Narratives* (New York: Harper and Row, 1987).

31. Ibid., 199.

32. Barbara E. Reid, *Choosing the Better Part? Women in the Gospel of Luke* (Collegeville, MN: Liturgical Press, 1996), 84.

33. Barbara E. Reid, "Review of *The Illegitimacy of Jesus: A Feminist Theological Interpretation of the Infancy Narratives,*

by Jane Schaberg," *Catholic Biblical Quarterly* 52, no. 2 (1990): 364–65.

34. Beverly Roberts Gaventa, *Mary: Glimpses of the Mother of Jesus* (Minneapolis: Fortress Press, 1999), 11.

35. Avital Wohlmann, "Pourquoi le Silence de l'Hebraisme d'Aujourd'hui au Sujet de Marie de Nazareth? Une Femme Juive Répond" [Why the silence today regarding the Jewishness of Mary of Nazareth? A Jewish woman responds], paper presented at the Sixth International Symposium on Mariology sponsored by the Pontifical Faculty, Rome, October 1986. Published in *Maria Nell' Hebraismo e Nell' Islam Oggi*, vol. 7, *Teologia e Spiritualità Mariana* (Rome: EDB, 1987), 9–38. I am grateful to Mary Stokes, BVM, for her assistance in translating this lecture from the French.

36. Ibid., 9.

37. Ibid., 10.

38. Sholem Asch, *Mary* (New York: G. P. Putnam's Sons, 1949).

39. Wohlmann, "Pourquoi le Silence . . . ," 26–31.

40. Gaventa, *Mary: Glimpses of the Mother of Jesus,* 130–31.

41. Beverly Roberts Gaventa and Cynthia L. Rigby, eds., *Blessed One: Protestant Perspectives on Mary* (Louisville, KY: Westminster John Knox, 2002).

42. Kathleen Norris, "Foreword," in ibid., ix.

43. Gaventa and Rigby, *Blessed One,* 1–2.

44. Elizabeth A. Johnson, *Truly Our Sister: A Theology of Mary in the Communion of Saints* (New York: Continuum, 2003).

45. Ibid., xv.

46. See ibid., chaps. 3–4.

47. Elizabeth A. Johnson, "Galilee: A Critical Matrix for Marian Studies," *Theological Studies* 70, no. 2 (June 2009): 327–46.

48. Johnson, *Truly Our Sister*, 216–17.

49. Elizabeth A. Johnson, *Friends of God and Prophets: A Feminist Theological Reading of the Communion of Saints* (New York: Continuum, 1999).

50. See John Farina, "The Study of Spirituality: Some Problems and Opportunities," *U.S. Catholic Historian* 8 (November 1989): 15–32.

51. Louis Bouyer, *The Spirituality of the New Testament and Fathers*, trans. Mary P. Ryan (New York: Seabury Press, 1963), viii.

52. Gordon S. Wakefield, "Spirituality," in *Westminster Dictionary of Christian Spirituality* (Philadelphia: Westminster Press, 1983), 361.

53. Jean Leclerq, "The Distinctive Characteristics of Roman Catholic American Spirituality," *Louvain Studies* (Spring 1983), 296.

54. Asch, *Mary*.

55. Ann Johnson, *Miryam of Nazareth: Woman of Strength and Wisdom* (Notre Dame, IN: Ave Maria Press, 1984); *Miryam of Judah: Witness in Truth and Tradition* (Notre Dame, IN: Ave Maria Press, 1987); *Miryam of Jerusalem: Teacher of the Disciples* (Notre Dame, IN: Ave Maria Press, 1991). Unfortunately, she spells out YHWH in the first volume, something not acceptable to most Jews.

56. Mary Catherine Nolan, *Mary's Song: Living Her Timeless Prayer* (Notre Dame, IN: Ave Maria Press, 2001).

57. Robert Ellsberg, *Blessed Among All Women: Women Saints, Prophets, and Witnesses for Our Time* (New York: Crossroad, 2005), 23.

58. Carol Frances Jegen, ed., *Mary According to Women* (Kansas City, MO: Leaven Press, 1985).

59. Doris Donnelly, ed., *Mary, Woman of Nazareth: Biblical and Theological Perspectives* (New York: Paulist Press, 1989).

60. Rien Poortvliet, *He Was One of Us* (Grand Rapids, MI: Baker Books, 1974).

61. Catherine O'Brien, "Mary in Film," in Boss, *Mary: The Complete Resource*, 532–36.

### 5. Searching for the Jewish Jesus to Find the Jewish Mary

1. Raymond E. Brown, *The Community of the Beloved Disciple* (New York: Paulist Press, 1979), 22–23.

2. Brown, *The Community of the Beloved Disciple*, 40–43, 66–69. In a presentation on the Gospel of John at Temple Beth Israel in Phoenix, Arizona, in 1972, Brown offered these reflections

to a group of priests, nuns, ministers, and rabbis. In the 1980s he shared with the writer that that was the first time he had lectured in a synagogue on anti-Judaism in the Gospel of John.

3. Adam H. Becker and Annette Yoshiko Reed, eds., *The Ways That Never Parted: Jews and Christians in Late Antiquity and the Early Middle Ages* (Minneapolis: Fortress Press, 2007).

4. This document and all official church documents are available on the vatican.va website.

5. James C. Turrow and Raymond E. Brown, "Canonicity," in *Jerome Biblical Commentary* (Englewood Cliffs, NJ: Prentice Hall, 1968), 515–34.

6. Raymond E. Brown, "A Heritage from Israel," *America* 128 (March 10, 1973): 221.

7. See Mary Christine Athans, "Anti-Semitism? Or Anti-Judaism?" in *Introduction to Jewish-Christian Relations*, ed. Michael Shermis and Arthur Zanonni (New York: Paulist Press, 1991), 123–24.

8. Wolfgang S. Seiferth, *Synagogue and Church in the Middle Ages: The Encounter of Jews and Christians* (New York: Charles Scribner's Sons, 1967), 12–14.

9. Martin Luther, *On the Jews and Their Lies, 1543*, trans. Martin H. Bertram, vol. 47, Luther's Works (Minneapolis: Fortress Press, 1971).

10. Johann Gottleib Fichte, *J. G. Fichte Werke*, ed. Fritz Medicus (Leipzig: Verlag von Felix Meiner, 1908), 4:105.

11. Alan T. Davies, "The Aryan Christ: A Motif in Christian Anti-Semitism," *Journal of Ecumenical Studies* 12, no. 4 (Fall 1975), 574.

12. Houston S. Chamberlain, *The Foundations of the Nineteenth Century*, trans. John Lees (London: John Lane, 1910).

13. Davies, "The Aryan Christ," 569–79. See also Susannah Heschel, *The Aryan Jesus: Christian Theologians and the Bible in Nazi Germany* (Princeton, NJ: Princeton University Press, 2008).

14. Jaroslav Pelikan, *Jesus Through the Centuries: His Place in History and in Culture* (New Haven, CT: Yale University Press, 1985), 20.

15. N. T. Wright, *Jesus and the Victory of God* (Minneapolis: Fortress Press, 1996), 18–20.

16. Norman Perrin, *Rediscovering the Teaching of Jesus* (New York: Harper and Row, 1967), 212–13.

17. Martin Kähler, *The So-Called Historical Jesus and the Historic, Biblical Christ*, 4th ed. (Minneapolis: Fortress Press, 1964; originally published in 1892).

18. Albert Schweitzer, *The Quest of the Historical Jesus*, trans. W. Montgomery (Minneapolis: Augsburg Fortress Press, 1906, 1910, 2001).

19. Rudolph Bultmann, *The History of the Synoptic Tradition*, trans. John Marsh, enl. ed. (Peabody, MA: Hendrickson, 1931, 1994).

20. Perrin, *Rediscovering the Teaching of Jesus,* 43.

21. Wright, *Victory of God,* 489.

22. See ibid., 29.

23. J. Ed Komoszewski, M. James Sawyer, and Daniel B. Wallace, *Reinventing Jesus: How Contemporary Skeptics Miss the Real Jesus and Mislead Popular Culture* (Grand Rapids, MI: Kregel Publications, 2006), 39–40, 49; N. T. Wright, "Jesus Seminar Critically Examined," *Setting Scholars Straight About the Bible*, Part V of the series "Deliver Us from the Jesus Seminar," March 5, 2007, available on the jesusseminar.blogspot.com website.

24. Wright, *Victory of God*, 83–89.

25. Matthew Hoffman, *From Rebel to Rabbi: Reclaiming Jesus and the Making of Modern Jewish Culture* (Stanford, CA: Stanford University Press, 2007), 2.

26. Ibid., 21–22.

27. David Novak, *Jewish-Christian Dialogue: A Jewish Justification* (New York: Oxford University Press, 1989), 75–76.

28. Samuel Sandmel, *We Jews and Jesus* (New York: Oxford University Press, 1973), 51.

29. Geiger became the primary advocate for the Reform movement in Judaism, Graetz for the Conservative movement.

30. Susannah Heschel, *Abraham Geiger and the Jewish Jesus* (Chicago: University of Chicago Press, 1998), 2.

31. Joseph Klausner, *Jesus of Nazareth: His Life, Times, and Teaching*, trans. Herbert Danby (New York: Bloch Publishing, 1989; originally published in English in 1925).

32. Joseph Klausner, *Jesus of Nazareth: His Life, Times, and Teaching*, trans. Herbert Danby (New York: Macmillan, 1925), 414.

33. Stephen S. Wise, *Jewish Daily Bulletin* (December 13, 1925), 1, as quoted in Novak, *Jewish-Christian Dialogue*, 78.

34. Michael J. Cook, *Modern Jews Engage the New Testament: Enhancing Jewish Well-Being in a Christian Environment* (Woodstock, VT: Jewish Lights, 2008); Amy-Jill Levine, *The Misunderstood Jew: The Church and the Scandal of the Jewish Jesus* (San Francisco: HarperSanFrancisco, 2006).

35. Beatrice Bruteau, *Jesus Through Jewish Eyes: Rabbis and Scholars Engage an Ancient Brother in a New Conversation* (Maryknoll, NY: Orbis Books, 2001); Philip A. Cunningham et al., eds., *Christ Jesus and the Jewish People Today: New Explorations of Theological Interrelationships* (Grand Rapids, MI: Eerdmans, 2011); Amy-Jill Levine and Marc Zvi Brettler, eds., *The Jewish Annotated New Testament: New Revised Standard Version Bible Translation* (New York: Oxford University Press, 2011).

36. "Pharisee," "pharisaical," *Webster's Ninth New Collegiate Dictionary* (Springfield, MA: Miriam Webster, Inc., 1983), 881.

37. Jacob Neusner, *The Rabbinic Traditions About the Pharisees Before 70*, 3 vols. (Leiden: Brill, 1971); idem, *From Politics to Piety: The Emergence of Pharisaic Judaism*, 2nd ed. (New York: KTAV Publishing House, 1979); Ellis Rivkin, *A Hidden Revolution: The Pharisees' Search for the Kingdom Within* (Nashville, TN: Abingdon, 1978).

38. See Eugene J. Fisher, *Faith Without Prejudice: Rebuilding Christian Attitudes Toward Judaism*, vol. 4 in Shared Ground Among Jews and Christians series (New York: Crossroad, 1993); John T. Pawlikowski, *Christ in the Light of the Christian-Jewish Dialogue* (New York: Paulist Press, 1982); Clark M. Williamson, *Has God Rejected His People? Anti-Judaism in the Christian Church* (Nashville, TN: Abingdon Press, 1982); E. P. Sanders, *Jesus and Judaism* (Philadelphia: Fortress Press, 1985); John P. Meier, *A Marginal Jew: Rethinking the Historical Jesus*, 4 vols. (New York: Doubleday, 1991); Anthony J. Saldarini, *Pharisees, Scribes, and Sadducees in Palestinian Society: A Sociological Approach* (Wilmington, DE: Michael Glazier, 1988).

39. Edward Kessler, "Mary: The Jewish Mother," *Irish Theological Quarterly* 76, no. 3 (2011): 215.

40. Harvey Falk, *Jesus the Pharisee: A New Look at the Jewishness of Jesus* (Mahwah, NJ: Paulist Press, 1985).

41. Lawrence H. Schiffman, "The Jewishness of Jesus: Commandments Concerning Interpersonal Relations," in *Jews and Christians Speak of Jesus*, ed. Arthur E. Zannoni (Minneapolis: Fortress Press, 1994), 39.

42. More recently, the commission stated: "At the time of Jesus, there were no doubt Pharisees who taught an ethic worthy of approval." For discussion, see Philip A. Cunningham, "The Pontifical Biblical Commission's 2001 Study on The Jewish People and Their Sacred Scriptures in the Christian Bible: Selected Important Quotations with Comments" (April 24, 2002), available on the people.sju.edu website.

43. William Scott Green includes the Dead Sea Scrolls as a source. He believes that the reference in some of the Qumran documents to "Those Who Seek Smooth Things" is another name for the Pharisees. William Scott Green, "What Do We Really Know About the Pharisees and How Do We Know It?" in *In Quest of the Historical Pharisees*, ed. Jacob Neusner and Bruce C. Chilton (Waco, TX: Baylor University Press, 2007), 411–13.

44. John Bowker, *Jesus and the Pharisees* (Cambridge: Cambridge University Press, 1973), 2.

45. Saldarini, *Pharisees, Scribes, and Sadducees in Palestinian Society*, 220–21.

46. Edward Kessler, "Midrash," in *A Dictionary of Jewish-Christian Relations*, ed. Edward Kessler and Neil Wenborn (Cambridge: Cambridge University Press, 2005), 293–94.

47. Nahum N. Glatzer, *Hillel the Elder: The Emergence of Classical Judaism* (New York: B'nai B'rith Hillel Foundation, 1957), 27.

48. See David Stern, *Parables in Midrash: Narrative and Exegesis in Rabbinic Literature* (Cambridge: Harvard University Press, 1994).

49. David Flusser, "Hillel and Jesus: Two Ways of Self-Awareness," in *Hillel and Jesus: Comparative Studies of Two Major Religious Leaders*, ed. James H. Charlesworth and Loren L. Johns (Minneapolis: Fortress Press, 1997), 94.

50. For the English translation of sections of the Talmud cited in parenthesis within the text of the present volume, see Isidore Epstein, ed., *The Babylonian Talmud*, 26 vols. (London: Soncino Press, 1935–59), available on the halakhah.com website.

51. Fisher, *Faith Without Prejudice,* 46.

52. Cecil Roth, ed., *The Concise Jewish Encyclopedia* (New York: New American Library, 1980), 305.

53. Fisher, *Faith Without Prejudice,* 52–55.

54. Pawlikowski, *Christ in the Light of the Christian-Jewish Dialogue*, 81–89.

55. Roth, *The Concise Jewish Encyclopedia*, 518–19.

56. Fisher, *Faith Without Prejudice*, 47.

57. Luis Alonso Schökel, "Readings on Justice in the Old Testament," course notes (Summer 1974).

58. Pawlikowski, *Christ in the Light of the Christian-Jewish Dialogue*, 83.

59. Lee I. Levine, *The Ancient Synagogue: The First Thousand Years* (New Haven, CT: Yale University Press, 2000), 19–20.

60. Elizabeth A. Johnson, *Truly Our Sister: A Theology of Mary in the Communion of Saints* (New York: Continuum, 2003), 167–68.

61. Ellis Rivkin, "The Internal City," *Journal for the Scientific Study of Religion* 5, no. 2 (Spring 1966): 236.

62. Bernadette J. Brooten, *Women Leaders in Ancient Synagogues,* Brown Judaic Studies 36 (Chico, CA: Scholars Press, 1982), 1.

63. See ibid., 5. One example is a marble plaque from Smyrna, Ionia, probably second century CE, on which the inscription translated from the Greek reads: "Rufina, a Jewess, head of the synagogue, built this tomb for her freed slaves and the slaves raised in her house. No one else has the right to bury anyone (here). If someone should dare to do so, he or she will pay 1500 denars to the sacred treasury and 1000 denars to the Jewish people. A copy of this inscription has been placed in the (public) archives."

64. Ibid., 103–38.

65. Anthony J. Saldarini, "Pluralism of Practice and Belief in First-Century Judaism," in Zannoni, *Jews and Christians Speak of Jesus*, 24.

66. Neusner, *From Politics to Piety*, 83.

67. Rivkin, *A Hidden Revolution*, chap. 4.

68. Pawlikowski, *Christ in the Light of the Christian-Jewish Dialogue*, 88.

69. Rivkin, *A Hidden Revolution*, 294.

70. Josephus, *Against Apion* II: 288–95, quoted in Rivkin, *A Hidden Revolution*, 295.

71. Rivkin, *A Hidden Revolution*, 310.

72. John T. Pawlikowski, *Jesus and the Theology of Israel* (Wilmington, DE: Michael Glazier, 1989), 55.

73. Elisabeth Schüssler Fiorenza, *Transforming Vision: Explorations in Feminist Theology* (Minneapolis: Fortress Press, 2011), 230–38.

74. To explore such parallels, see Michael Hilton and Gordon Marshall, *The Gospels and Rabbinic Judaism: A Study Guide* (Hoboken, NJ: Ktav Publishing, 1988).

75. Levine, *The Misunderstood Jew*, 43.

76. Pawlikowski, *Christ in the Light of the Christian-Jewish Dialogue*, 88–89.

77. Kevin J. Madigan and Jon D. Levenson, *Resurrection: The Power of God for Christians and Jews* (New Haven, CT: Yale University Press, 2008), xi–xii, 22.

78. Pawlikowski, *Christ in the Light of the Christian-Jewish Dialogue*, 89.

79. Rivkin, *A Hidden Revolution*, 307.

80. Madigan and Levenson, *Resurrection*, 201.

81. "The Amidah Prayer," Hanefesh: National Assembly of Jewish Students, hanefesh.com website.

82. Pawlikowski, *Christ in the Light of the Christian-Jewish Dialogue*, 103–7.

83. David Flusser, "A New Sensitivity in Judaism and the Christian Message," *Harvard Theological Review* 61, no. 2 (April 1968): 126.

84. Tal Ilan, *Integrating Women into Second Temple History* (Tübingen: Mohr Siebeck, 1999).

85. Ibid., 4

86. Ibid., 81.

87. Ross Shepard Kraemer, *Her Share of the Blessings: Women's Religions Among Pagans, Jews, and Christians in the Greco-Roman World* (New York: Oxford University Press, 1992), 100.

88. Ilan, *Integrating Women into the Second Temple History*, 80–81.

89. See Elisabeth Schüssler Fiorenza, *In Memory of Her: A Feminist Theological Reconstruction of Christian Origins* (New York: Crossroad, 1983).

90. Tal Ilan, "Paul and Pharisee Women," in *On the Cutting Edge: The Study of Women in Biblical Worlds*, ed. Jane Schaberg, Alice Bach, and Esther Fuchs (New York: Continuum, 2004), 82, quoting and commenting on Schüssler Fiorenza, *In Memory of Her*, 115.

91. Ilan, "Paul and Pharisee Women," 84–86.

92. Ibid., 94.

93. Liam M. Tracey, "Pentecost," in Kessler and Wenborn, *A Dictionary of Jewish-Christian Relations*, 339.

### *6. Jewish Spirituality and Hebrew Prayer*

1. Arthur Green, ed., *Jewish Spirituality: From the Bible Through the Middle Ages*, vol. 13 in *World Spirituality: An Encyclopedic History of the Religious Quest* (New York: Crossroad, 1987), xiii.

2. Roger LeDeaut, "Worship and Religious Practice," in *The Spirituality of Judaism*, ed. Roger LeDeaut, Annie Jaubert, and Kurt Hurby (St. Meinrad, IN: Abbey Press, 1977), 25, 29.

3. *Pesikta d'Rab Kahana*, 157b, trans. S. Schecter, in S. Schecter, *Aspects of Rabbinic Theology* (New York: Macmillan, 1909), quoted in Evelyn Garfiel, *Service of the Heart: A Guide to the Jewish Prayer Book* (North Hollywood, CA: Wilshire Book Company, 1978), 23.

4. Markus Holland McDowell, "'As I Prayed Many Things'": Patterns of Prayer in the Portrayal of Jewish Women in the Literature of the Second Temple Period" (Fuller Theological Seminary, 2004). This dissertation was published as *Prayers of Jewish Women: Studies of Patterns of Prayer in the Second Temple Period* (Tübingen: Mohr Siebeck, 2006).

5. Raymond E. Brown et al., eds., *Mary in the New Testament* (Philadelphia: Fortress Press, 1978), 150–52.

6. Jaroslav Pelikan, David Flusser, and Justin Lang, *Mary: Images of the Mother of Jesus in Jewish and Christian Perspectives* (Minneapolis: Fortress Press, 2005), 12.

7. Translations of the *Spiritual Exercises* that I have found especially helpful are George Ganss, *The Spiritual Exercises of St. Ignatius: A Translation and Commentary* (St. Louis: Institute of Jesuit Sources, 1992); and David L. Fleming, *Draw Me into Your Friendship: A Literal Translation and a Contemporary Reading of the Spiritual Exercises* (St. Louis: Institute of Jesuit Sources, 1996). Among other helpful volumes are David Lonsdale, *Eyes to See, Ears to Hear: An Introduction to Ignatian Spirituality* (Maryknoll, NY: Orbis Books, 2003); and Michael Ivens, *Understanding the Spiritual Exercises: Text and Commentary* (Heresfordshire: Inigo Enterprises, 1998).

8. John O'Malley, "Early Jesuit Spirituality: Spain and Italy," in *Christian Spirituality: Post-Reformation and Modern*, ed. Louis Dupre and Don E. Saliers, vol. 18 on *World Spirituality: An Encyclopedic History of the Religious Quest* (New York: Crossroad, 1989), 5.

9. Jacob Neusner, *A Midrash Reader* (Minneapolis: Augsburg Fortress Press, 1990), 5.

10. Marc Rastoin, "From Windfall to Fall: The Conversos in the Society of Jesus," in *Friends on the Way: Jesuits Encounter Contemporary Judaism*, ed. Thomas Michel (New York: Fordham University Press, 2007), 8–19.

11. The practice of a thirty-six day retreat developed when it seemed beneficial to offer a four-day introductory session preceding the thirty-day Ignatian retreat and two days after the retreat reflection and debriefing, so that the retreatants could benefit more from the experience.

12. The earliest known version of the book of Esther was written in Hebrew. The prayer used in this meditation comes from a longer Greek version (often referred to as "Additions to Esther"), which, according to some experts, was also originally written in Hebrew or in Aramaic not later than 93 CE. Josephus paraphrases the additions, suggesting that first-century Jews would have been familiar

with this prayer. See David Noel Freedman, ed., "Esther, Additions To," *Anchor Bible Dictionary*, vol. 2 (New York: Doubleday, 1992), 630–32.

13. Fleming, *Draw Me into Your Friendship*, 96–97.

14. Ibid., 96.

15. See Ivens, *Understanding the Spiritual Exercises*, 95.

16. Garfiel, *Service of the Heart*, 221.

17. Joseph H. Hertz, *The Authorized Daily Prayer Book*, rev. (New York: Bloch Publishing, 1946), 344–45.

18. The origin of the *Dayeinu* (or *Dayyenu*) continues to be a subject of controversy among scholars. See Paul F. Bradshaw and Lawrence A. Hoffman, eds., *Passover and Easter: Origin and History to Modern Times*, Two Liturgical Traditions (Notre Dame, IN: University of Notre Dame Press, 1999); see especially Israel J. Yuval, "Easter and Passover as Early Jewish-Christian Dialogue," 98–124. Yuval refers to the fact that L. Finkelstein dates the *Dayyenu* to as early as 198–167 BCE. E. Goldschmidt does not accept his thesis. However, Melito of Sardis (120–85 CE) composed what appears to be a parody on the *Dayyenu,* "About Easter," in the second century CE, by which one could infer that the hymn was known in Jewish circles possibly in the first century CE. See Yuval, "Easter and Passover as Early Jewish-Christian Dialogue," 103–5.

19. Herbert Bronstein, ed., *A Passover Haggadah, The New Union Haggadah,* 2nd rev. ed. (New York: Penguin, 1978), 52–53.

20. Hertz, *The Authorized Daily Prayer Book*, 745–49, 746n.

# Bibliography


Altholz, Josef L. *The Churches in the Nineteenth Century*. New York: Bobbs-Merrill, 1967.

Anderson, H. George, J. Francis Stafford, and Joseph A. Burgess, eds. *The One Mediator, the Saints, and Mary*. Lutherans and Catholics in Dialogue. Minneapolis, MN: Augsburg, 1992.

Asch, Sholem. *Mary*. New York: G. P. Putnam's Sons, 1949.

Athans, Mary Christine. "Anti-semitism? or Anti-Judaism?" In *Introduction to Jewish-Christian Relations*, edited by Michael Shermis and Arthur Zanonni. New York: Paulist Press, 1991.

———. "Mary in the American Catholic Church." *U.S. Catholic Historian* 8, no. 4 (Fall 1989): 103–16.

Bancy, Alain, Maurice Jourjon, and the Dombes Group. *Mary in the Plan of God and in the Communion of Saints*. New York: Paulist Press, 1999.

Beattie, Tina. "Mary in Patristic Theology." In Boss, *Mary: The Complete Resource*, 75–105.

Becker, Adam H., and Annette Yoshiko Reed, eds. *The Ways That Never Parted: Jews and Christians in Late Antiquity and the Early Middle Ages*. Minneapolis, MN: Fortress Press, 2007.

Becker, Carl L. *The Heavenly City of the Eighteenth Century Philosophers*. New Haven, CT: Yale University Press, 1932.

Boff, Leonardo. *The Maternal Face of God*. San Francisco: Harper and Row, 1987.

Boss, Sarah Jane, ed. *Mary: The Complete Resource*. London: Continuum, 2007.

Bouyer, Louis. *The Spirituality of the New Testament and Fathers*. Translated by Mary P. Ryan. New York: Seabury Press, 1963.

Bowker, John. *Jesus and the Pharisees*. Cambridge: Cambridge University Press, 1973.

Braaten, Carl E., and Robert W. Jenson. *Mary, Mother of God*. Grand Rapids, MI: Eerdmans, 2004.

Bradshaw, Paul F., and Lawrence A. Hoffman, eds. *Passover and Easter: Origin and History to Modern Times*. Two Liturgical Traditions. Notre Dame, IN: University of Notre Dame Press, 1999.

Bronstein, Herbert, ed. *A Passover Haggadah: The New Union Haggadah*. 2nd rev. ed. New York: Penguin, 1978.

Brown, Raymond E. "Biblical Reflections on Crises Facing the Church." New York: Paulist Press, 1975.

———. *The Community of the Beloved Disciple*. New York: Paulist Press, 1979.

———. "A Heritage from Israel." *America* 128 (March 10, 1973): 121.

———. *The Virginal Conception and Bodily Resurrection of Jesus*. New York: Paulist Press, 1973.

Brown, Raymond E., Karl P. Donfried, Joseph A. Fitzmyer, and John Reumann, eds. *Mary in the New Testament*. Philadelphia: Fortress Press, 1978.

Bruteau, Beatrice. *Jesus Through Jewish Eyes: Rabbis and Scholars Engage an Ancient Brother in a New Conversation*. Maryknoll, NY: Orbis Books, 2001.

Bultmann, Rudolph. *The History of the Synoptic Tradition*. Translated by John Marsh. enl. ed. Peabody, MA: Hendrickson, 1921.

Calvin, Jean. "Commentarius in Harmonium Evangelicam." In *Corpus Reformatum*, vol. 45 (Braunschweig: Brunsvigae, 1901).

———. *La Nativité* 7, no. 28. Paris: Revue Réformée, 1956.

Carr, Anne E. "Mary in the Mystery of the Church: Vatican Council II." In *Mary According to Women*, edited by Carol Frances Jegen, 5–32. Kansas City, MO: Leaven Press, 1985.

Chamberlain, Houston S. *The Foundations of the Nineteenth Century*. Translated by John Lees. Vol. 1. 2 vols. London: John Lane, 1910.

Charlesworth, James H. *Jesus Within Judaism: New Light from Exciting Archeological Discoveries*. New York: Doubleday, 1988.

Cook, Michael J. *Modern Jews Engage the New Testament: Enhancing Jewish Well-being in a Christian Environment*. Woodstock, VT: Jewish Lights, 2008.

Culp-Hill, Kathleen, trans. *Songs of Holy Mary of Alfonso X, The Wise: A Translation of the* Cantigas De Santa Maria. Tempe, AZ: Arizona Center for Medieval and Renaissance Studies, 2000.

Cunneen, Sally. *In Search of Mary: The Woman and the Symbol.* New York: Ballantine, 1996.

Cunningham, Philip A., Joseph Sievers, Mary C. Boys, Hans Hermann Hendrix, and Jesper Smartvik, eds. *Christ Jesus and the Jewish People Today: New Explorations of Theological Interrelationships.* Grand Rapids, MI: Eerdmans, 2011.

D'Agostino, Peter R. *Rome in America: Transnational Catholic Ideology from the Risorgimento to Fascism.* Chapel Hill: University of North Carolina Press, 2004.

Davies, Alan T. "The Aryan Christ: A Motif in Christian Anti-Semitism." *Journal of Ecumenical Studies* 12, no. 4 (Fall 1975): 569–79.

DeCock, Mary. "Our Lady of Guadalupe: Symbol of Liberation." In *Mary According to Women*, edited by Carol Frances Jegen, 113–41. Kansas City, MO: Leaven, 1985.

Denaux, Adelbert, and Nicholas Sagovsky, eds. *Studying Mary: Reflections on the Virgin Mary in Anglican and Roman Catholic Theology and Devotion.* ARCIC Working Papers. London: T & T Clark, 2007.

Denziger, Heinrich, and John F. Clarkson, eds. *The Church Teaches: Documents of the Church in English Translation.* St. Louis: B. Herder, 1955.

Dolan, John P. *Catholicism: An Historical Survey.* Woodbury, NY: Barron's Educational Series, 1968.

Donnelly, Doris, ed. *Mary, Woman of Nazareth: Biblical and Theological Perspectives.* New York: Paulist Press, 1989.

Donovan, Mary Ann. *One Right Reading? A Guide to Irenaeus.* Collegeville, MN: Liturgical Press, 1997.

Ellsberg, Robert. *Blessed Among All Women: Women Saints, Prophets, and Witnesses for Our Time.* New York: Crossroad, 2005.

Epstein, Isidore, ed. *The Babylonian Talmud.* 26 vols. London: Soncino Press, 1935.

Falk, Harvey. *Jesus the Pharisee: A New Look at the Jewishness of Jesus.* Mahwah, NJ: Paulist Press, 1985.

Farina, John. "The Study of Spirituality: Some Problems and Opportunities." *U.S. Catholic Historian* 8 (November 1989): 15–32.

Fichte, Johann Gottleib. *J.G. Fichte Werke.* Edited by Fritz Medicus. Vol. 4. Leipzig: Verlag von Felix Meiner, 1908.

Fisher, Eugene J. *Faith Without Prejudice: Rebuilding Christian Attitudes Toward Judaism*. Revised and expanded edition. New York: Crossroad, 1993.

Fisher, Eugene J., and Leon Klenicki, eds. *Pope John Paul II on Jews and Judaism: 1979–1986*. Washington, DC: USCC, 1987.

Flannery, Austin, ed. *Vatican II: Conciliar and Post-Conciliar Documents*. New York: Costello, 1975.

Fleming, David L. *Draw Me into Your Friendship: A Literal Translation and a Contemporary Reading of the Spiritual Exercises*. St. Louis: Institute of Jesuit Sources, 1996.

Flusser, David. "Hillel and Jesus: Two Ways of Self-Awareness." In *Hillel and Jesus: Comparative Studies of Two Major Religious Leaders*, edited by James H. Charlesworth and Loren L. Johns. Minneapolis, MN: Fortress Press, 1997.

———. "A New Sensitivity in Judaism and the Christian Message." *Harvard Theological Review* 61, no. 2 (April 1968): 107–27.

Freedman, David Noel, ed. "Esther, Additions To." In *Anchor Bible Dictionary*, 2:630–32. New York: Doubleday, 1992.

Freund, W. H. C. *The Early Church*. Philadelphia: Fortress Press, 1965.

Ganss, George. *Ignatius of Loyola: The Spiritual Exercises and Selected Works*. New York: Paulist Press, 1991.

———. *The Spiritual Exercises of St. Ignatius: A Translation and Commentary*. St. Louis: Institute of Jesuit Sources, 1992.

Garfiel, Evelyn. *Service of the Heart: A Guide to the Jewish Prayer Book*. North Hollywood, CA: Wilshire Book Company, 1958.

Gaventa, Beverly Roberts. *Mary: Glimpses of the Mother of Jesus*. Minneapolis, MN: Fortress Press, 1999.

Gaventa, Beverly Roberts, and Cynthia L. Rigby, eds. *Blessed One: Protestant Perspectives on Mary*. Louisville, KY: Westminster John Knox, 2002.

Gebara, Ivone, and Maria Clara Bingemer. *Mary, Mother of God, Mother of the Poor*. Translated by Phillip Berryman. Maryknoll, NY: Orbis Books, 1987.

Glatzer, Nahum N. *Hillel the Elder: The Emergence of Classical Judaism*. New York: B'nai B'rith Hillel Foundation, 1957.

Graef, Hilda. *Mary: A History of Doctrine and Devotion*. Combined ed. Notre Dame, IN: Ave Maria Press, 2009.

———. *Mary: A History of Doctrine and Devotion*. Vol. 1, *From the Beginnings of the Eve of the Reformation*. Vol. 2, *From the Reformation to the Present Day*. New York: Sheed and Ward, 1963, 1965.

Green, Arthur. *Jewish Spirituality: From the Bible Through the Middle Ages*. Vol. 13 of *World Spirituality: An Encyclopedic History of the Religious Quest*. 18 vols. New York: Crossroad, 1987.

———. "Shekhinah, the Virgin Mary, and the Song of Songs: Reflections on a Kabbalistic Symbol in Its Historical Context." *American Jewish Studies Review* 26, no. 1 (2002): 1–52.

Green, William Scott. "What Do We Really Know About the Pharisees and How Do We Know It?" In *In Quest of the Historical Pharisees*, edited by Jacob Neusner and Bruce C. Chilton, 409–24. Waco, TX: Baylor University Press, 2007.

Halsey, William H. *The Survival of American Innocence: Catholicism in an Era of Disillusionment 1920-1940*. Notre Dame, IN: University of Notre Dame Press, 1967.

Hennesey, James J. "A Prelude to Vatican II: American Bishops and the Definition of the Immaculate Conception." *Theological Studies* 25, no. 3 (1964): 409–19.

Hertz, Joseph H. *The Authorized Daily Prayer Book*. New York: Bloch Publishing, 1974.

Heschel, Susannah. *The Aryan Jesus: Christian Theologians and the Bible in Nazi Germany*. Princeton, NJ: Princeton University Press, 2008.

———. "Feminism in Jewish-Christian Dialogue." In *Introduction to Jewish-Christian Relations*, edited by Michael Schermis and Arthur E. Zannoni, 232–40. New York: Paulist Press, 1991.

Hilton, Michael, and Gordon Marshall. *The Gospels and Rabbinic Judaism: A Study Guide*. Hoboken, NJ: Ktav Publishing House, 1988.

Hoffman, Matthew. *From Rebel to Rabbi: Reclaiming Jesus and the Making of Modern Jewish Culture*. Stanford, CA: Stanford University Press, 2007.

Holmes, J. Derek, and Bradford W. Bickers. *A Short History of the Catholic Church*. New York: Paulist Press, 1984.

Hopkins, Gerard Manley. *Poems and Prose of Gerard Manley Hopkins*. London: Penguin Classics, 1985.

Houselander, Caryll. *The Reed of God*. Westminster, MD: Christian Classics, 1944.

Idilby, Ranya, Suzanne Oliver, and Priscilla Warner. *The Faith Club: A Muslim, A Christian, A Jew—Three Women Search for Understanding*. New York: Free Press, 2006.

Ignatius of Loyola. "Autobiography." In *Ignatius of Loyola: The Spiritual Exercises and Selected Works*, edited by George Ganss, 65–111. Mahwah, NJ: Paulist Press, 1991.

Ilan, Tal. *Integrating Women into Second Temple History*. Tübingen: Mohr Siebeck, 1999.

———. "Paul and the Pharisee Women." In *On the Cutting Edge: The Study of Women in Biblical Worlds*, edited by Jane Schaberg, Alice Bach, and Esther Fuchs, 82–101. New York: Continuum, 2004.

Ivens, Michael. *Understanding the Spiritual Exercises: Text and Commentary*. Heresfordshire: Inigo Enterprises, 1998.

Jegen, Carol Frances. "Mary Immaculate: Woman of Freedom, Patroness of the United States." In Jegen, *Mary According to Women*, 143–63.

Jegen, Carol Frances, ed. *Mary According to Women*. Kansas City, MO: Leaven Press, 1985.

Johnson, Ann. *Miryam of Jerusalem: Teacher of the Disciples*. Notre Dame, IN: Ave Maria Press, 1991.

———. *Miryam of Judah: Witness in Truth and Tradition*. Notre Dame, IN: Ave Maria Press, 1987.

———. *Miryam of Nazareth: Woman of Strength and Wisdom*. Notre Dame, IN: Ave Maria Press, 1984.

Johnson, Elizabeth A. *Friends of God and Prophets: A Feminist Theological Reading of the Communion of Saints*. New York: Continuum, 1999.

———. "Galilee: A Critical Matrix for Marian Studies." *Theological Studies* 70, no. 2 (June 2009): 327–46.

———. *Truly Our Sister: A Theology of Mary in the Communion of Saints*. New York: Continuum, 2003.

Johnson, Trevor. "Mary in Early Modern Europe." In Boss, *Mary: The Complete Resource*, 363–84.

Kähler, Martin. *The So-Called Historical Jesus and the Historic, Biblical Christ*. 4th edition. Minneapolis, MN: Fortress Press, 1964.

Karidoyanes Fitzgerald, Kyriaki. "Mary the Theotokos and the Call to Holiness." In Braaten and Jenson, *Mary, Mother of God*, 80–99.

Kenneally, James J. "Eve, Mary and the Historians." *Horizons* 3 (1976): 187–202.

Kessler, Edward. "Mary: The Jewish Mother." *Irish Theological Quarterly* 76, no. 3 (2011): 211–23.

———. "Midrash." In Kessler and Wenborn, *A Dictionary of Jewish-Christian Relations*, 293–94.

Kessler, Edward, and Neil Wenborn, eds. *A Dictionary of Jewish-Christian Relations*. Cambridge: Cambridge University Press, 2005.

Klausner, Joseph. *Jesus of Nazareth: His Life, Times, and Teaching*. Translated by Herbert Danby. New York: Bloch Publishing, 1989.

Komoszewski, J. Ed, M. James Sawyer, and Daniel B. Wallace. *Reinventing Jesus: How Contemporary Skeptics Miss the Real Jesus and Mislead Popular Culture*. Grand Rapids, MI: Kregel Publications, 2006.

Kraemer, Ross Shepard. *Her Share of the Blessings: Women's Religions Among Pagans, Jews and Christians in the Greco-Roman World*. New York: Oxford University Press, 1992.

Kselman, Thomas A., and Stevan Avella. "Marian Piety and the Cold War in the United States." *Catholic Historical Review* 72, no. 3 (July 1986): 403–24.

LeClercq, Jean. "The Distinctive Characteristics of Roman Catholic American Spirituality." *Louvain Studies* 9 (Spring 1983): 295–306.

LeDeaut, Roger. "Worship and Religious Practice." In *The Spirituality of Judaism*, edited by Roger LeDeaut, Annie Jaubert, and Kurt Hurby. St. Meinrad, IN: Abbey Press, 1977.

Levine, Amy-Jill. *The Misunderstood Jew: The Church and the Scandal of the Jewish Jesus*. San Francisco: HarperSanFrancisco, 2006.

Levine, Amy-Jill, and Marc Zvi Brettler, eds. *The Jewish Annotated New Testament: New Revised Standard Version Bible Translation*. New York: Oxford University Press, 2011.

Levine, Lee I. *The Ancient Synagogue: The First Thousand Years*. New Haven, CT: Yale University Press, 2000.

Lonsdale, David. *Eyes to See, Ears to Hear: An Introduction to Ignatian Spirituality*. Maryknoll, NY: Orbis Books, 2003.

Luther, Martin. "Sermon on the Afternoon of Christmas Day, 1530." In *Martin Luther's Basic Theological Writing*, edited by Timothy F. Lull and William R. Russell, 171–75. 3d ed. Minneapolis: Fortress, 2012.

———. *On the Jews and Their Lies, 1543*. Translated by Martin H. Bertram. Vol. 47 of *Luther's Works*. Minneapolis, MN: Fortress Press/Augsburg Fortress Press, 1971.

———. *Works of Martin Luther*. Translated by A. T. W. Steinhaeuser. Philadelphia: Holman, 1930.

Madigan, Kevin J., and Jon D. Levenson. *Resurrection: The Power of God for Christians and Jews*. New Haven, CT: Yale University Press, 2008.

Maunder, Chris. "Mary in the New Testament and the Apocrypha." In Boss, *Mary: The Complete Resource*, 11–46.

McBrien, Richard P. *Catholicism*. 2 vols. Revised edition. San Francisco: HarperSanFrancisco, 1994.

McDowell, Markus Holland. *Prayers of Jewish Women: Studies of Patterns of Prayer in the Second Temple Period*. Tübingen: Mohr Siebeck, 2006.

———. "'As I Prayed Many Things': Patterns of Prayer in the Portrayal of Jewish Women in the Literature of the Second Temple Period." Fuller Theological Seminary, 2004.

McGuckin, John. "The Early Cult of Mary and Inter-Religious Contexts in the Fifth-Century Church." In *The Origins of the Cult of the Virgin Mary*, edited by Chris Maunder, 1–22. London: Burns and Oates, 2008.

Meier, John P. *A Marginal Jew: Rethinking the Historical Jesus*. Vol. 1, *The Roots of the Problem and the Person*. New York: Doubleday, 1991.

Neusner, Jacob. *A Midrash Reader*. Minneapolis, MN: Augsburg Fortress Press, 1990.

———. *From Politics to Piety: The Emergence of Pharisaic Judaism*. 2nd ed. New York: KTAV Publishing House, 1979.

———. *The Rabbinic Traditions About the Pharisees Before 70*. 3 Vols. Leiden: Brill, 1971.

Newman, John Henry. *The New Eve*. Oxford: Newman Bookshop, 1952.

Nolan, Mary Catherine. *Mary's Song: Living Her Timeless Prayer.* Notre Dame, IN: Ave Maria Press, 2001.

Novak, David. *Jewish-Christian Dialogue: A Jewish Justification.* New York: Oxford University Press, 1989.

O'Brien, Catherine. "Mary in Film." In Boss, *Mary: The Complete Resource*, 532–36.

O'Malley, John. "Early Jesuit Spirituality: Spain and Italy." In *Christian Spirituality: Post-Reformation and Modern*, edited by Louis Dupre and Don E. Saliers. Vol. 18 of *World Spirituality: An Encyclopedic History of the Religious Quest.* New York: Crossroad, 1989.

Origen. *Contra Celsum.* Translated by Henry Chadwick. London: Cambridge University Press, 1980.

Parlby, Geri. "The Origins of Marian Art in the Catacombs and the Problems of Identification." In *The Origins of the Cult of the Virgin Mary*, edited by Chris Maunder, 41–56. London: Burns and Oates, 2008.

Pawlikowski, John T. *Christ in the Light of the Christian-Jewish Dialogue.* New York: Crossroad, 1982.

———. *Jesus and the Theology of Israel.* Wilmington, DE: Michael Glazier, 1989.

Pelikan, Jaroslav. *Jesus Through the Centuries: His Place in History and in Culture.* New Haven, CT: Yale University Press, 1985.

———. *Mary Through the Centuries: Her Place in the History of Culture.* New Haven, CT: Yale University Press, 1996.

Pelikan, Jaroslav, David Flusser, and Justin Lang. *Mary: Images of the Mother of Jesus in Jewish and Christian Perspectives.* Minneapolis, MN: Fortress Press, 2005.

Perrin, Norman. *Rediscovering the Teaching of Jesus.* New York: Harper and Row, 1967.

Plaskow, Judith. "Christian Feminism and Anti-Judaism." *Cross Currents* 28, no. 3 (Fall 1978): 306–9.

Pontifical Biblical Commission. *The Jewish People and Their Sacred Scriptures in the Christian Bible.* Boston: Pauline Books, 2002.

Poortvliet, Rien. *He Was One of Us.* Grand Rapids, MI: Baker Books, 1974.

Price, Richard. "Theotokos: The Title and Its Significance in Doctrine and Devotion." In Boss, *Mary: The Complete Resource*, 56–73.

Radford Ruether, Rosemary. *Mary: The Feminine Face of the Church*. Philadelphia: Westminster John Knox, 1977.

———. "Misogynism and Virginal Feminism in the Fathers of the Church." In *Religion and Sexism: Images of Women in Jewish and Christian Traditions*, edited by Rosemary Radford Ruether, 150–83. New York: Simon and Schuster, 1974.

———. *Sexism and God-Talk: Toward a Feminist Theology*. Boston: Beacon, 1993.

Rastoin, Marc. "From Windfall to Fall: The *Conversos* in the Society of Jesus." In *Friends on the Way: Jesuits Encounter Contemporary Judaism*, edited by Thomas Michel. New York: Fordham University Press, 2007.

Reid, Barbara E. *Choosing the Better Part? Women in the Gospel of Luke*. Collegeville, MN: Liturgical Press, 1996.

Rivkin, Ellis. *A Hidden Revolution: The Pharisees Search for the Kingdom Within*. Nashville, TN: Abingdon, 1978.

———. "The Internal City." *Journal for the Scientific Study of Religion* 5, no. 2 (Spring 1966): 225–40.

Roth, Cecil, ed. *The Concise Jewish Encyclopedia*. New York: New American Library, 1980.

Rubin, Miri. *Mother of God: A History of the Virgin Mary*. New Haven, CT: Yale University Press, 2009.

Saldarini, Anthony J. *Pharisees, Scribes, and Sadducees in Palestinian Society: A Sociological Approach*. Wilmington, DE: Michael Glazier, 1988.

Sanders, E. P. *Jesus and Judaism*. Philadelphia: Fortress Press, 1985.

Sandmel, Samuel. *We Jews and Jesus*. New York: Oxford University Press, 1973.

Schaberg, Jane. *The Illegitimacy of Jesus: A Feminist Theological Interpretation of the Infancy Narratives*. New York: Harper and Row, 1987.

Schiffman, Lawrence H. "The Jewishness of Jesus: Commandments Concerning Interpersonal Relations." In *Jews and Christians Speak of Jesus*, edited by Arthur E. Zannoni. Minneapolis, MN: Fortress Press, 1994.

Schillebeeckx, Edward. *Mary, Mother of the Redemption*. Translated by N. D. Smith. New York: Sheed and Ward, 1964.

Schillebeeckx, Edward, and Catherina Halkes. *Mary: Yesterday, Today, Tomorrow*. Translated by John Bowden. New York: Crossroad, 1993.

Schökel, Luis Alonso. "Readings on Justice in the Old Testament." Course notes, Summer 1974.

Schüssler Fiorenza, Elisabeth. *In Memory of Her: A Feminist Theological Reconstruction of Christian Origins*. New York: Crossroad, 1983.

———. *Jesus: Miriam's Child, Sophia's Prophet: Critical Issues in Feminist Christology*. New York: Continuum, 1995.

———. *Transforming Vision: Explorations in Feminist Theology*. Minneapolis, MN: Fortress Press, 2011.

Schweitzer, Albert. *The Quest of the Historical Jesus*. Translated by W. Montgomery. Minneapolis, MN: Augsburg Fortress Press, 1906.

Seiferth, Wolfgang S. *Synagogue and Church in the Middle Ages: The Encounter of Jews and Christians*. New York: Charles Scribner's Sons, 1967.

Shinners, Jr., John. "Mary and the People: The Cult of Mary and Popular Belief." In *Mary, Woman of Nazareth*, edited by Doris Donnelly, 161–86. New York: Paulist Press, 1989.

Shoemaker, Stephen J. "Marian Liturgies and Devotions in Early Christianity." In Boss, *Mary: The Complete Resource*, 130–48.

Spalding, Martin John. "Introduction." *Ave Maria* I, no. 1 (1865): 3–8.

Stanton, Elizabeth Cady. "Has Christianity Benefitted Women?" In *Elizabeth Cady Stanton, Feminist as Thinker: A Reader in Documents and Essays*, edited by Carol DuBois and Richard Cándida-Smith, 243–53. New York: New York University Press, 2007.

Stern, David. *Parables in Midrash: Narrative and Exegesis in Rabbinic Literature*. Cambridge: Harvard University Press, 1994.

Stowe, Harriet Beecher. *Sunny Memories of Foreign Lands*. Vol. 2. 2 vols. Boston: Sampson, 1854.

Suenens, Leon J. *The Nun in the World*. Westminster, MD: Newman Press, 1963.

Swidler, Leonard. "Jesus Was a Feminist." *The Catholic World* 212 (January 1971): 177–83.

Tambasco, Anthony J. *What Are They Saying About Mary?* New York: Paulist Press, 1984.

Tavard, George. *The Thousand Faces of Mary*. Collegeville, MN: Liturgical Press, 1996.

Turrow, James C., and Raymond E. Brown. "Canonicity." In *Jerome Biblical Commentary*, 515–34. Englewood Cliffs, NJ: Prentice Hall, 1968.

Wakefield, Gordon S. "Spirituality." In *Westminster Dictionary of Christian Spirituality*, 61. Philadelphia: Westminster Press, 1983.

Walsh, James J. *The Thirteenth: The Greatest of Centuries*. New York: Fordham University Press, 1943.

Warner, Marina. *Alone of All Her Sex: The Myth and Cult of the Virgin Mary*. New York: Vintage, 1983.

Williamson, Clark M. *Has God Rejected His People? Anti-Judaism in the Christian Church*. Nashville, TN: Abingdon, 1982.

Wohlmann, Avital. "Pourquoi Le Silence De L'Hébraïsme D'Aujourd'hui Au Sujet De Marie De Nazareth? Une Femme Juive Répond." In *Maria Nell' Hebraismo e Nell' Islam Oggi*. Vol. 7 in *Teologia e Spiritualità Mariana*. Rome: EDB, 1987.

Wright, N. T. *Jesus and the Victory of God*. Minneapolis, MN: Fortress Press, 1996.

Yuval, Israel J. "Easter and Passover as Early Jewish-Christian Dialogue." In Bradshaw and Hoffman, *Passover and Easter,* 98–124.

# Index